HEAThER FoRD
JHU

THE PRICE OF FREEDOM

THE
PRICE OF
FREEDOM

SLAVERY AND MANUMISSION IN BALTIMORE

AND EARLY NATIONAL MARYLAND

T. Stephen Whitman

THE UNIVERSITY PRESS OF KENTUCKY

Publication of this volume was made possible in part by a grant
from the National Endowment for the Humanities.

Copyright 1997 by The University Press of Kentucky

Scholarly publisher for the Commonwealth,
serving Bellarmine College, Berea College, Centre
College of Kentucky, Eastern Kentucky University,
The Filson Club Historical Society, Georgetown College,
Kentucky Historical Society, Kentucky State University,
Morehead State University, Murray State University,
Northern Kentucky University, Transylvania University,
University of Kentucky, University of Louisville,
and Western Kentucky University.

Editorial and Sales Offices: The University Press of Kentucky
663 South Limestone Street, Lexington, Kentucky 40508-4008

Library of Congress Cataloging-in-Publication Data

Whitman, T. Stephen, 1950–
    The price of freedom : slavery and manumission in Baltimore and
early national Maryland / T. Stephen Whitman.
        p.   cm.
    Includes bibliographical references and index.
    ISBN 0-8131-2004-7 (acid-free paper)
    1. Slavery—Maryland.   2. Slavery—Maryland—Baltimore.
3. Slaves—Emancipation—Maryland.   4. Slaves—Emancipation—
Maryland—Baltimore.   5. Maryland—History.   6. Maryland—Race
relations.   7. Baltimore (Md.)—History.   8. Baltimore (Md.)—Race
relations.   I. Title.
E445.M3W45   1997
975.2′00496—dc20   96-27386

This book is printed on acid-free recycled paper
meeting the requirements of the American National Standard
for Permanence of Paper for Printed Library Materials.

Manufactured in the United States of America

To Dorothy J. and Aaron T. Whitman

CONTENTS

ILLUSTRATIONS

MAPS

TABLES *provide analysis of tables*

ACKNOWLEDGMENTS

I wish to thank those who have helped me with this work. My colleagues at Mount St. Mary's have given me time to work and a summer study grant that enabled me to use that time to write. The archivists and staff of the Maryland State Archives and the Maryland Historical Society have unfailingly done a superb job, not only in obtaining materials I wanted, but also in helping me to figure out what might aid my inquiries. Many fellow researchers at the archives have shared ideas, but I owe a special debt of gratitude to Lois Green Carr and Phoebe Jacobsen for their sustained interest, encouragement, and observations. Chapters 2 and 4 have appeared in different form as articles in the *Journal of Southern History* and *Social Science History* respectively; the editors' and anonymous referees' comments have been useful and enlightening. Stephanie Cole, Christine Daniels, Curt Johnson, Robert Olwell, Chris Phillips, James Rice, Stephen Sarson, James Sidbury, and Frank Towers have all read portions of this work and provided valuable comments. William Freehling's seminar on antebellum history first sparked my interest in slavery and manumission, an interest nurtured by his subsequent support and insights and by his invaluable suggestions on how to revise the work for publication. Jack Greene kindly invited me to present my work at an informal workshop on slavery in 1993; the comments of the participants, especially Wilma King's, gave me several new ideas to pursue. To Ronald Walters, who supervised this work at the dissertation stage, my thanks not only for his indefatigable efforts to sharpen my thinking and writing, but also for his even-tempered dealing with an advisee who might easily have exhausted his patience.

INTRODUCTION

During the first half century of American independence, Baltimore's population multiplied to make it the nation's third largest city. Within a single life span the mid-eighteenth-century village at the mouth of Jones' Falls Creek swelled to a city of eighty thousand souls, spreading northeastward from the Patapsco River to Fells' Point in a crescent-shaped swarm of houses, shops, mills, and shipyards. In this vibrant and tumultuous environment, with spurts of virtually volcanic growth punctuated by short but prostrating slumps, workers of all statuses, whether free, apprenticed, indentured, or enslaved, were sought out by merchants, manufacturers, and craftsmen. Until the prolonged hard times of the 1820s, entrepreneurs regarded bound workers as key assets in seeking steady production and profits from Baltimore's first flowering.

Maryland's blacks played a vital part in making both Baltimore's fortunes and their own. Arriving as slaves either purchased from or migrating with masters leaving the Eastern and lower Western Shores of Maryland, they soon seized opportunities to earn money for themselves as well as their masters. For many, hard labor and its earnings became tools with which to carve out autonomy within slavery and, ultimately, to propel themselves out of slavery through self-purchase or manumission granted after a further term of service. So widespread were such manumissions that by 1830 four-fifths of Baltimore's blacks were legally free, the largest group of free people of color in any U.S. city.

Meanwhile, blacks elsewhere in Maryland achieved freedom much more slowly, though still in impressive numbers. Nearly three-quarters of the state's rural blacks were still slaves in 1830. Before 1850 free persons of color outnumbered slaves only in Cecil and Caroline Counties, the former abutting on free Pennsylvania and the latter on northern Delaware, where slavery had become moribund. Thus, Baltimore's hinterlands remained strongly committed to slave labor even as blacks transformed the city into an island of freedom.

1

Understanding Maryland's and Baltimore's experience with slavery and emancipation requires locating Maryland and Baltimore in context, both spatially and temporally. On the eve of the American Revolution every colony of British North America had slaves, and as Jack Greene has noted, their numbers were everywhere on the increase, even in such unlikely milieus as New Hampshire.[1] But something happened over the next fifty years. By the 1820s slavery had become almost entirely southern, as states from Pennsylvania northward gradually abolished it. Accounting for this dramatic change in American society has generated a torrent of historical analysis and controversy.

One broad band of thinking, perhaps best exemplified by the work of David Brion Davis, stresses the development of antislavery sensibilities in seeking to explain the geographic contraction of slavery: in the late eighteenth century, large numbers of people first began to think and write that slavery was wrong, even indefensibly wrong, in a moral or religious sense.[2] These sensibilities, reinforced by republicanism in post-Revolutionary America, generated powerful social and political forces that swept slavery away in the North and excluded it from the Northwest. Even in the plantation South, where its vital economic importance sustained it, and where the ideology of republicanism could be invoked to defend the property rights of slaveholders against the intrusion of state power in the name of antislavery sentiment, slavery was challenged strongly enough to compel slaveholders to modify the exercise of patriarchal power over their chattels. By the early nineteenth century, masters developed paternalistic policies stressing mutual obligations between master and slave, as a reform of slavery designed to ameliorate its harshest aspects and improve its image. So, in broad outline, might we describe the impact of the rise of humanitarianism on slavery in America for the period of the 1770s to the 1820s.

But other historians have been far from satisfied with explanations invoking so strongly the power of ideas to change the world. Eric Williams and various continuators and modifiers of his work have centered their attention on a supposed transformation to capitalism rendering slavery anachronistic, as it became a less profitable form of exploitation than waged labor. According to this view slaveholders freeing chattels are not humanitarians, but rather entrepreneurs liquidating a devalued investment, and antislaveryites can become little more than visible hands working to adjust the world to its new master, the market.[3]

Still other historians have tried to deconstruct what they see as a false dichotomy between humanitarian and self-interested motivations as explanations for the regionalization of slavery in the early national

United States. Thomas Haskell has speculated that the habits and modes of action acquired by capitalistic entrepreneurs predisposed them toward a more humanitarian outlook, by engendering in them a greater sense of responsibility for the consequences of their actions and hence a greater sense of guilt for slave trading and slaveholding.[4] Alternatively, Joyce Chaplin has demonstrated that, at least in the deep South, planters could embrace humanitarian values without relinquishing their slaves; indeed, they came to believe that their role as masters was critical to civilizing and Christianizing their slaves.[5]

Yet another line of inquiry has refocused attention on how the American Revolution reshaped slavery where it survived, in the southern states. Sylvia Frey has shown compellingly how the chaos engendered by the war in the South battered slavery, providing African Americans with opportunities to escape from or strike back at their oppressors.[6] For Frey, the movement toward ameliorating slavery from the 1780s to the 1820s can be understood only as part of a strategy by slaveholders to regain control of black workers. According to this interpretation, although black agency could not destroy slavery, it did force numerous short-term concessions from masters, regarding maintenance, preservation of families, and access to organized religion.

Private, voluntary manumission has generally been understood as a midrange response to the rise of antislavery sentiment. Northern states abolished slavery by gradual emancipation, and the deep South preserved slavery in its full vigor, but in the Chesapeake relatively liberal manumission laws facilitated partial and halting efforts by portions of Delaware, Maryland, and Virginia to work their way out of slavery.[7] There is much to be said for seeing private manumission as slaveholders gradually weaning themselves from reliance on lifelong bound labor. Manumitters were presumably originally inspired by republican or religious antislavery ideas, for if their motive had been purely economic, they could have simply sold their chattels to dealers on their way to Kentucky or New Orleans. Also, granting immediate freedom to all of one's slaves might bring economic ruin for oneself. The compromise solution would be the gradual freeing of the slaves over as much as thirty years, while one sought new ways of creating and accumulating wealth.

If we go looking for such patterns of manumission in Maryland, we find them readily enough, notably among Quaker planters and merchants of the Eastern Shore, where many blacks gained freedom as early as the 1770s and 1780s.[8] The Quakers may be said to have designed a model informing later manumissions: Both dealing in and holding slaves for life were moral wrongs; the slaveholder's duty to God and the care of his own soul required him to free himself of this taint. At the same time, the responsibility to maintain his family argued against immediate emancipation, as did the obligation to prepare slaves for the challenges of free life. Gradual manumission could achieve all of these aims. A model, but not the only one.

Characterizing manumission primarily as an exit from slavery, as an attempt to maximize spiritual or ideological gains while minimizing economic losses associated with one's divorce from slaveholding, fails to explain two significant features of Maryland's social and economic geography in the early national period. First, manumission enjoyed great prominence at the same time that slavery also grew and flourished, especially in Baltimore. Second, many slaveholders acquired more slaves after manumitting slaves. To understand these developments we must go beyond models that focus solely on slaveholders' motivations. Weighing the complexities of slaveholders' actions is indeed critical. But it is equally necessary to appreciate the actions and behavior of the blacks who were seeking to become free. Only by mapping both the economic and ideological consequences of black-white interaction can we gain a more complete sense of the processes that resulted in Maryland's unusual mixture of free and enslaved African Americans.

Early national Maryland's slaves wrested freedom from their masters in a bewildering variety of unequal power struggles. These were balanced by momentary harmonies of interest, mixtures of exploitation and kindness, and long, patient bargaining interspersed with violent episodes. The fascinating and often inspiring processes by which slaves won liberty could and did operate both in Baltimore and in rural Maryland and indeed can be found in virtually any slaveholding society: even in the heyday of the Cotton Kingdom, a few blacks in the deep South managed to become free. But far more blacks did so in Baltimore and some of Maryland's rural counties than in any other slave state, Quaker-dominated Delaware excepted. This book examines the ties between Baltimore's growth and the economic stagnation in southern and eastern Maryland, in order to understand how blacks could work their way out of slavery.

The story begins with the spread of slavery in Baltimore roughly between 1770 and 1815 and flows into its supplanting by free black labor, from about 1800 to 1830. The first two chapters, dealing with slaves and their work in shipyards, craft shops, and an early chemical factory in Baltimore, show how masters' need to secure reliable labor led to the spread of slavery in the city and how that very process created opportunities for blacks to seek manumission. They also speak to the question of how the presence of slaves and bound white laborers contributed to the growth of urban manufacturing in the early national period. The next three chapters, depicting master-slave interactions and the resulting reshaping of slavery in Maryland, portray manumission's ambiguous role in preserving, modifying, and destabilizing both the relations of masters and slaves and slavery itself. In these pages I analyze the strategies of masters for perpetuating control and the corresponding efforts by blacks to gain autonomy: blacks both negotiated over manumission, acknowledging the legitimacy of slavery, and resisted overtly through flight. I also seek to show how the workings of manumission helped generate new forms of dependency in which former slaves became enmeshed.

The concluding chapter grapples with the role of antislavery and republican ideology in shaping white attitudes in Baltimore, not only toward slaves and slavery, but also toward the community of freed African Americans who eventually replaced slaves as a prime component of the city's wage labor force. Here the aim is to achieve a fuller understanding of how and why manumission could not propel a more complete liberation of Maryland's slaves and to see how a partial transition from bound to free black labor fed into an emerging free labor ideology in the 1820s, with a heightened emphasis on race-based ideas of political economy.

In summary, the story of early-nineteenth-century Maryland suggests not only that the spread of slavery, industrial and urban growth, and selective manumission were able to coexist but also that they might have temporarily reinforced one another. These factors, and the shifts that destroyed the fragile balance among them, resulting in the waning of slavery in the city, further inform (1) the differing responses of South and North to possible industrialization, (2) the causes of slavery's weakness in many southern cities, and (3) the function of manumission during and after the First Emancipation in the upper South.

Most work on manumission itself, as opposed to the larger studies of antislavery discussed above, has proceeded from one of two vantage points. Those interested in the slaveholder's perspective have assessed manumitters' religious, humanitarian, or economic motivation. Alternatively, scholars interested in African American history have often treated manumission as a kind of prologue or springboard from which to delve into a study of life in free black communities. The best recent work, studies by Shane White and by Gary Nash and Jean Soderlund, has departed from this pattern and affords excellent in-depth analyses of manumission in states legislating *post-nati* emancipation, New York and Pennsylvania, respectively.[9] But understanding the transmutations of slavery in Baltimore and rural Maryland before 1830, by focusing

MD

on manumission in a slave state, can also help in recasting our understanding of how blacks came to be free, or at least in framing more contingent evaluations of that process.

This work also departs from two common focal points of examinations of slavery: the plantation and the antebellum period. Much of the best historical writing of the past two generations has developed subtle understandings of agricultural slave labor and its impact on regional growth and development, or of the many-sided nature of master-slave relations, to mention only two prominent topics, but slavery in urban settings has received less attention. Discussions of American urban or industrial slavery have tended to categorize it as exotic, anomalous, and marginal. The most common approach has been to take the "failure" of urban or industrial slavery as a given and to look for explanations of the phenomenon. That maintaining masterly control over slaves, or keeping them constantly employed and hence maximally profitable, was more difficult in towns than on plantations is no longer in doubt. It has proved easy to move from such distinctions to conclusions that urban slavery was foredoomed or performed fundamentally different functions in society, such as status display for the wealthy, rather than that of a wealth-generating system of labor.

In delving into the causes underlying Baltimore's early move toward a greater use of slave labor, with its subsequent evolution into an almost entirely free labor city, accounting for the city's place in its regional economy and polity is important. The expansion of slavery in Baltimore was fueled in part by shifts in the labor regime of the surrounding counties. Mono-cropping of tobacco began to give way to a mixed agriculture relying more strongly on wheat; the result was less need for year-round field laborers and increased availability of bound workers to employers in Baltimore. These changes flowed in part from interruptions in trade patterns caused by European wars of the late eighteenth and early nineteenth centuries. These disruptions in trade stimulated urban manufacturing of import substitutes while depressing the export of tobacco. Both Baltimore's interactive role with its hinterland and its somewhat dependent status vis-á-vis modifications in the transatlantic economy helped drive internal shifts in the city's patterns of labor usage.

This book thus attempts to gauge both macro- and microeconomic forces affecting slavery and manumission in Maryland. Such an approach, although it can be extremely valuable in sketching a multicausal explanation for slavery's eventual marginalization in Baltimore, is not without pitfalls. For example, one must avoid the temptation to assume too much congruence between the impulses of large economic forces and the actions of individual slaveholders. Such an assumption would be overly reductive, ignoring the many noneconomic factors that inform human decisions, and would also tend to depict African Americans, enslaved or free, as passive victims or beneficiaries of white action—a wildly inaccurate portrayal.

Moreover, even within the idealized world in which rational economic calculation determines action, there are, and were in early national Baltimore, conflicts between economic theory and practice. Even people who are relatively unaffected by motives of humanity, religion, or republicanism may fail to engage in maximally effective economic behavior. The final chapter on the political economy of slavery, antislavery, and free black workers attempts to come to grips with this phenomenon.

1

SLAVERY IN EARLY NATIONAL
BALTIMORE AND RURAL MARYLAND

The story of blacks gaining freedom in Baltimore begins with the arrival of slaves from the countryside and their employment in craft work and manufacturing. Those slaves, either owned or hired from their owners, found that their masters valued and rewarded their willingness to come to the city and their productive service even to the point of granting their freedom.

Understanding how and why blacks came or were brought to Baltimore and how that process led to freedom requires an examination of the ebbs and flows of the economy and the society both in the city and in the countryside. Two rural Maryland counties, Dorchester and Prince George's, will serve as examples of their regions. Dorchester County, on Maryland's sandy Eastern Shore, was a rural, mixed-agriculture region in the early 1800s with a few small towns, including a modest commercial center at the county seat of Cambridge. Prince George's County, south of Baltimore and east of Washington City, typified lower Western Shore tobacco growing counties. Almost entirely rural, its relatively richer soils allowed the profitable cultivation of tobacco long after that crop had ceased to dominate Eastern Shore agriculture. Both counties thus featured different local economies from that of Baltimore and offer different perspectives on bound labor as well. Prince George's remained tied to tobacco and slaves throughout the early national and antebellum periods. Dorchester, like most of the Eastern Shore, shifted to a mixed-agriculture regime and gradually decreased its reliance on slavery after 1800, supplementing it with an equally mixed bag of labor forms, including tenancy, indentured servitude, labor rendered dependent by debt, and waged work.

Slaves began to live and work in Baltimore in the third quarter of the eighteenth century. It was an inconsequential hamlet before 1750, but with the opening up of the Maryland and Pennsylvania backcountry, the town grew up around mills on the Jones' Falls Creek and the adjacent harbor, as an entrepôt for wheat, corn, and livestock. In 1768 Baltimore became the seat of Baltimore County, a thirty-mile-wide swatch of land extending from the city and the Chesapeake Bay northward to the Pennsylvania border. By 1800 rural manufacturers clustered at mills on several of the county's smaller rivers that empty into the Chesapeake, while residents of the upper county, north and west of Baltimore city, grew grain and raised cattle in a landscape also dotted with flour mills, sawmills, and iron forges.

Reflecting their diverse paths of development, the three counties exhibited different histories respecting their usage of slaves (see table 1). Slavery's growth in the city of Baltimore outpaced that of Maryland at large between 1790 and 1810, but over the next twenty years a gradual decline prevailed, accelerating after 1830. In outlying Baltimore County a modest increase in slavery before 1800 ceased thereafter.[1] Likewise in Dorchester slavery dwindled rapidly after 1830, following a slow diminution that had begun as early as 1790, when the county recorded its peak slave population. Prince George's, on the other hand, with more slaves than any other Maryland county, showed little change in slave population throughout the early national and antebellum periods. In both of the latter counties and their respective regions, masters did not welcome growth in the slave population, preferring to hire or sell off surplus "hands," both locally and to southwestern slave traders.

Dorchester's slight loss in slave numbers from 1790 to 1810 paralleled downturns in Eastern Shore counties such as Kent, Queen Anne's, and Somerset. Prince George's static demography was replicated by sister tobacco-growing counties of the Western Shore: Anne Arundel, Calvert, Charles, and Saint Mary's Counties collectively showed a modest 5 percent increase in slaves over these decades.

Considered as a unit, Baltimore County and Baltimore city registered a 60 percent increase between 1790 and 1810, well within the range of Maryland's fast-growing northern tier: slave population more than doubled in Washington and Allegany Counties and increased by more than 50 percent in Frederick County, about 30 percent in Harford County, and some 25 percent in Montgomery County. Growth in slaveholding accompanied the opening up of previously untilled farmlands, as slaves took on the onerous tasks of clearing land and improving farmsteads.

But slavery expanded much more vigorously in late-eighteenth- and early-nineteenth-century Baltimore city than in its outlying county or in Maryland generally: the city's numbers nearly quadrupled, from 1,255

TABLE 1

Slave Population in Baltimore, Dorchester, and Prince George's Counties, 1790-1860

(Units of 100)

	1790	1800	1810	1820	1830	1860
Baltimore Co.	59	68	66	67	66	32
Baltimore-City	12	28	47	44	41	22
Dorchester Co.	53	46	50	52	50	41
Prince George's Co.	112	122	114	112	116	125

NOTE: Prince George's County figures include a correction of 1810 census data, in which 2,200 slaves were mistakenly counted as free persons of color in the county. I am indebted for this information to Prof. Steven Sarson of the University College of Swansea, Wales.

to 4,672, while in the rest of the county slavery increased by less than 15 percent. In fact, the city's growth in slaveholding exceeded that of any other county in the state; at the same time the increase in outlying Baltimore County was lower than that of any other northern or western county.[2]

Baltimoreans purchased many slaves from rural owners. Between 1790 and 1810 city dwellers bought more than eight times as many slaves from elsewhere as they sold to owners outside the city. Better than one quarter of all sales of slaves in the county before 1810 sent a rural slave to the city.[3] Slaveholders moving to town with their chattels also swelled the slave population. James Piper, a onetime Kent County planter-merchant who later operated a ropewalk in Baltimore with slave workmen, and Seth Sweetser, an Annapolitan who took his boot-making business and four slave craftsmen with him to the city, typify such migrations. Rural slave sellers, whether pressed by the debt and credit crises of the mid-1780s or by longer-term needs to reshape labor forces, supplied both new and old Baltimoreans with laborers relatively cheaply. Planters were pruning their holdings of slaves as they shifted from the year-round labor intensity of tobacco growing to crop mixes with seasonal peaks of labor demand, such as wheat, corn, and fruits and vegetables.[4]

City dwellers also brought slaves to Baltimore from outside the state. Although Maryland had banned importing slaves "by land or water" in 1783, Maryland residents could obtain exemptions for domestic transactions. A slaveholder had only to file a declaration identifying the slaves and specifying that their labor was intended for his use only rather than for resale. More than 300 slaves came to Baltimore in this fashion during the 1790s, mostly from Virginia, even as the practice of manumission spread.[5] In 1792 the legislature authorized slaveholders fleeing Saint Domingue to bring their slaves into Maryland, a measure repealed in 1797, as fears grew that the "French negroes" would foment a slave insurrection.[6] French émigrés had meanwhile declared the importation of 133 slaves. A few more slaves entered the city with masters who chose to leave New York after passage of that state's *post-nati* emancipation law in 1799.[7] Finally, slaveholders secured dozens of private bills from the Maryland legislature to bring in still more slaves.[8]

The enslaved men and women who entered Baltimore in such large numbers from the 1780s to 1820 engaged in many kinds of work, often for new masters, in both senses of the phrase: slaves dealt with owners previously unknown to them, and many of the owners had not held slaves before acquiring them in Baltimore. A look at these slaveholders, focusing on their work, their level of wealth, and the relationship between slavery and the economic environment in which these masters operated will help to sketch in more of the background to blacks' ability to propel themselves from slavery to freedom in Baltimore.

Merchants, ship captains, public officials, and professionals such as doctors, lawyers, and bankers made up the majority of urban slaveholders, but hundreds of craft workers and manufacturers also had slaves residing in their households between 1790 and 1820.[9] The breadth and depth of slaveholding in the crafts is an important element in the phenomenon of urban manumission. First, it compels caution in generalizing about artisans or mechanics as an antislavery element rendering slavery unstable in a city setting. The spread of slavery in Baltimore's workshops from 1790 to 1810, coincident with the rise of manumission, raises questions whether connections between these two supposedly antithetical processes exist. One potential connection is that most manumissions freed African Americans only after a term of service, during which time they could be bought and sold at prices discounted below those prevailing for lifelong slaves. Purchasing such workers might have been highly appealing to craftsmen seeking to expand their command of labor as cheaply as possible.

Slaveholding in the crafts peaked around 1810, when 325 people, 19 percent of all those who could be matched from the census rolls to the city directory, held slaves. A higher proportion of practitioners held slaves in 1810 than in 1790, 1800, or 1820, in nearly two-thirds of the crafts. Most of the remaining occupations showed the broadest participation in slaveholding in 1800; only four did so in 1820 or later.[10] Slaveholding thus expanded in Baltimore's craft and industrial sector in tandem with the city's growth until the second decade of the nineteenth century.

Both the share of all Baltimore slaveholders who worked in the crafts and the share of slaves held by artisans and manufacturers also peaked in the period from 1810 to 1820. In 1790 workers in crafts and industry made up 24 percent of slaveholders with identifiable occupations and held 23 percent of the slaves. By 1800 those proportions had increased markedly: craftsmen composed 33 percent of identifiable slaveholders and held 27 percent of the slaves. In 1810 they were 35 percent of the slaveholders and held 33 percent of the slaves. But by 1820 only 22 percent of the slaveholders practiced a craft, holding 21 percent of the slaves.[11]

Slaves were thus pulled into Baltimore during its rapid growth after 1780 by overlapping and mushrooming labor needs on the part of merchants, craftsmen, and manufacturers. Attracted by the ability to retain bound laborers in a boom town, even people of moderate wealth could obtain slave labor without committing themselves to lifelong ownership of slaves: throughout the period African Americans serving as term slaves pending manumission were commonly bought and sold for one-third to one-half less than slaves for life.

The rise in slavery in Baltimore's workshops coincided with a decline in skilled work by slaves and white apprentices in the surrounding countryside. Whereas runaway ads placed by Prince George's and Anne Arundel County masters in the *Maryland Gazette* described nearly a quarter of male slaves in the 1780s and 1790s as possessing artisanal skills, that proportion fell to less than one-tenth by the second decade of the nineteenth century.[12] A study of Saint Mary's County likewise found fewer skilled male slaves after 1810, a change attributable to changing market conditions: Baltimore-made goods increasingly undersold local products, reducing the utility of rural slave artisans.[13] Concomitantly, many of those artisans may have been sold to Baltimore, hired their own time there, or even run away to the city, simultaneously building up Baltimore's craft labor base and reducing the out-counties' capacity for craft production. As for apprentices, both the volume and the proportion of rural indentures promising to train children in craft skills were lower after 1815 than previously.[14]

Thus Baltimore drained its hinterlands of skilled slaves, many of whom then produced manufactures in the city's shops. The competition engendered by the distribution of those goods in rural Maryland subsequently rendered rural craft work and the associated training of slaves less profitable. Eventually, with fewer rural African Americans learning craft skills, the continued recruitment of slaves for Baltimore's craft shops became more difficult: the scarcity of skilled slaves in rural counties after 1810 may have triggered the decline in slavery's share of the Baltimore craft labor market.

The prevalence of manumission in Baltimore must therefore be contemplated against the backdrop of slave migration to the city. One might be tempted to think that late-eighteenth- or early-nineteenth-century manumission was a sign that supply of slaves exceeded demand, or that slavery had become unprofitable. Clearly, such a view is highly unsatisfactory, if not for rural Maryland, then certainly for the city. An alternative view, which sees gradual manumission as a tactic of employers to encourage the entry of free laborers into a labor market, also fails to account for the active recruitment of slaves for craft work. It has been suggested that white craft workers especially disliked working alongside slaves who were bound for life and that craft masters used manumission to reduce this stigma. At the same time gradual manumission would retain the services of the bound laborers until the shift to a free labor market was completed. But if the masters had had this strategy in mind, they would not have continued to purchase slaves for craft work.[15]

In fact, one of the prime attractions of Baltimore, for both skilled and unskilled blacks, lay precisely in its reputation as a place where a slave could gain freedom through self-purchase or delayed manumission in return for rendering highly productive labor. Thus, Baltimore's growth, fed by voluntary and involuntary black migration, altered rural labor, choking off slavery-based craft work in the countryside. But the city could only temporarily fuel manufacturing growth with rural craft slaves; as that process shut itself down by the 1820s, new sources of labor had to be found: white immigrants and an ever-growing free black population would take the place of slaves. Nonetheless, slave-buying artisans and manufacturers played an important part in this slow transformation of Maryland's economy and labor force.

Of course, not all the slaves in craft work were owned by those who employed them; slave hiring from merchants, rentiers, and professionals offered a short-term, if expensive, source of bound workers. Hiring or hiring out slaves was the principal means by which a slaveholder could temporarily adjust his or her supply of labor power. Of course, in this situation a slave's willingness to work as a hireling would be worth encouraging with incentives and rewards. Shifts in the need for slave labor could arise from changes in one's economic activities or from the evolution of one's family structure. Advertisers seeking to hire or sell slaves routinely assured readers that they were moved not by the slave's bad character or work habits, but by "want of employment" for the worker or by a plan to "retire from business." Whatever the realities, advertisers clearly expected such explanations to be plausible to prospective customers familiar with Baltimore's volatile economic climate.[16]

Slaves were hired, or hired themselves, for farm labor, craft or manufacturing work, and domestic service.[17] Because no transfer of title to property occurred, far fewer hiring contracts survive than do records of slave sales or manumissions, making it difficult to estimate the extent of the practice. In Baltimore between 1790 and 1820, one-sixth of slave advertisements expressed a desire to hire or hire out slaves. Just under 10 percent of runaway ads noted that the fugitive had been hired out.[18] Slave hiring had become common enough by the years between 1810 and 1820 for several Baltimore concerns to play the role of employment agency. Alexander Stuart and Jacob G. Smith advertised that they had "a number of Negroes to Hire, by the day, week, month, or year. Also, several young ones, of each sex, which [they would] place in genteel families, for two or three years, for their victuals and clothes."[19] Finally, the passage of a law in 1817 barring slaves from "going at large" to hire their own time suggests that the practice was widespread.[20]

In other southern cities many widows, innkeepers, and lawyers hired out their slaves, who comprised their principal taxable property. For example, an 1813 assessment list showed thirty-eight slaveholding women identified as widows in the city directory. Twenty-one of these women held more than a quarter of their property in slaves; for twelve of the widows slaves composed a majority of their holdings. One of them, Ann Crow, hired out Sam, a man of unstated age who was rated at $125. Crow also owned Sarah, a woman over thirty-six years old, rated at $40. Her only other taxable property was $12 worth of furniture; what Sam and Sarah earned probably was Crow's economic mainstay.[21]

Inns and taverns frequently served as points of rendezvous for slave hiring or brokering, allowing vendors of such laborers to capitalize on the flow of people and information that swirled through the doors. No doubt the innkeeper's ability to hire out his or her own slaves served as a hedge against slow times, an option that may have been particularly attractive for artisans operating a small inn or tavern as a sideline.[22] Baltimore's largest slaveholder in 1813, John Gadsby, employed his thirty-six slaves in operating his Indian Queen Hotel, but it is not likely that Elizabeth Winkle needed the unremitting labor of six slaves to keep a tavern worth less than one hundred dollars, exclusive of the slaves.[23] She may instead have hired them out, or allowed them to hire their own time. Account books of Baltimore manufacturers record such short-term transactions. For example, David McKim, a factory operator of the 1820s, noted payments to Mme. DeLozier "for her hands" and to attorney Simon Wilmer in amounts suggesting that one or two of his slaves had helped McKim deal with a short-term surge in work at his chemical plant.[24]

Baltimore's professions included many men who might have been slave rentiers. The 1813 tax list records thirteen lawyers and eleven doctors who held four or more slaves composing at least a quarter of each man's wealth; slaves represented a majority of the wealth of nine of them. From bankers, brokers, cashiers, clerks, and insurance company officers came another twelve men whose holdings were strongly concentrated in slaves. All told, more than seventy slaveholders in these occupations had significant property holdings in slaves, which made them plausible candidates to have engaged in slave hiring.[25]

Slaveholding merchants, storekeepers, and sea captains, as well as artisans, may also have rented out bound workers. A court case of 1798 illustrates slave hiring by a seamstress. In that year Martha Hay sued Captain Conner over the loss of a slave named Perry. Hay, a widow managing the estate of her children, had hired Perry to Conner, "to perform a Voyage from Baltimore to Hamburg and thence back to Baltimore, as a Cook on board the Ship Mary," for twenty dollars a month. On the return voyage Perry escaped at Martinique and was not retaken. Hay sought to recover Perry's value from Conner and dwelt on the importance of Perry's income to the maintenance of her children.[26] This case illustrates the role slave hiring could play and the difficulty of detecting it in the documentary record. Captain Conner does not appear to have been a slaveholder, yet he employed slaves on his ship.[27] Only Perry's successful escape created the circumstances that allowed his work to reach our attention. All told, it seems reasonable to conclude that slave hiring affected the lives of significant numbers of Baltimore's slaves and masters.

Slaveholders like Martha Hay and Ann Crow were not rich, and that made them fairly typical of Baltimore slaveholders. The evidence from Baltimore's 1813 tax list, which itemized slaves by age and sex and defined the portion of an owner's wealth they represented, suggests that many people of moderate wealth relied on slave labor.[28] In all, 3,367 resident property holders, including 1,135 masters and their 2,740 slaves, appeared in the 1813 assessment lists. Most of these slaveholders had one to three slaves, who commonly represented about one-quarter of an owner's total worth, despite assessment rules that often undervalued slaves by 60 or 70 percent by fixing a maximum value of $125 for a slave.[29] Baltimore slaveholders thus almost certainly held a larger proportion of their real total wealth in slaves than is reflected in the 1813 assessments.

One of the more striking aspects of this picture is the relatively equal likelihood that Baltimoreans possessing any taxable wealth would hold slaves, regardless of how rich they were. To be sure, a majority of the very richest citizens owned slaves, compared with only one in eight of those on the bottom rung of the taxable wealth ladder. But Baltimoreans holding as little as $140 of property were about three-quarters as likely to be slaveholders as those worth five or six times as much. Table 2 illustrates this proposition.

This fairly flat distribution of slaveholding across most strata of wealth does not fit well with a view of urban slaveholding oriented strongly toward status display. Were such an attitude a key factor, a stronger link might have appeared between great wealth and slaveholding. Moreover, the slave or slaves owned by property holders worth less than one thousand dollars represented a very substantial portion of their total taxable wealth; it may be doubted that people held a quarter or a half of their property in a nonproductive house servant, as opposed to a worker whose labor could yield income or accumulation of capital.

One way to explore this question further is to revisit the question of whether merchants, professionals, and others not directly engaged in production were significantly more likely to hold slaves than artisans were. Table 3 breaks down the 1813 taxables into craftsmen and manufacturers on the one hand, and all other wealth holders on the other.[30]

Craftsmen and manufacturers were nearly as likely to hold slaves as others of similar wealth; only the middle quintile shows a disproportionately larger cohort of slaveholders among the other wealth holders. Perhaps the most telling thing about table 3 is that about two in five Baltimore craftsmen who could own slaves—who had enough property to choose—did so.[31]

These data are incompatible with an opinion that artisans or mechanics were averse to slavery. The aversion may have been real enough on the part of apprentices and journeymen facing competition from slave workers, but those craft practitioners who had property, and from whose ranks employers of craft labor sprang, had a much more mixed reaction.

TABLE 2

Slaveholding and Wealth: Proportions of Slaveholders
by Deciles of Taxable Wealth, Baltimore, 1813

Decile Ranking	Mean Wealth	Median Wealth	% Holding Slaves
First	$4,553	$3,310	59
Second	1,488	1,447	45
Third	900	890	39
Fourth	603	600	37
Fifth	411	400	33
Sixth	290	285	25
Seventh	204	200	30
Eighth	141	140	28
Ninth	100	94	19
Tenth	53	52	12
Overall	874	336	34

NOTE: This group includes 3,367 wealth holders.

Baltimore's slaveholders, whether craftsmen or not, held fewer slaves than rural Marylanders did: statewide, the average slaveholder owned seven or eight persons, but Baltimore's owners held an average of two or three slaves. Between 1790 and 1820 the mean holding among slave-owning craft workers hovered around 2.5, as did that of all other slaveholders.[32] For all four censuses, 80 to 90 percent of slaveholders owned four or fewer slaves, and only 1 or 2 percent Baltimoreans reached the "large planter" standard of owning 20 or more slaves. See table 4.

More than four-fifths of Baltimore slaveholders, regardless of occupation, held fewer than five slaves at any given period. Correspondingly, most slaves were part of small groups: In 1790, 8 percent of slaves were part of holdings of ten or more chattels; in 1820 the ratio was 12 percent, whereas in all four decades a majority of slaves were owned as part of a holding of one to three persons.

This relative stability may be related to turnover in the ranks of the slaveholders. Less than one-third (29 percent) of the slaveholders in the 1790 census for Baltimore town could be verified as Baltimore slaveholders in 1800. In 1810 and 1820 only 23 percent of those in the

TABLE 3

Slaveholding and Wealth: Craftsmen and Manufacturers
versus Other Wealth Holders, Baltimore, 1813

Wealth	Crafts/Mfg.		Others	
Quintile	N	% Slaveholders	N	% Slaveholders
First	115	63	366	68
Second	145	42	271	47
Third	148	28	278	43
Fourth	141	36	266	38
Fifth	115	22	200	21
Total	664	38	1,381	46

prior census still lived in Baltimore and owned slaves.[33] Manufacturers and craftsmen were more likely than the norm, however, to remain slaveholders from one decade to the next, at least before 1820.[34] In 1800 half of the craftsmen (31 of 60) who had identifiably owned slaves in 1790 were still Baltimore slaveholders at work at their craft. In 1810 34 percent (71 of 210) of those who had owned slaves in 1800 again appeared as slaveholders. By 1820, however, only 22 percent (66 of 310) of slaveholders who had engaged in craft or industrial work ten years earlier retained slaves, a decrease that fits with other signs of slavery's weakening in Baltimore after 1815. The higher persistence rates between 1790 and 1810 corroborate other evidence that slaveholding grew stronger among the crafts before 1810 and did not begin to lose vitality until 1820.[35]

Black men and women thus participated extensively in the early-nineteenth-century city's craft and manufacturing work. Slavery in late antebellum Baltimore increasingly fettered women working as domestics or menials, but the picture is very different prior to 1830. To be sure, as early as 1820, female slaves outnumbered men by 2,368 to 1,989, a ratio of 119:100. And by 1860 nearly two-thirds of Baltimore's dwindling slave population was female. These patterns have lent support to the view that Baltimore's slaves were primarily female at all stages of the city's development. But data from slave transactions suggests otherwise. Before 1830 only 52 percent of slaves sold were women or girls.[36] Similarly, manumissions exhibited a ratio of only 103 females to 100 males, and declarations of slaves brought into Baltimore city from outside the state actually exhibit a 99:100 ratio.[37] Taken to-

TABLE 4

Numbers of Slaves Held by Craftsmen and Manufacturers, in Comparison to Slaveholders of Other Known Occupations in the City of Baltimore, 1790-1820

		Slaveholders					
			Percent owning				
Occupation	Year	N	1	2-4	5-9	10-19	20+
Craft & mfg.	1790	60	48	40	8	2	2
Others	1790	188	39	45	15	1	<1
Craft & mfg.	1800	210	45	43	10	1	1
Others	1800	435	36	48	14	2	0
Craft & mfg.	1810	325	46	44	8	2	<1
Others	1810	612	43	42	12	2	1
Craft & mfg.	1820	299	49	40	8	2	1
Others	1820	1069	47	42	9	1	<1

gether, the court documents identify 1,601 slaves, of whom 775 were males and 826 were females, a female-to-male ratio of 107:100.

Patterns of slave employment in the crafts, whether of men or women, can be discerned by examining how many artisans and manufacturers owned slaves in selected trades. Elsewhere in the South, black women worked in tobacco manufacturing as well as in hatting, tailoring, baking, and other food processing and clothing-related trades; most other trades relied on male workers.[38]

Slaves were most valuable in enterprises requiring uninterrupted labor over sustained periods: brick making, rope making, and shipbuilding would be prime examples. Few businesses flourished as much as brick making during Baltimore's rapid commercial and residential expansion. The admixtures of clay and sand in local soils provided ideal materials, especially in the southern and western regions of the city, and the frequent fires that swept away wooden structures were a good advertisement for brick construction.[39] Slaves who shaped and fired bricks by the tens of thousands were the brick makers' mainstays, as a 1798 brick makers' petition to the Baltimore City Council asserted: "If any of you gentlemen have been at our brickyard, you have no doubt observed four black Men for one white man . . . because of the extream hard labor." In an early instance of what would become a

popular theme in discussions of Baltimore's labor market, the petitioners urged the council to repeal an ordinance regulating brick size and
shape, arguing that doing so would lessen the harshness of labor and
"incourage poor white men and boys to come to the brickyard for
imployment." The repealing ordinance was approved, but in 1813 brick
makers still relied heavily on slaves. Ten of seventeen brick makers
found in the tax list owned slaves, including nineteen men and three
boys.[40] Six of these slaveholders were in the top quintile of wealth
holding and were worth well over $1,000, but the other four were
middling men worth from $120 to $520, three of whom held a majority of their taxable worth in slaves.

   Twenty-two adult male slaves toiled at a ropewalk owned by William and Robert Patterson, composing the second largest group of slaves
in Baltimore in 1813. Shipbuilders, who also worked with some of the
largest groups of slaves, included more than thirty slaveholders in all.[41]
The ship building and fitting industry enjoyed a peak period in early
Baltimore as construction was spurred by naval warfare, both to build
merchant vessels to replace those lost to warships or privateers, and
(after 1812) to fit out American privateers. Half of the shipbuilders
held 25 percent or more of their wealth in slaves, five of them a majority thereof. However, crafts allied with shipbuilding, such as sail making, block and pump making, and rigging, had fewer than ten
slaveholders collectively; only two sail makers and one block maker
can be identified as slaveholders on the 1813 tax rolls. Only Benjamin
Buck, a sail maker with assessable wealth of $494, who owned three
slaves, appears to have had a substantial proportion of his wealth in
slaves.

   This phenomenon illustrates another important feature of the economics of slaveholding. Shipbuilders orchestrated a host of activities,
including design; construction; fitting out the vessel with its masts, spars,
ropes, and blocks; and caulking, painting, and other finishing work.
Operating the way general contractors do in today's construction business, they employed (or owned) some labor directly and subcontracted
out other work, to riggers, for example. As the prime mover in the
operation, the shipbuilder controlled the flow of work and was well
placed to estimate ongoing labor needs, an ability that was important
to investing efficiently in slaves and avoiding the maintenance of idle
laborers. Subcontractors faced more uncertainty about the existence of
the steady work that would make slave owning pay. Put another way,
the shipbuilder could reasonably hope to find some kind of work—
caulking, rough carpentry, or the like—to keep slaves fully employed at
all times; the rigger could not.

Differing degrees of specialization, technical knowledge requirements of the craft, and scale of operation shaped different labor strategies for these two occupations. The rigger carried on a single specialized activity requiring a fairly high degree of knowledge and skill, and
he operated on a small scale. He had little to gain by exploiting slave
labor. The shipbuilder, operating in a larger and more diversified fashion, could and did profit from slave workers, who provided him with a
core of cheap labor augmented by more expensive wage labor as the
volume of work dictated.[42]

Other factors appear to have been at work in the metalworking
trades. Blacksmiths did not rely heavily on slave labor: about one-third
of those who appear on the tax rolls held slaves, but only four of twenty-
nine could be positively identified as owning an adult male worker.[43]
Those who did hold male slaves were in the top two quintiles of wealth,
suggesting that scale of operation may have borne on the utility of
slave labor. Their ranks included Thomas Worrell, the richest of the lot
at an assessed value of $2,370 and owner of nine slaves, and Thomas
Perkins, assessed at more than $1,000, with four slaves. Specialized
operators may also have seen more opportunities to exploit slaves profitably; Richard Chenowith, who owned an adult male worker, listed
his occupation as "blacksmith" but advertised himself in the Baltimore
newspapers as a maker of ploughs and other farm implements. If
Chenowith was in fact producing enough plows, harrows, and seed
drills to warrant segmenting his production work into discrete jobs, he
would have been better placed to exploit slaves for at least some of his
labor needs. Chenowith was still on the make in 1813; by 1819 he
reported his occupation as "patent plough maker" and owned three
male slaves.[44]

Nail making also shows links between slaveholding, specialization,
and operational scale. Anyone familiar with Adam Smith's example of
pin making to illustrate productivity gains associated with division of
labor can imagine how nail making could lend itself to the same process.[45] In fact, the two richest nail manufacturers in Baltimore, Enoch
Betts and Richardson Stewart, were major slaveholders: Betts owned
eleven slaves and Stewart seven, including three men and two boys.
Slaves composed more than four-fifths of Betts's wealth; even for the
much richer Stewart they were a substantial one-fifth of his holdings. A
third nail manufacturer, Bernard Coskery, no longer in business by 1813,
had owned fourteen slaves at the time of the 1810 census.[46]

Whether specializing or not, wealthier ironworkers were much more
likely to own slaves: a majority of those in the top two quintiles of
wealth were slaveholders, as opposed to only one in fourteen in the

lower ranks, a pattern contrary to the generally weak correlation between level of wealth and slaveholding. One explanation may be that
entry into metalworking required larger amounts of capital than many
other crafts. A cordwainer or a carpenter could practice his trade with
a set of hand tools, but a blacksmith needed a forge and fairly expensive appurtenances, such as bellows, anvils, and tools for shaping and
handling hot iron. The absence of slaveholding among less wealthy
blacksmiths may mean that these craftsmen lacked the wealth to have
acquired ownership of all the tools and structures needed to practice
their craft, or that they had no capital with which to acquire slaves
after doing so.[47] Only when they had passed beyond the unusually
high threshold of wealth necessary for metalworking could they begin
to consider the option of owning labor power as well.

By contrast, in trades where high capital requirements did not pose
a barrier to entry, there was not that marked variation in slaveholding
between wealthy and less wealthy practitioners. Bakers, carpenters,
painters, potters, and soap and candle makers were in this category.[48]
In these trades masters of modest means could profit from slaveholding
if demand for their product or service was high and inelastic. Bread
comes readily to mind as such a product, and in fact 54 percent of the
bakers on the 1813 tax rolls owned slaves. This proportion is nearly
half again as large as the 38 percent average for all crafts. Slaveholding
bakers ranged in wealth from three who had total assessable wealth
under $250 to three well-off "biscuit bakers," that is, makers of ships'
bread. Soap and candle makers, manufacturing minor household staples,
also tended to hold slaves fairly commonly.

The construction trades, however, had fewer slaveholders than the
crafts as a whole. Carpenters, painters, and bricklayers, relying on out-
door construction work, were idled in the winter and could lose work
days to foul weather throughout the year. Moreover, demand for their
services could fluctuate dramatically with the changing fortunes of Baltimore generally. Maintaining slaves might be only sporadically and
unpredictably profitable for them; slaveholders were rare in these trades
even among the wealthiest practitioners.[49]

Thus, in the construction sector manufacturers of producer goods
(brick makers, stonecutters, and nail makers) owned slave labor power
more often than did makers of finished goods (carpenters, bricklayers,
painters). This pattern also appeared in the leather trades, where tanners and curriers were nearly twice as likely to be slaveholders as boot
makers, cordwainers, or glovers.[50] Though there were no iron makers
operating within the city limits of Baltimore by 1813, those in the environs were much more oriented toward slave labor than the blacksmiths

and foundries they supplied.[51] Larger concerns could more generally ensure profitable uses for slaves than could smaller counterparts. If it can be granted that overall taxable wealth predicted scale of operation, then most tanners had bigger operations than most cordwainers, most brick makers than most bricklayers, and most iron makers than most blacksmiths. In each case the supplier had more opportunities to divide labor, assign some tasks to slaves, keep them fully employed, and reap profits.

Also, makers of producer goods often found themselves locked into lengthy production cycles, with little short-term flexibility to reduce production levels and work complement in response to demand shifts. Iron makers sought to keep their furnaces in blast for as long as iron ore, limestone, and charcoal could be hauled to the furnace to keep the process going, generally somewhere between five months and a full year. Tanners might need two years or more to transform raw animal hides into usable leather. Even if the market for iron or tanned hides turned bad, the producer had little choice but to see a production run through and make the best of things. Free labor could then be added to a slave or servant base in good times and dismissed when business slowed. Surviving business records are too scanty to indicate conclusively the extent to which large-scale entrepreneurs employed such strategies, but the link between slaveholding and large-scale operation is suggestive.

Finally, slaves often performed work that white laborers avoided because of its noxiousness or social stigma, or both. Slaves thus toiled as servants, chimney sweeps, and washerwomen. But manufacturing work could also acquire a low status that channeled slaves in and free whites out. Thus, tobacco manufacturing, like the working of the tobacco crop in the Chesapeake, relied heavily on slaves. Eleven of twelve tobacco, snuff, or cigar manufacturers in Baltimore owned slaves, ranging from three men in the lowest quintile of wealth to Baltimore's richest businesswoman, Jeanne de Volunbrunn, whose twenty-two slaves made the cigars she sold.[52]

Finally, as a major port city, Baltimore was home to large numbers of seamen, whose ranks included enslaved sailors, often owned by ship captains. In wartime, privateers sometimes had slave crewmen, as evidenced by lawsuits over the ownership of prize shares garnered by enslaved sailors. So black workers percolated into virtually all the city's laboring ranks. To be sure, many slaves cooked food, kept house, or cared for their masters' horses. But many others worked for and with large and small producers, who sought efficient laborers who would generate high-quality, high-volume output.

Finding positive incentives to ensure steady production preoccupied urban masters and those who hired their slaves. Reliance on the negative incentive of physical coercion, however brutally effective it might be on the plantation, carried far more risks in the forge or in the protofactory. Beaten craft slaves could sabotage much more valuable property than vengeful field hands could, and in any case it was more difficult to employ the whip or the fist to exact skilled labor. Accordingly, to squeeze more work from their slaves, city slaveholders appealed to blacks' interests more than to their fears. Slaves might be allowed to choose a master to whom to be hired; once at work, they might be able to earn cash for working overtime or surpassing output quotas. The ultimate incentive would be the opportunity to liberate oneself through self-purchase, or perhaps a manumission granted in return for faithful service. Here lay openings that blacks would exploit to gain autonomy.

In Baltimore the number of gradual manumissions rose dramatically following the Revolutionary War in tandem with the vigorous expansion of slavery. As early as the 1790s, many enslaved craft workers were entitled to freedom by a deed of manumission taking effect after service for a term of years. While serving out their time, these term slaves could be bought and sold, and in fact a quarter to a third of slave sales advertisements and bills of sale in Baltimore concerned men and women promised liberty in the future.[53]

Urban craftsmen and manufacturers were attracted by the cost of term slaves, typically one-third to one-half less than the cost of slaves for life. Such discounts often made purchasing a term slave less costly than annual hiring or owning slaves for life. An employer prepared to resell term slaves within a year or so could actually obtain labor at no cost other than food, shelter, and the opportunity costs of capital for the period of ownership.[54] The average savings available to the purchaser of term slave labor are difficult to isolate because many other variables influenced slave prices besides term of ownership, such as age or physical condition, skills possessed, and reputation as a good worker or a runaway. But examination of a large volume of slave sales in Baltimore indicates that term slaves generally could be bought for 30 to 50 percent less than slaves for life of comparable age, sex, and vigor. Put concretely, a normally healthy young adult male slave for life sold for $300 to $375 in Baltimore about 1810; a comparable slave with a term of six to ten years to serve would cost from $150 to $250, while an annual hire might run $45 to $60. The discount for female term slaves was slightly greater than for males, although not dramatically so.[55] Under these circumstances gradual manumission lowered the cost barriers and the risks associated with owning human chattels and helped account for the spread of slavery among urbanites of relatively modest wealth.

Manufacturers and craft masters could also seek bound labor for limited terms from apprentices, indentured servants, or German redemptioners. These institutions embraced both white and free black youths and may have served as models for structuring gradual manumission. The migration of German servants fell drastically from the 1790s onward because of the turmoil of the Napoleonic Wars in Europe, but craft and orphan apprenticeship flourished. About eighteen hundred male apprentices were learning their trades at any one time in early-nineteenth-century Baltimore, a number approaching that of the male slave population. They composed an important source of labor in their own right, and their availability for any given trade affected participation of African American workers in that occupation.[56]

Juxtaposing the occupational concentrations of apprentices with those of slavery in the crafts illuminates entrepreneurs' labor strategies and the work preferences of whites and free blacks.[57] In many trades the relative costs and potential gains of purchasing bound adult laborers dictated a strong preference for slavery. In other work the all but free acquisition and low maintenance costs of bound children gave apprentices a major competitive advantage.[58]

In shipyards virtually no boys served as apprentice ship carpenters or joiners, but sail makers had more apprentices than the average, across craft occupations.[59] The shipbuilders, who could afford slaves, used them, while the less wealthy sail makers took on apprentices. Brick makers, bakers, and soap and candle makers, who commonly held slaves, employed relatively few apprentices.[60] In the metalworking trades high proportions of masters had apprentices. Ninety boys who were bound out in the years sampled between 1800 and 1820 served eighty-one different blacksmiths, suggesting that the craft was still characterized by small, independent operators, teaching the secrets of their trade to one boy at a time. A blacksmith apparently could afford to keep and board an apprentice but did not find it profitable to purchase a slave.

In still other situations masters reached out for bound labor of all kinds. William Camp, a cabinetmaker, appeared in the 1810 census as head of a twenty-six-person household that included two white boys, ages ten to fifteen, eleven white men, ages sixteen to twenty-five, and two slaves. Camp had a dozen or more apprentices under his direction at a time, and he also continued to acquire slaves; the 1813 tax lists showed him with four slaves, including two adult men, and in 1815 Camp purchased Ashberry, a twenty-two-year old man who had five years to serve before his delayed manumission went into effect.[61] Other leading cabinetmakers, as well as chair makers, hatters, tanners, and cordwainers, commingled apprentices and slaves in large operations.[62] These employers were segmenting labor, as evidenced by indentures limiting instructional obligations to certain aspects of a trade. Joseph Cox, a hatter, promised to teach one apprentice "the pulling and cutting branch" of his trade, while another was to learn "the finishing branch." Richard K. Heath, tanner and currier, taught his apprentices tanning or currying, but not both. James Sloan taught some apprentice cordwainers only to make uppers or heels; only a few learned all branches of the trade.[63] All three men owned male slaves of working age.

Apprenticeship could also be a way station from slavery to freedom, defining the framework of control for a prospectively freed slave. Thus, Juliet, age seventeen, bound herself to Thomas Graham for eleven years "in consideration of [his] having paid two hundred dollars for her freedom." Graham secured an unusually long term of service for his investment, while Juliet derived the intangible but considerable benefit of becoming at once a legally free person, lessening the danger of being sold, should Graham die before the expiration of her term.[64] Indentures could bind a series of family members to the same master, as part of the emancipation process. In 1810 Charles Brown, a freedman who had served as an indentured servant with Sarah Bennet to earn freedom for his wife, Lucy, bound out two daughters, born while Lucy was still a slave, to serve Bennet until their sixteenth birthdays. Brown surrendered control of his children but gained their immediate legal freedom.[65] An indenture could also provide an alternative to debtor's prison: Jacques Zacharie bound himself to Charles Pressoir for six years in 1805, with the agreement that on payment of $450 Pressoir would "manumit" Zacharie.[66] In each of these examples a master and a dependent person agreed to blur the line dividing slavery and freedom by entering into a contract for labor service according to which the weaker party surrendered practical control over his or her life for a time as a way of escaping permanent dependence.

Masters could also agree among themselves to indenture slaves, as a form of long-term hire. Thus, John Duret bound out Joseph Baptist for six years to Joseph Leclair, a hairdresser, to learn Leclair's trade and to receive nominal freedom dues of six dollars at the expiration of his indenture. But Duret also specified that Baptist was "to be returned to me" at that time. Duret received no payment from Leclair; presumably, he bound out Baptist to enhance his long-term value by having him trained in a skilled occupation, with no maintenance costs while Baptist learned. An indenture could also be a disguised slave sale: Stephen Comte, an emigrant from Saint Domingue, could not legally sell slaves he had recently brought with him into the state. But he could indenture forty-year-old Negro Ann to Peter Rescaniere, a slaveholding baker, for twenty-five years, in return for two hundred dollars.[67]

More commonly, and more humanely, indentures promised skill training and education to term slaves. When Noah Richardson indentured his grandson, John, a twelve-year-old scheduled to become free at twenty-three, he ensured that John Mowbray would not only teach young John coopering but would also provide him with twelve months of schooling and freedom dues.[68] Elizabeth Edwards, a white woman who inherited slaves in 1812, manumitted all of them prospectively, and arranged for George, age fourteen, as well as sixteen-year-old John and eighteen-year-old Morris, to be bound out to blacksmiths or shoemakers. As a female head of household, Edwards may have felt uncomfortable managing three nearly grown young men; although she sent them from her home, there is no indication that she bound out or sold female slaves whose manumissions she had also put in train. Edwards used apprenticeship to find masters preferable to herself for controlling three teenage boys.[69]

Nevertheless, in Baltimore apprenticeship remained a nearly all-white institution, its counterpart for blacks being slavery for a specified term of years pending a promised manumission. A substantial proportion of Baltimore's free blacks had been born as slaves and had gained their freedom as young or middle-aged adults. Very few recorded manumissions freed a male slave during his most productive years, between the ages of fourteen and thirty; accordingly, this age cohort of free black men was disproportionately small. The infrequency of free black bindings by Baltimore masters who otherwise avidly pursued bound labor contrasts sharply with the practice of rural farmers and craftsmen elsewhere in Maryland.

From the Eastern Shore, where free blacks were numerous, both whites and blacks migrated to Baltimore in search of greater economic opportunity.[70] Large numbers of planters needing a reserve supply of agricultural workers for wheat and fruit harvests turned to binding free black boys as apprentice farmers, and girls as house servants, in tandem with reducing numbers of slaves owned. In Talbot County a quarter of all indentures bound free blacks, over four times the proportion in Baltimore; even in slavery-oriented Prince George's County, one-fifth of the indentures were of free blacks.[71]

Where medium-term binding of children worked to a master's advantage, the power of the law was invoked to retain laborers who might otherwise leave the county and who would be difficult to replace, given the lack of migration to Maryland's farm country.[72] In dynamically growing Baltimore, masters had little or no need to risk a commitment to free blacks as craft apprentices or as house servants, particularly when a stronger hold on such persons as term slaves was readily available. The gradual accretion of law permitting the binding of ever-larger classes of free black youth had little impact on the number of free black apprentices in Baltimore, further confirming the idea that lack of demand for their services, under the terms of apprenticeship, was at least as important as a putative lack of supply of boys available to be indentured.[73]

But an economic rationale cannot fully explain why craftsmen, willing to use black slaves serving a term of years, would hesitate over black apprentices. The purchase price of an adolescent male term slave, at two hundred dollars or more, doubled or tripled the outlays for an apprentice's freedom dues and education, which might amount to fifty to one hundred dollars, and a person in either status would need to be fed, clothed, and housed. Thus, masters expended more to work with term slaves than with black or white apprentices. If free blacks were readily available to perform casual labor in the crafts and manufacturing, why did reliance on term slavery persist? Alternatively, what set of attitudes dictated the employment of white and black free and bound labor, with only the category of black apprentices being ruled out?

One possibility is that white craft workers objected to the presence of free blacks with status equal to them. In fact, whites and blacks worked together in virtually all the crafts and industries of Baltimore, and very little evidence, at least prior to 1830, suggests that whites found the presence of black workers demeaning, per se. But whites did expect and demand to be placed in a legally and socially superior status relative to all blacks, slave or free.

Hence, rapid growth in the number of free blacks in Maryland was accompanied by legislation registering their subordinate status. Free people of color were barred from voting or holding elective office at the very end of the eighteenth century, as pressure was mounting to broaden the franchise for white men.[74] In the same vein, revamped court procedures permitted slaves and free people of color to give evidence against each other, but not against whites, narrowing the social distance between free and enslaved blacks while increasing it between black and white freemen.[75] The Maryland penitentiary routinely segregated white and black prisoners, and even barred free blacks from serving there at one point.[76] And by 1818 the state's apprenticeship laws required higher educational benefits for white than for black children.

Though jealously protected, white racial superiority was not threatened by the mere presence of blacks in the workplace, and black apprentices posed no problem in largely segregated work settings, such as barbershops or naileries. But as craft apprentices, entitled to the same benefits and status as white coworkers, free blacks were socially unacceptable. The rapid spread of the use of term slaves in Baltimore's workshops after 1790 may be partly cause and partly consequence of white concerns about status as measured by blacks' possession of the attributes of freemen.

One indicator of this sentiment is that masters who indentured large numbers of apprentices bound disproportionately fewer free blacks than those who worked with a single apprentice. The absence of black apprentices in the protofactories of men like William Camp and Joseph Cox, who bound a dozen or more apprentices at a time and owned several slaves, is suggestive. Had revulsion toward free blacks originated solely with masters, there would be no reason to expect that masters binding many apprentices would enter into a different proportion of free black indentures than those binding one boy at a time.[77] Although few masters bound black children to do craft work in Baltimore, in rural counties the occasional black boy bound to a shoemaker or a carpenter provided needed labor without infringing social codes that demanded black subordination, because he in all likelihood worked alone.[78]

Changes in the apprenticeship laws may also have had differential impact in Baltimore and rural Maryland. The revised law of 1818, which allowed the binding of any free black child not "at service or learning a trade, or employed in the service of their parents" facilitated court-directed bindings of free black children in rural counties.[79] In Baltimore, orphans' court judges took advantage of the new authority to waive the requirement that free black apprentices be taught to read and write, so long as the apprentices' freedom dues were then increased. By commuting masters' education obligations, the 1818 law may have made free black apprentices more attractive to Baltimore masters, increasing their bindings and reducing the number of free black children who might become public charges. But this relaxation of benefits owed to free blacks did little to alter their underrepresentation in apprenticeship: in the 1820s free blacks still made up only 9 percent of indentured children, a 3 percent increase over the preceding decade but less than half of the free black population share of the city, which reached nearly one-fifth by 1830.

Still another possibility is that the scarcity of free black craft apprentices reflected an aversion on the part of black parents to placing

by wage work speaks less to bound labor's supposed inflexibility than it does to long-term increases in the supply of laborers. Where individual circumstances still favored industrial slavery, it survived in Baltimore into the 1820s and 1830s, not merely in dying local industries like iron making, but in endeavors marked by new technology and investment, such as chemical production.

2

INDUSTRIAL SLAVERY IN BALTIMORE

Chemical manufacturing began in Maryland around 1810, with local producers of alum, pigments, and dyes springing up to supply Baltimore's first cotton and woolen mills. When, in the mid-1820s, the firm of J.K. McKim and Sons decided to enter the chemical business, they erected a new factory and purchased slaves as operatives. The records of the McKim-led Maryland Chemical Works provide a rare, in-depth portrait of the operations of industrial slavery in Baltimore and of the importance of prospective manumission in making and keeping slave workers productive.

More than twenty years ago, Robert S. Starobin in his pathbreaking *Industrial Slavery in the Old South* contended that slaveholding industrialists were able "to create a fairly stable work force by means of sophisticated incentives"; he characterized industrial slavery as a largely successful institution, at least on its own exploitative terms.[1] Starobin's massive array of evidence challenged earlier dismissals of industrial slavery that had called it an exotic, aberrant, or insignificant variation of slavery as an institution of agricultural labor. That view had been perhaps best expounded by Richard C. Wade, who argued that diffusion and fragmentation of the master's exclusive control of the slave in urban settings rendered urban and, by implication, much industrial slavery, unsuccessful.[2] Likewise thrown into doubt by Starobin's work was the view that enterprises reliant on slave labor must necessarily be inhospitable to technological innovation.

Starobin placed his findings in time by noting that "campaigns for industry became most intense when southerners felt least secure within the Union" and singled out the years from the late 1820s to the early 1830s, and the late 1840s and 1850s, as peak times in the development of industrial slavery.[3] Claudia Dale Goldin's analysis of the late antebellum decline in urban slavery dovetailed neatly with Starobin's chronology, as she advanced the view that urban entrepreneurs moved away from slavery when high demand for slaves in the agricultural South-

Maryland by Dennis Griffith, 1794, depicting the nineteen counties of Maryland as they existed during the late eighteenth and early nineteenth centuries. Engraved by J. Thackara and J. Vallance, Philadelphia, published 1795. Maryland Historical Society

west drove up the price of slaves beyond their worth as urban workers in the mid-1830s and again in the 1850s.[4] Subsequently, however, Fred Bateman and Thomas Weiss have shown that industrial slavery remained highly profitable even in the late antebellum years when slave prices were highest and that southerners did, in fact, fail to take optimal advantage of entrepreneurial opportunities in industry. They concluded that the slaveholders' exceptional aversion to risk best explained the South's failure to industrialize.[5] Charles B. Dew indicates the force of risk aversion by suggesting the incompatibility between slave labor and technological innovation. In a recent article on iron making, Dew argued that "slave labor, once it was trained and functioning in the traditional ways of making iron, exerted a powerful, conservative influence on the technology of the southern iron industry" because allocating the labor of skilled slaves by using task systems froze in place unchanging production quotas and negated potential gains in productivity that might have resulted from changes in iron production technology.[6]

These analyses return to the question of whether slavery and slaveholding—at least in the industrial sphere—were economically irrational. This case study looks at a chemical plant in the late 1820s, the first of Starobin's boom periods but near the end of slavery's prominence in Baltimore. In that decade the distance between northern and southern industrial activity had not yet become unbridgeable. In some industrial sectors, such as cloth manufactures, the South already lagged far behind. But in other realms, such as chemical manufacturing, American industrialization, both North and South, had barely begun.

The Maryland Chemical Works was a Baltimore firm that manufactured industrial chemicals, pigments, and medicines with a mixed slave and free work force between 1825 and 1835. Situated at a regional transportation and marketing hub and blessed with strong capital backing and access to credit, the company did not fall afoul of the financial and marketing problems that plagued many startup industries in the South. Because such extraneous factors were not present to affect the composition of the workforce, it is possible to assess the pros and cons of industrial slavery at the Maryland Chemical Works without encountering issues unrelated to the shop floor. Moreover, since both advanced technology and slave workers were present, some observations can be made on the utility of Dew's comments on the potential pitfalls of such enterprises.

Labor cost and labor productivity were the most important elements in shaping the firm's employment strategies toward slaves. In addition, the slaves gained leverage from the firm's reliance on them, and they sought greater compensation and more autonomy, which required frequent adjustments and responses by management. Ultimately, the unanticipated need to negotiate with their own chattels exacted a business cost in time and trouble and, perhaps more critically, a psychic cost that led the owners to limit their commitment to industrial slavery, an outcome that helps to explain both the South's general slowness to industrialize in the early nineteenth century and Baltimore's virtual abandonment of slavery in its industries.

The business arrangements that supported the Maryland Chemical Works began in 1825 when John K. McKim, Jr., a Baltimore merchant, launched his sons, David and Richard McKim, in business by funding their joint enterprise with Howard Sims, a chemical manufacturer. Sims borrowed money from McKim to expand his plant and in return entered into a partnership with David and Richard McKim "in the art or business of manufacturing and vending Chemicals, Medicines, Paints and various articles necessary to the useful arts."[7] David McKim led the Maryland Chemical Works for the next eight years, during which time slaves played a key role in producing the factory's prize-winning industrial chemicals.[8] The interplay between McKim's entrepreneurial goal to maintain a mixed slave and free work force and the varied objectives of the slave hands illuminates with rare clarity the transmutation and adaptation of slavery at its geographic, social, and economic margin.[9]

During 1826 and 1827 David McKim bought fifteen adult male slaves for the company.[10] Concomitantly, he expanded the plant dramatically, installing a twenty-four-horsepower steam engine; adding new buildings, including a dwelling for the slaves; and walling in the entire plant complex.[11] Then, in anticipation of the slave hiring season at the beginning of 1828, McKim announced to slave owners, and perhaps to slaves allowd to hire their own time, that he "Wanted on hire by the year TEN or FIFTEEN healthful able bodied NEGRO MEN, from 18 to 35 years of age. To orderly and well recommended men liberal wages will be given."[12] Within weeks thirteen newly hired slaves were at work, swelling slave numbers to twenty-eight, two-fifths of all manufacturing hands at the chemical works.[13] Over the next five years, David McKim tested the feasibility of slave labor in a factory setting, carefully monitoring his labor costs and production levels and gradually reshaping his workforce accordingly. In a curiously mixed outcome, McKim diminished the proportion of slaves among his workers but relied on those who remained to provide the skill and continuity needed for stable production of chemicals. McKim's careful attention to the composition of the workforce reveals the long-range utility of industrial slave labor in the volatile economy of early-nineteenth-century America. Uncertain demand for products made total reliance on a slave workforce in large enterprises an unsound economic strategy because employment levels often had to be adjusted to changing markets. However, high turnover among white wage workers disrupted production and encouraged employers to retain slave workers.

The firm manufactured approximately thirty medicines, pigments, dyes, and industrial chemicals, but it was best known for its alum, used by cloth manufacturers as a mordant to set dyes in cloth.[14] These goods were marketed nationally through commission merchants in major ports and were also sold directly to local manufacturers, painters, and druggists.[15] As a corporation, the Maryland Chemical Works barely broke even during the period from 1827 to 1833, which is covered by the surviving records, but large profits accrued to the McKims as merchants. Operating the family firm of J.K. McKim and Sons, they not only garnered commissions on goods sold to or on behalf of the firm but also earned interest on working capital advanced to the firm.[16]

The manufacture of chemicals began with workers separating metallic ore from rock in which it was embedded by calcining, crushing, grinding, and sifting. The ore was purified by cooking or saturating it repeatedly in chemical baths to draw off unwanted elements. More cooking or steeping then induced reactions with desirable elements to make up the final product, generally a metal sulfate or oxide. Total processing time varied enormously: some pigments could be made in a few days, but the manufacture of alum could take six months or more of steady labor.[17] Slaves worked in all the production routines of the factory but were especially prominent in alum making.

The Maryland Chemical Works produced large volumes of very pure alum, using a lengthy sequence of operations that transformed reddish clay into snowy white alum crystals.[18] Workers first shoveled the clay into a long, low furnace, where it was roasted continuously for several days and nights in order to increase its porosity and oxidize commingled iron compounds. After cooling, the clay was transferred to lead-lined cisterns and there dissolved in a heated sulfuric acid bath, agitated almost constantly by workers to speed up the decomposition of the clay.[19]

The acid-sodden clay was then removed to a covered shed to dry, evaporation being helped along by repeated rakings.[20] After that it was hauled to lixiviate in a water-filled cistern in order to extract soluble alum particles. Periodically the resulting mother liquor was drawn off to a holding tank while workers cleaned out the exhausted clay and added a fresh batch. Then the mother liquor would be pumped back into the refilled cistern. Three or four such "washings" brought the mother liquor to its alum-absorbing capacity.

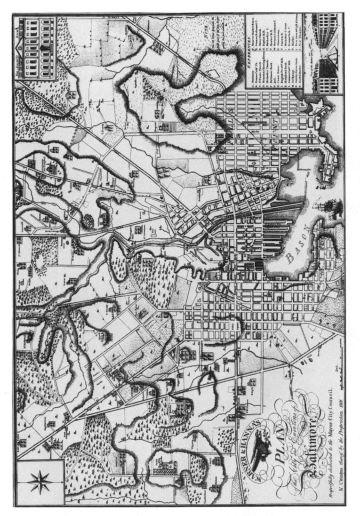

Baltimore as a city of about thirty thousand people, c. 1801. The three original settlements—Fell's Point to the east, Old Town to the north, and Baltimore Town to the west and southwest—have already grown together. Warner and Hanna's Plan of the City and Environs of Baltimore, 1801. Engraved by Francis Shallus, Philadelphia. Maryland Historical Society

This super-charged liquid was next evaporated for seven or eight days in a low-temperature furnace and gradually cooked down to a viscous state. When the liquor was sufficiently syrupy, workers sluiced it into yet another container and fluxed or precipitated it into alum flour by bringing it into contact with potassium chloride, in the form of soap-boiler's waste, with more stirring to reduce chemical reaction time.[21] The alum flour was reliquified in a steam-filled cistern and transferred to conical casks to recrystallize. After four to five days, workers loosened the hoops of the "cone" and removed the leaded staves, revealing a tapering column of crusted alum with a core of partially crystallized liquor. Ten days to two weeks of air drying ensued, to foster further crystallization; workmen then pierced the sides of the cone with axes to allow the remaining liquor to flow out.[22] The now finished alum was milled, sieved, and packed in casks or boxes, ready for sale. Throughout the six-to-eight-month process, laborers stoked furnaces, agitated alum broth, raked up drying alum heaps, and shoveled alum from furnace to cistern and back again, day and night, seven days a week.

David McKim thus needed steady labor over many months to produce his factory's top-selling chemical, and in fact the firm operated year round, obviating one potential disadvantage of industrial slave labor in the early nineteenth century. McKim had no reason to fear that capital invested in slaves would be underutilized, because there was little slack time during which slaves might have been unproductive. Only heavy capital expenditures could ensure such full-time operations: without the steam engine, the covered factory buildings, and the large stockpiles of raw materials kept on hand, the Maryland Chemical Works might well have been forced to shut down from time to time, in which case an investment in slaves would have become less attractive.[23] In this regard investment in advanced factory technology and production setting may have been necessary in order to make slave labor profitable.

Another potential economic objection to industrial slave labor, the risk of capital loss through accidental death or injury in the workplace, clearly received little weight in David McKim's plans. Though the plant was noxious, it was not especially dangerous. Slaves might not thrive in the heat, dust, and fumes they worked with, but they faced a low level of risk in comparison to the perils of mining, railroad construction, and canal building. These enterprises, despite the constant danger of explosions and cave-ins, relied heavily on hired slaves in the upper South of the 1820s.[24] In short, McKim probably felt no qualms on this score and expected to persuade owners to hire slaves to him, as he was in fact able to do.[25]

Unrelenting physical labor in the heat of the furnaces may have been regarded as an urban equivalent of plantation field labor. Blacks were thought to have greater tolerance for working in heat, and perhaps in McKim's view that putative trait recommended slaves for the chemical works.[26]

A need for year-round labor is one component of a production system reliant on slaves; a significant market demand for slave-made goods is also necessary in order to provide a return on the investment in owning and maintaining a workforce. Here, too, circumstances seemed favorable in the late 1820s: Baltimore's expanding industrial base included mills turning out cloth, paper, gunpowder, glass, soap, starch, and paints, all of which needed industrial chemicals to make their goods.[27] In addition McKim could ship goods cheaply from Baltimore's wharves to other seaboard cities.

But perhaps the biggest incentive for acquiring slaves came from the turnover of free laborers, which routinely exceeded 100 percent per year. Although some turnover of unskilled laborers was expected and even welcomed, hiring two or three workers per year per job must have impeded production, a problem that could be addressed by obtaining bound labor.[28] For all these reasons, then, David McKim committed the firm extensively to slave labor from 1826 through 1828. The firm bought slaves, contracted with owners for the hire of others, and dealt directly with a few slaves who hired their own time.[29]

Compensation for both free workers and slaves was based principally on the number of hours they worked; relatively few jobs had pay pegged to units of production. Free workers typically earned $.75 per day or $4.50 per six-day week, with overtime paid at the same rate. Slaves also worked a six-day week but were paid money only for overtime work, which was called "extras" and usually was expressed and paid for as units of time rather than of production. Because of the nature of most work in the chemical plant, few jobs easily resolved themselves into tasks with measurable output. Workers in furnaces or foundries might be paid by the weight of iron produced in a day or the number of stove plates cast, but a chemical worker could hardly be paid by the amount of alum made, when the process took months and many different workers to complete.[30] Given the need for continuous monitoring of the cooking, bathing, and drying of chemicals, most extras were earned by Sunday or nighttime tending of furnaces, cisterns, and vats.

The Maryland Chemical Works' pay book indicates that about fifteen slaves worked at the chemical plant on average; altogether forty-six slaves appear by name. As a method of reducing worker turnover, slave labor unquestionably succeeded: while two-thirds of the wage

TABLE 5

Free and Slave Workers: Employment Duration at the Maryland Chemical Works

Workers' Length of Employment	Free		Slave	
	N	%	N	%
1 Week or less	89	(25)	0	(0)
2-4 Weeks	71	(20)	3	(7)
5-12 Weeks	77	(21)	3	(7)
13-26 Weeks	37	(10)	6	(13)
6 Months to 1 year	38	(10)	8	(17)
1-2 Years	32	(9)	13	(28)
2-3 Years	10	(3)	3	(7)
3 Years or more	9	(2)	10	(22)
Total	363		46	

NOTE: Percentages are rounded and may not add to 100.

Table 5 characterizes employment duration of wage and slave workers who appeared in the Maryland Chemical Works Pay Book from September 15, 1827, to April 28, 1832. Slave totals do not include unnamed "hands" whose owners received payment for their occasional services. Free workers' totals do not include salaried plant managers, such as Howard Sims or his successors.

workers stayed less than three months and six-sevenths worked less than a year, a majority of the slaves spent a full year or more at the works. The slaves made up only one-ninth of all workers at the factory but performed about one-third of all labor. To the extent that longer service rendered workers more valuable, the importance of the slaves was heightened: 40 percent of the workmen whose experience exceeded two years and 53 percent of those who labored three years or more were slaves, as shown in table 5.

But these data conceal an uneven pattern of slave usage by the McKims: the plant had as many as thirty and as few as seven slaves on the books at different times. As a proportion of the total workforce, slaves declined from a high of 42 percent in 1827 to 14 percent in 1831. Despite the slaves' contribution to reducing turnover, the firm relied less on slave labor and more on free workers over time. The number of slaves declined steadily from twenty-eight to eight between 1828 and 1831 and then leveled off for the last year and a half of the records. In comparison, the number of free workers fluctuated much

TABLE 6

Number of Slaves and Free Workers at the Maryland Chemical Works				
Date	Free Workers	Slaves	Total	% Slaves
Sept. 1827	28	20	48	42
Jan. 1828	42	28	70	40
Jul. 1828	41	21	62	34
Jan. 1829	43	17	60	28
July 1829	40	14	54	26
Jan. 1830	36	14	50	28
July 1830	37	13	50	26
Jan. 1831	34	8	42	19
July 1831	42	7	49	14
Jan. 1832	32	7	39	18
Apr. 1832	32	7	39	18

less, being usually no more than five workers over or under an average figure of thirty-seven or thirty-eight.[31] A gradual but steady reduction in the overall factory workforce was thus effected principally by lessening the number of slaves.

David McKim chose to reduce but not to eliminate slave labor, and he did so by decreasing the number of slaves hired by the factory.[32] Thirteen of the twenty-eight slaves employed in January of 1828, or 46 percent, were hired, but all of the seven or eight at the plant in 1831 and 1832 were owned.[33] McKim's continued reliance on owned slaves and his declining use of annually hired slaves argues that he sought to use slave labor not as cheap, undifferentiated labor but as increasingly skilled and experienced workers. The switch away from hired slave labor further underlines that, unlike many southern industries reliant on slave labor, the Maryland Chemical Works was not tightly constrained by lack of capital. Had McKim been financially pressed, he might have sold slaves to get cash and then met subsequent needs for slave labor through increased hiring.

One could speculate that McKim chose to hold on to his slaves for reasons having nothing to do with their work output or skills, perhaps because a downturn in slave prices prevented him from recouping his investment. But prices for adult male slaves sold in Baltimore in the late 1820s and early 1830s were slightly higher than what McKim's slaves had cost. He had paid an average of $295 in 1826 and 1827 for male slaves varying in age from seventeen to twenty-nine; average Baltimore prices for comparable slaves were $320 for the period 1828 through 1831.[34]

Further evidence that McKim based his decision whether to retain slaves on their contributions in the workplace arises from slave records in the pay book, which show that, of slaves owned by the factory, McKim kept his best workers and sold the others.[35] His chief evaluation criteria were slave absenteeism and willingness to perform extras.

One baseline against which to measure slaves was the absence rate of free white workers, which amounted to just under one-tenth of all work days.[36] Perhaps to McKim's surprise, the slaves missed work 9.4 percent of the time, virtually the same rate as that of the free laborers, 9.6 percent.[37] To the extent that McKim's decision to shift to slave labor in 1827 reflected dissatisfaction with wage laborer turnover and absences, the fact that slave laborers appeared for work no more frequently than freemen may have made McKim reconsider the size of his slave force. Nonetheless, although McKim could discharge unsatisfactory workers, slave or free, the only good workers he could be assured of keeping were those he owned.[38]

A second look at the absentee data shows that slaves missed slightly more than half of their lost work days because of illnesses lasting a week or more. But one- or two-day absences also occurred with what must have been an irritating frequency for David McKim, accounting for over 4 percent of their scheduled work days.[39] McKim hired substitutes for workers recuperating from extended periods of illness or from accidents; obtaining replacements for short stints was no doubt more difficult and probably disrupted production disproportionately more than hiring longer-term replacements.[40]

In fact, slaves who frequently missed work for a short term did not stay long at the factory. Among slaves employed for less than eighteen months, 63 percent exhibited above-average short-term absenteeism compared to 21 percent of slaves who labored there for more than eighteen months. Free workers showed a comparable pattern. Of thirty who stayed more than eighteen months, twenty-four or 80 percent missed work less often than the median for their group.[41]

Two of three long-staying slaves with above-average absence rates, William Adams and Perry Tilghman, had one extended illness each but were otherwise steady workers.[42] More positively, both Tilghman and Adams worked extras frequently, which McKim also valued highly. Tilghman earned cash by working extras in 86 percent of the weeks

Business card of the Maryland Chemical Works, 1828. The card is addressed to Samuel Thomas, the firm's Philadelphia agent. From the ephemera collection of the Maryland Historical Society

when he was healthy. Adams earned extras in 90 percent of the weeks in which he was not sick, frequently by casting lead.[43]

David McKim consistently evaluated an employee's worth, regardless of race, in terms of steady work with infrequent absences. In fact, a group of about fifteen veteran workers, roughly half slaves, became the core of employees upon whom he relied for stable output. Their efforts were supplemented by thirty to thirty-five casual laborers, whose composition over the years was increasingly white. These laborers typically left after six months or less and were quickly replaced. White and black veterans performed different but complementary roles in keeping production going in this potentially chaotic atmosphere.

Longtime white workers tended to specialize in one production process in the plant and gradually commanded higher wages.[44] Veteran slaves displayed more versatility in tasks they undertook. Of ten slaves who stayed longer than three years at the factory, eight did three or more different jobs; six worked four or more jobs. These men may have functioned as all-purpose trouble-shooters, filling gaps occasioned by frequent departures of white laborers.[45]

The firm's records reveal nothing about McKim's motives for not channeling his veteran slave hands into specialized work routines. Possibly the high volume of white turnover precluded that option. Alternatively, McKim might have felt that specialization paid dividends only when a seasoned worker could lead a crew of men (this may have been what fattened the pay envelopes of the veteran whites); if so, specializing his slaves would have done no good unless McKim could put them in charge of all-slave crews, for clearly no white man would take direction from a slave. The slave crew option, in turn, would not have been likely to appeal to an entrepreneur who was, in general, reducing his commitment to slave labor over time.

This admittedly speculative chain of inferences sketches a potential drag on the efficiency of mixed free and slave labor enterprises: the difficulty of retaining and advancing good workers to more productive and responsible duties without falling afoul of race-based strictures. McKim may have been making the best of an unalterable situation in using his slaves as versatile gap fillers in a mostly free white labor force. It is worth noting that by this strategy, knowingly or not, McKim reduced the risk of experiencing what happened among the ironworkers described by Charles Dew: that slave-dominated workforce was able to limit the pace of production by turning customary task-based output quotas into production ceilings.[46]

In contrast to McKim's treatment of his good hands, James Jacobs's encounter with the Maryland Chemical Works illustrates the dismissal

In this context the notion that a slave could refuse work seems less bizarre. Still, one might ask why McKim could not invoke the threat of physical punishment. How could a slave, subject to the coercion of his master, refuse to work extra time? In fact, Winder and the others might have exercised considerable leverage in this realm.

Alum making required work or oversight twenty-four hours a day for weeks and months at a time. Workers regulated the heat of furnaces; they stirred reducing or lixiviating baths; they raked heaps of alum to speed its drying. Perhaps two or three workers made the rounds of such chores nightly. Each had to be reasonably diligent to keep up the pace of production and avoid ruining batches of chemicals. An idle or disaffected worker could do a great deal of harm in such a setting. From a manager's standpoint, the slaves at the plant must have seemed suited for night work. They were experienced and they knew the business better than most white employees; in fact, in many cases they would be seeing to the same cisterns, vats, and evaporating beds they tended during the day. Retaining wage laborers was difficult even for day work and was probably almost impossible for night work, but the slaves housed at the plant could be made to work at night. They could not be compelled to do good work, however, without hiring a night manager. Even then, there was no guarantee of the night manager's reliability.[56]

If active cooperation of slaves in night work could be enlisted, they could work largely unsupervised, calling the plant manager, who lived at the plant, only when an emergency arose.[57] Faced with the choice of incurring the added cost of hiring a night manager or motivating his slaves to do good work unsupervised, David McKim chose to pay his slaves for extra work, as many other slaveholders did, both industrialists and planters. Presumably, he hoped thereby to engage their interest, at least quasi-voluntarily, in the nighttime operation of the plant.[58] He soon came to rely heavily on slave overwork, prizing those who could be counted on to do such work and being sufficiently aggravated by the likes of Winder or Jacobs to sell them. But by increasing the demands on his slaves, McKim became more dependent on them. Not only could James Winder force a change in his situation by "shirking," but McKim's most reliable slaves could also turn the tables on him, successfully ratcheting up their compensation by demanding higher rates of pay for extras. McKim had purchased slaves in part to render himself immune to the turmoil occasioned by the frequent departures of independent-minded free workers; now he discovered that owning workers transformed but did not eliminate his labor problems. Unable to quit, the slaves could use their value both as a form of capital and as experienced workers to negotiate for improvements in their lot.

Pay for extras was present in the earliest records of the plant, an extra being a unit of time equal to one day.[59] Industrial concerns with mixed slave and free workforces often paid slave overwork at the same rate as basic pay for white wage laborers, but the Maryland Chemical Works rewarded slaves only twenty-five cents for each extra, rather than the seventy-five cents per day paid white workers.[60] McKim valued slaves who worked extras partly because the incremental cost of such labor was very cheap. Slaves worked extras far more often than their white counterparts, which fits and supports this view. The typical slave worked some extra hours in more than 70 percent of his work weeks, whereas for white workers the rate was 20 to 25 percent.

The need to obtain reliable night workers goes far to explain these developments. McKim's use of veteran slaves as all-purpose workers fits hand in glove with a heavy usage of them for night work. As the workers with the broadest familiarity with the plant's production routines, a slave night crew could carry out the needed work with fewer men.

But McKim may have unwittingly started an interactive process that led him away from his planned extensive utilization of slave labor; he imposed a work regime that many of his slaves would not or could not bear, rendering him more dependent on those slaves who cooperated. McKim increased his exploitation of slaves by paying them for extras because the twenty-five cents he paid for an extra day or night's labor was considerably less than the basic daily cost of feeding, clothing, and sheltering a slave.[61] Thus, McKim's practice of keeping slaves who worked many extras and were seldom absent was economically sound.[62]

McKim's unwillingness to pay slave overwork any more than one-third the rates paid free workers may, however, have unwittingly contributed to the gradual elimination of hired slaves from his workforce. The slaves, like McKim, undoubtedly had their own expectations about hired work and would have had no economic reason to relish working in a factory that may have paid far less than other employers for overwork, their one source of cash income. Hired slaves who were unhappy with their work could seek to improve their lot in several ways. They could ask their owner to terminate the hire and place them elsewhere, at once or in the next hiring year; they could engage the owner's pecuniary interest by offering to hire their own time at a higher rate than their present hirer was paying; or they could seek to be discharged by the hirer by absenting themselves from work, malingering, or feigning illness.[63]

McKim's system of overwork incentives thus had several important ramifications. By basing overwork on time, rather than output, he reduced the danger of incentive goals becoming production ceilings through the customary expectations of slave workers, the fate that befell southern iron makers in Charles Dew's view.[64] McKim paid slaves less for overwork than white counterparts. But the lower overwork pay may have intensified some discontented slaves' efforts to leave the plant and may have caused the slave workers to use the incentive system to control the pace of production.

The plant's pay book records several experiences with hired slaves that suggest a malfunctioning incentive system. In 1828 Stephen Dorsey, a hired slave with a good work record in just over a year at the plant, began "hiring his own time" according to a pay book marginal note. The firm no longer provided Dorsey with food, clothing, and lodging and no longer paid Dorsey's master for his labor. Instead, Dorsey began to earn a weekly wage from the firm and paid his master for the right to hire out his time in a separate transaction. Two weeks after this shift of status first appeared in the pay book, Stephen Dorsey had quit after missing seven days out of twelve while hiring his own time. It is tempting to conclude that Dorsey wanted the autonomy of hiring his own time so that he could quit, presumably after skipping work for a few days to give himself time to find a better-paying job.

At least two other slaves, Donald Fender and Moses Murphy, were hired to the plant for a year and compiled exemplary work records but did not return in the ensuing year. Fender in fact worked extras every week in the year but one, which represented the highest rate over a sustained period of all the slaves in the pay book. McKim probably sought to rehire Fender and Murphy, but it may well be that they persuaded their masters to send them elsewhere.[65] An adverse reaction to the unfairness of the extras pay may also have influenced the refusal of James Winder and James Jacobs to work extras.

Further evidence that McKim found himself hampered by his insistence on underpriced extras appears in the pay book starting in 1829. In that year the firm began to pay its slaves $.375 per extra for unusually noxious duties.[66] McKim did not increase the wages of his white employees, so these raises for extra work were not made to match other pay adjustments. Rather, he may have been obliged to acknowledge his dependence on his own slaves by granting an increase in the rate of extra pay.[67] Those earning the new, higher rates were precisely the veteran slaves who been at the works since 1827, whose skill and experience became ever more critical as McKim encountered difficulties with other slave workers.[68]

By 1831 McKim had stabilized the factory workforce at forty to forty-five hands, including a nucleus of seven or eight long-serving slaves and about thirty-five white laborers.[69] Financial conditions continued to improve for the veterans: in the week of January 21, 1832, six slaves began drawing a regular weekly wage of fifty cents, whether or not they worked extras, which continued to be paid at twenty-five cents apiece, over and above the fifty-cent base pay.[70] Inasmuch as slaves continued to work and earn large numbers of extras after this development, the January change was not merely one of accounting routine. Rather, the slaves were now formally receiving some small proportion of the fruits of their labors as a cash wage.[71]

For David McKim an additional three and a half dollars a week to reward or placate seven veteran hands probably represented a prudent investment, a sound move to help protect the health of his sixty-thousand-dollar-a-year chemical business. For the men, fifty cents a week represented a doubling of their weekly cash income.[72] What McKim might easily have seen as a minor concession may have been a significant victory for the men who made his fortune for him. Or McKim may have viewed the need to pay his own slaves as a further complication in the intricate business of making a success out of industrial slavery, while the slaves may have regarded the fifty cents a week as a pittance that underlined their still virtually uncompensated servitude. The whole episode demonstrates how protean slavery could be: experienced, knowledgeable wage laborers, working independently in a prize-winning plant in a new industry, able to influence their compensation, were nonetheless slaves.

Although some of them were slaves for life, McKim had also bought men who were slaves "for a term of years," after which they would be free, as provided for by a manumission by deed or will. Scipio Freeman, who toiled at the Maryland Chemical Works for the full five years recorded in the pay book, was one such man. McKim bought Freeman in January 1827 for two hundred dollars, a low price for a healthy twenty-three-year-old male slave. But, as William Wilmer explained in the bill of sale, he was selling "my negro man Scipio to serve from the first of January 1827 to the first of January 1835, . . . after which he is to be free. . . . this Scipio was born February 4, 1804 . . . and was left by the will of Philip Taylor of Kent County to be free at the age of 31 years."[73]

Freeman missed work only 4 percent of the time, less than half the normal rate, and worked 460 extras, more than any other slave; he worked the night shift about twice a week on average.[74] Then in 1830 Freeman began to earn another dollar or more per week by digging or hauling alum clay at four or six cents a barrow load.[75] Scipio Freeman was trying to give truth to his name: he was buying his way out of slavery.

No record of Freeman's self-purchase survives, but the 1833 city directory identifies a free black laborer named Scipio Freeman living in Federal Hill on Johnson Street, near the Maryland Chemical Works. It is almost surely the case that Freeman's unrelenting toil allowed him, at four cents per load of clay dug and twenty-five cents per extra for each sleepless night among the alum cisterns, to buy his freedom two years or so before his scheduled manumission.[76]

Scipio Freeman overlooked nothing in his drive to amass his purchase price. When, late in 1830, David McKim ceased buying food for the men and instead began paying a free black woman $1.50 per slave per week for boarding, the pay book noted almost immediately that Scipio Freeman was receiving $1.50 directly and "boarding himself." For the remaining nineteen months of the pay book, Freeman took his $1.50 and cut corners, hard as that must have been on a slave rations stipend, to save more money.[77]

Scipio Freeman's market value, as an adult male slave with two years to serve in 1833, would have ranged from $100 to $120.[78] McKim may of course have pegged Freeman's manumission price higher, incorporating a premium for consenting to emancipate Freeman ahead of schedule.[79] If McKim charged no premium, and if Freeman bought his freedom solely from his own resources, Freeman must have saved about a third of all the money he received from the firm, despite boarding himself for the last year and a half of that period.[80] Freeman must have been self-disciplined to have saved so much from endeavors generating less than a dollar a week before 1830 and three to four dollars a week once he began boarding himself and digging clay.

Freeman had to work six days and two extras and dig about thirty loads of clay to earn $3.50 a week, which was $1.00 less than the weekly wage for unskilled free labor. These figures convey why David McKim cooperated with Freeman's efforts at self-purchase. From 1830 to 1832 Freeman worked half again as much as a typical wage laborer, yet he cost McKim about 15 percent less than the laborer's $4.50 a week. Moreover, when McKim sold Freeman his freedom, he probably recouped half or more of his original $200 outlay for the slave. Six years of labor at Freeman's volume might have cost McKim as much as $2,000 in wages to white laborers; his actual costs were about $800 less.[81] Cheap labor could be extracted from a slave in return for the prospect of manumission. But had Freeman done no more than the "lazy" slave for life James Winder did, he would have generated about $1,250 worth of labor in six years, at a cost of about $400 less, an outcome far less favorable to David McKim than the actual result.[82]

McKim must have believed initially that the inducement of cash would spur slaves to work long and hard, since he secured slave labor of all kinds for the plant. But the hired slaves produced less than those owned by McKim, because they missed work more often and worked fewer extras. After four and one-half years, McKim employed only the slaves he owned, and his outstanding producer for the whole period was the soon-to-be-manumitted Scipio Freeman. Freeman may not have been typical, but for David McKim he represented the ideal of the productive slave laborer's response to cash incentives. In order to better understand McKim's incentive system, it may be useful to turn to the companion question of how much slave labor cost the firm.

The journal of the Maryland Chemical Works included among its debit accounts a line item for slave expenses. In 1828 David McKim kept minute records of money spent on slave upkeep, from which the basic maintenance cost for slaves can be reconstructed. McKim spent about eighty-five cents a week per man on food, mainly duplicating the monotonous fare of the plantation: the men ate chiefly bacon and cornmeal, augmented by molasses and coffee. McKim also regularly purchased small amounts of milk, bread, and vegetables. Seasonal variations played their part in the slaves' diet: McKim bought barrels of herring and, in the spring, shad, as bacon substitutes. Less often, generally when a man was sick, he supplied small amounts of sugar, lemons, oranges, pepper, and mustard. Occasional ledger entries record the purchase of a gallon or two of whiskey and a few hands of tobacco.

Early in 1828 McKim distributed clothing and shoes to all the men except those hiring their own time, at a cost of about nineteen dollars per slave.[83] His only other clothing expenditure for the year was to hire Rebecca Demby, a free black, at $1.50 a week to wash the slaves' clothing and blankets.[84] McKim entered in his 1828 books an expense of $477 for construction of the Negro House. Other minor shelter expenses included a few dollars for "straw for the Negro House." Perhaps the men needed to restuff straw mattresses, or possibly the Negro House was strewn with rushes that required periodic freshening.

Miscellaneous expenses included a medical retainer fee of one hundred dollars paid in January to Dr. Winkelman, presumably both for McKim's slaves and to satisfy masters who may have required that medical attention be available before leasing their slaves to a chemical plant.[85] Other fees indicate the need for coercion in a slave society: McKim purchased fetters from a blacksmith and paid a white laborer a reward of $2.625 for retrieving the slave runaway Allan Henson, in September 1828. All told, McKim's direct expenses totaled $2,217.49, for slaves who were present at the plant for a total of 1,175 weeks, or 22.6 work years. Annual direct costs thus equaled $98.12 per slave.

TABLE 8

Annual Cost per Slave at the Maryland Chemical Works, 1829

Type of Cost	Slaves Owned for a Term of Yrs.	Slaves Owned for Life	Hired Slaves
Direct costs	98.12	98.12	98.12
Capital opportunity	12.00	21.00	3.30
Hire costs	—	—	55.00
Depreciation	25.00	14.00	—
Taxes	3.00	3.00	3.00
Runaway costs	—	35.00	50.00
Death costs	—	35.00	—
Annual total	$138.12	$206.12	$209.42
Weeks worked	47.1	47.1	47.1
Cost per week	$2.93	$4.38	$4.45

The explanation that David McKim was simply unaware of the potential cost advantages is not adequate either. His sedulous recording of six-cent expenditures for lemons, the dogged itemization of the exact number of pounds of bacon bought and the per-pound price for each and every order, and the logging of half and quarter extras worked all bespeak the cost-conscious entrepreneur who knew fully what he was spending to procure labor power and cared to save a penny if he could.[93]

The slaves themselves had changed McKim's outlook, by a rash of runaway attempts that must have made it nearly impossible for him to take the serene long view. McKim clearly took no comfort from the marginally lower slave labor costs in a "bad" year like 1829; he could have little confidence of making slavery pay at the rate of ten or twenty cents per week saved after a year in which he had lost at least eight hundred dollars of slave property.

The first escape attempt took place in August 1828, when Allen Henson ran. Henson was recaptured in two days with the aid of a white coworker, George Rea, a plumber, and McKim responded carefully. Henson was not fined for running off, and he continued to earn extras, but McKim ordered locks and fetters, possibly to restrain Henson when he was not working.[94]

In the first week of February 1829 James Winder tried his unsuccessful run; the very next week twenty-year-old Joseph Smith, a slave for life owned by the firm, made the first successful getaway. Then in late March two hired slaves cooperated in a runaway attempt. Nicolas Ford escaped; Hall Brittain, who did not run but assisted Ford, was fired and sent back to his master.[95] Ford had come to the plant to replace Joseph Smith.

Smith had just entered his prime as a worker; David McKim lost at least the $275 he had paid for the then-seventeen-year-old slave in 1826.[96] Nicolas Ford, whose age and condition are not known to us, could easily have cost McKim more, unless the circumstances of the escape forced Ford's owner to absorb the loss.[97] Whether or not McKim had to pay Ford's owner, the escape probably made future hiring more difficult for McKim, because slaveholders would have begun to judge the plant an unsafe place to which to rent their human property.

That possibility took on another dimension when in mid-July 1829 one of McKim's most reliable workers, William Sewell, fell sick. Despite Doctor Winkelman's ministrations, Sewell remained ill for over a week and then died suddenly on July 26, 1829.[98] Coming on the heels of the disturbances of the spring, Sewell's death propelled McKim to try new ways of managing his slaves.

First, McKim loosened his purse strings to diversify the slaves' diet and make life at the factory more bearable. He had already begun to buy sugar, pepper, oranges, lemons, vinegar, and mustard more frequently after the attempted escapes of the winter and spring; after Sewell's death he expanded the provision of food treats. This new-found awareness of the importance of food culminated in 1830 in McKim's decision to board the slaves out, a concession of autonomy that probably mattered more to the men than what they ate, and which may well have originated with the idea of using better rations to buy peace with the slaves.

Second, McKim began to pay time-and-a-half extras in the summer of 1829. More than likely the veteran slaves had a hand in the establishment of this practice, possibly by voicing objection to extra work associated with Sewell's illness and death, possibly by unspoken resistance in the form of poorly done extras.

Finally, in 1829 David McKim committed himself to a permanent reduction in the number of slave workers. In July he sold off Henson and Edward Norris, to be followed in early 1830 by James Winder. Twenty slaves had been at the plant in the spring of 1829, but McKim let the figure drift down to fourteen by the year's end and hired only enough new slaves at the New Year in 1830 to replace departing hires.[99]

McKim, by becoming more selective, hoped to reduce the risks that had cost him so much in 1829.

Thus did the Maryland Chemical Works' uncharacteristically heavy resort to slave labor in a new industry gradually wind down. Some of the black men confined in the plant were willing enough to participate vigorously in McKim's program of exploitation: Scipio Freeman apparently judged the reward of a hastened manumission as the best available alternative. He accepted being underpaid as the price of gaining more rapid entry into a less constrained wage market. Others, like James Jacobs or James Winder, refused to respond to McKim's incentives and chose to take their chances with a new owner. Some hired slaves used their leverage with their masters to avoid extended service at the factory. Still others bid for freedom directly through escape. Collectively, their actions prodded David McKim toward a broader use of free labor and toward the creation of a hybrid, quasi-free labor regime for those slaves who remained.

In the end, McKim had perhaps transformed his own modes of determining what constituted a good labor force. The cost-conscious plant owner of 1826 through 1828, buying and hiring cheap slave labor and grinding maintenance costs down wherever possible, had become more production conscious, winnowing out unproductive workers and providing growing, though still woefully small, compensation to his loyal slave hands by 1831 and 1832. By then slaves made up a far smaller share of the men at the factory than they had five years earlier, but in tandem with a few key white hands, they provided experience that the free workforce largely lacked. The firm no longer depended so much on slave brawn to turn out alum and Prussian blue; it may have depended more on slave brains.

The Maryland Chemical Works suffered from some of the problems discussed in Richard Wade's *Slavery in the Cities*—slave absenteeism and runaways. The chemical company's cost data suggest that slavery was still cheaper than free labor, even in a year like 1829. The company operated during a time of relatively low slave prices, at least compared to those in the 1850s, and in that sense it does not speak to Goldin's slave price–driven model for the decline of urban slavery. But it is worth noting that even a doubling of slave prices would have left slave labor marginally cheaper at the plant, unless accompanied by the extremely high losses of a year like 1829.[100] As for Fred Bateman and Thomas Weiss's risk aversion explanation, the actions of David McKim provide only partial confirmation: McKim certainly sought to minimize his risk of slave losses by his selective retention of slaves who worked hard and

Slaves were key workers in Baltimore's shipyards, as this scene suggests. "Fardy and Auld's shipyard, Federal Hill," attributed to William Hare, 1854. The Peale Museum, Baltimore

who were "safe property," in the argot of the day, but he persisted in using slave labor even after absorbing significant losses. Finally, although the Maryland Chemical Works was not constrained by antiquated technology because of using slave workers, McKim's trials in operating a successful overwork incentive system obliquely support Charles Dew's point about the difficulty of innovating to increase productivity of slave workers.

Of course, no one case can confirm or deny these competing and sometimes overlapping theories. Nonetheless, this case study suggests that the intricacy of managing a mixed slave and free labor work force may have limited or constrained the development of industrial slavery. David McKim devised a cost-effective way to extract labor profitably from workers whose differing legal statuses—free, slave for life, slave for a term of years, or hired slave—gave them different motivations and responses to his wage and cost incentive systems. McKim adjusted the incentive scheme and other aspects of slave compensation and remade his workforce. His final muted use of industrial slaves may well exemplify a more widespread response to the unforeseen difficulties of commingling slavery and industrial capitalism.

As an episode in the history of slavery in Baltimore, the events at the chemical factory occurred at the very end of fifty years of widespread employment of slaves in crafts and industry. David McKim's constant struggle to reshape his workforce and secure steady labor through rewards, slave sales, and accelerated manumission by self-purchase represented but a few examples of the tactical battles masters and slaves waged throughout the early national period. McKim's difficulties are one indicator of how contestation of the terms of slavery, often focused on the operations of gradual manumission, had transformed the institution in Baltimore, limiting masters' power over their chattels, and giving slaves a powerful weapon in their pursuit of autonomy.

3

THE BLACK DRIVE FOR AUTONOMY AND
MASTERS' RESPONSES

When James Gunn advertised for the return of a runaway slave, twenty-four-year-old John Scott, he advised that if Scott "returns before my departure for Georgia I will give him his freedom at age 31." Whether Scott took Gunn's offer is unknown, but this ad neatly brings together three powerful influences on the operations of slavery in Maryland: the master's power to remove the slave from home and family by sale or migration, the slave's ability to counteract this threat by running off, and the possibility of resolving conflict by concessions of autonomy.[1]

Although the threat of sale was hardly a lever of control uniquely employed by Maryland masters, their slaves could combat that threat with two unusual advantages.[2] First, they had an uncommonly good setting for attempted escapes. Nearby Pennsylvania beckoned, both from all the counties of Maryland's northern tier and from the upper Eastern shore. Slaves could also seek aid from Baltimore's free blacks in finding temporary hiding places while hatching more complete escape plans. Second, slaves could pursue liberty through the courts, by filing petitions for freedom: during the 1780s and 1790s several hundred blacks were emancipated via this procedure. These potentialities constituted powerful counterweights to the master's power, the effects of which can be detected not only in the manner in which masters sought to retrieve runaways but also in their exercise of such defining acts of slavery as the buying and selling of human beings and the disposition of their labor. The time period here examined is that of slavery's growth in Baltimore, from the Revolutionary War until around 1815, and the beginning of its decline as a labor institution, from 1815 to 1830. In the earlier part of this period, slaveholders had been able to contain challenges to their control by judiciously softening some of the harshness of slavery. However, as the city of Baltimore and its environs became a haven for runaways, many of whom found it unnecessary to flee slave territory to gain at least a measure of freedom, masters needed different means to appease their slaves. The attempts by slaves to gain freedom over their masters' objections and the masters' countering strategies, especially conceding to slaves a voice in their hire or sale and offering them delayed freedom, assumed central importance in blacks' efforts to gain autonomy. What drove masters to such concessions was the need to secure slaves' cooperation in maintaining predictable and uninterrupted employment, production, and profit. Uprooting them to Baltimore, after all, had flowed from the perception that slaves could generate more output as urban laborers, craftsmen, and domestics than in the stagnating agricultural economy of the late eighteenth century. But Baltimore masters soon discovered, as rural planters had long known, that matching one's supply of slave laborers to the demand for their services could be a serious problem. Both urban and rural masters engaged extensively in hiring slaves out by the year or the month. In that way they could generate income from laborers who might otherwise be underemployed, while retaining ownership of these persons in anticipation of further shifts in labor costs that would once again make directly exploiting their slaves more profitable than hiring them out.[3]

But the more slave sellers or hirers sought to fine tune their capitalization of labor by assigning slaves to new jobs or new masters, the greater the risk that the slaves would resist through flight, especially if removal to the Southwest loomed as a possibility. Runaway ads testify to the frequency with which recently purchased or hired slaves ran off. One slaveholder noted querulously that he had paid two hundred dollars for the runaway "not three weeks ago," and that the "rogue" had already run off twice.[4] Overall runaway rates dropped during most of Baltimore's boom years, but the general consolidation of control had to be recreated every time a slave encountered a new master.

To avoid disruptive slave resistance to sale or hiring, some buyers and sellers informally surrendered a degree of their theoretically unlimited powers and attempted to co-opt slaves by allowing them to choose the locale, work, or master to whom they would be assigned. A promise of eventual freedom, often made in concert with sale for a term of years to a new master, represented the ultimate concession of autonomy but certainly not the only one masters made.

Transactions of this sort have been cited as examples of slavery's early-nineteenth-century "amelioration," emphasizing mutual obligation rather than compulsion as the keynote of the master-slave relationship, supposedly driven by slaveholders' humanitarian motives as well as a self-conscious redressing of slavery's tarnished image in a republican society. Although these influences no doubt played their part, slaveholders also pursued their self-interest through such new ways of managing human property. The upsurge in gradual emancipations, so noticeable in the early 1800s, was only the most visible product of the negotiated concessions of masterly authority that constituted slavery's amelioration.

The roots of such changes are to be found in the difficulties experience in maintaining plantation slavery from the late 1770s onward in Maryland. During the Revolution, military action in the Chesapeake offered frequent opportunities for slaves to flee to British troops or ships, or indeed to the Continental army, in the hope of gaining freedom as soldiers or camp followers.[5] The passage of French troops through Maryland both before and after the Yorktown campaign afforded more chances for escape.[6] Other runaways took advantage of the general breakdown of civil authority during the war to make off on their own to Baltimore, to Pennsylvania, or to sea. Conditions were especially unstable on the disaffected Eastern Shore, where Revolutionary Whigs struggled to preserve even a shadowy semblance of order.[7] The difficulties of controlling slaves in such circumstances were no doubt extraordinary, especially for Quakers and Methodists, who generally classed themselves as neutrals and accordingly had few allies to call upon if their slaves decamped. It is tempting to speculate that the very real threat of slaves defecting successfully, as well as emerging religious sensibilities, played a part in moving some of these Eastern Shore masters to make the first large-scale promises of delayed emancipation to slaves in the late 1770s and early 1780s.

After the war a new threat to slaveholding appeared, or rather reappeared, in the form of slaves' petitions seeking freedom by legal action. Maryland's judges did not embrace freedom petitions as a tool to rule in toto against the legitimacy of slavery, as jurists in Massachusetts and New Hampshire did, even during the state's greatest openness to antislavery views in the economically depressed 1780s. Instead, cases in Maryland centered on the particular claims of blacks seeking to prove free female ancestry to win liberty. The long-term reliance on white indentured servants in colonial Maryland meant that large numbers of slaves could hope to advance claims to having had white forebears.

In Maryland's most celebrated case, Mary Butler obtained her freedom in 1787 by proving descent from Eleanor or "Irish Nell" Butler, who had come to Maryland in 1681 as the servant of the proprietor, Lord Baltimore, and then had married an enslaved black. Under the Act concerning Negroes of 1663, her marriage made Butler and her children slaves for life.[8] When the proprietor learned of her enslavement, he swiftly secured a new law, in 1681, banning marriages between female servants and slaves. The law imposed a staggering fine of ten thousand pounds of tobacco on any master permitting such a marriage and freed the woman and her issue. The 1681 law also formally repealed the 1663 act, but it noted that all "matters and things relating in the said act to the marriage of negroes and free-born women and their issue, are firm and valid until this present time of the repeal thereof."[9] Lord Baltimore then returned to England, but back in Maryland Nell Butler and her descendants were treated as slaves, because her marriage had occurred while the punitive law of 1663 was still in force.

In 1770 William and Mary Butler filed petitions for freedom, arguing that the 1681 act should be construed to effect their liberation, as Lord Baltimore had presumably intended. Mary Butler was a great grand-daughter of Nell Butler, and she and William were parents of the 1787 petitioner. The provincial court ruled against them, construing the savings clause of the 1681 statute to preserve the property rights of Nell Butler's master and his descendants. The court noted, "The construction is good in a political point of view. Many of these people, if turned loose, cannot mix with us and become members of society. What may be the effects cannot perhaps be fully pointed out; but as much inconvenience may reasonably be expected, their title to freedom ought to be made out very clearly."[10] The pre-Revolutionary provincial court thus narrowed the road to freedom via petition, reflecting attitudes that would evolve little in the remaining century of slavery's life in Maryland. Blacks, even if free, "cannot mix with us and become members of society." Given the perceived immutability of racial barriers, and the "inconvenience" that whites might experience from widespread black freedom, it should be granted only electively for meritorious individuals.

Mary Butler's successful freedom petition of 1787 must be understood against this background. Her attorney sought a flat affirmation that descent from a white woman entitled one to freedom. The defendant contended that the long possession of Nell Butler's descendants as slaves was proof of title and urged that the 1770 opinion be upheld. The appeals court affirmed Mary Butler to be free, but not solely because she was descended from Nell Butler. Rather, the court found that as no documentary proof existed that Nell Butler had ever been convicted of marrying a slave, she could not have forfeited her freedom.[11] By the same token, mere descent from a white woman did not automatically grant freedom.[12] The court seized on a procedural point that only minimally disturbed property rights.

In another landmark case filed in 1791, the brothers Mahoney sought to prove descent from an admitted negro woman named Ann Joice, arguing that she had become free by residing in England with her master in the late 1670s and that her descendants ought also to be free. After eleven years of litigation, the court of appeals denied freedom, ruling that because Ann Joice had never formally been declared free, slavery "reattached" to her when she accompanied her master to Maryland. Another avenue of legal assault on slaveholding was blocked.[13]

In both the Butler and the Mahoney cases, the courts admitted hearsay evidence on the ancestry of freedom petitioners, under the doctrine that the general reputation of the petitioner's neighborhood as to his or her descent would often be the only reliable evidence. This attitude did open new legal strategies to blacks, who filed a spate of cases trying to show descent from white women or Indians.[14] In a different vein, runaway bondmen could improve their chances of passing as free by "claim[ing] to be descended from the famous and prolific Nell Butler," as one slaveholder wryly noted in a 1792 advertisement for a runaway.[15]

Aiding freedom petitioners constituted a major activity of the "Maryland Society for promoting the abolition of slavery, and the relief of poor negroes and others unlawfully held in bondage," a group with some 250 members in the 1790s, mostly merchants and professionals from Baltimore and its environs.[16] In one controversial case the society sustained the efforts of Jonathan and David Fortune to establish their freeborn lineage through two years of litigation, eliciting a shrill complaint from the Fortunes' ostensible owners, Ezekiel and Edward Dorsey of Anne Arundel County. The Dorseys told a Maryland House of Delegates committee of having expended more than 250 pounds in contesting the Fortunes' freedom petitions, more than the slaves were worth. Agreeing wholeheartedly with the Dorseys' self-serving portrayal of themselves as innocent victims of "improper interference" with their slaves, the Committee of Grievances flayed the abolition society for that classic sin against true republican values, the exercise of arbitrary power: "From the numbers, wealth, influence, and industry of the society, with their extensive connexions, an individual has but a slender chance of encountering them; and that if interest only was to be considered, he had better content to give up a slave. . . . their conduct has been unjust and oppressive."[17] Three years later the assembly rallied to protect powerless slaveholders, requiring that costs of unsuccessful petitions be paid before appeals could be filed.[18] Subsequent laws would strike directly at antislavery advocates for blacks, by making petitioners' attorneys responsible for the costs and fees of unsuccessful freedom suits. The legislature thus shored up the power of the master; it gave him or her a freer hand in dealing with black desires for freedom.

Despite these restrictions, freedom petitions afforded some men and women leverage with which to bargain for eventual freedom. Slaves rapidly informed themselves about and took advantage of their petition rights. The Butler case had originated in Saint Mary's County, at the southern tip of Maryland's Western Shore, but the torrent of white complaints about petitioners centered on Baltimore and nearby counties such as Anne Arundel and Prince George's only a few years afterward. Slaves also were quick to challenge masters who transported them into or out of Maryland in violation of the state's ban on slave importation, knowing that such masters might have legally forfeited title to such slaves.[19]

Moreover, masters knew that contesting a freedom suit might not end their troubles. Courts could order a petitioner removed from a slaveholder's control for months or even years pending resolution of a petition, with attendant loss of the slave's labor. And victory in court could bring on new difficulties, as Gassaway Rawlings, an Anne Arundel County planter, learned. He first advertised to recover his slave Ephraim in 1797, noting that he was contesting a freedom petition. In October of 1800 Rawlings sought Ephraim again, declaring that he had run away immediately after the courts rejected his petition.[20]

Faced with such possibilities, some masters chose to manumit freedom petitioners. Although the Reverend John Ashton finally triumphed in court over the Mahoneys in 1802, at least six of the seven brothers were freed by 1808, either by Ashton or by Charles Carroll of Carrollton. It is not clear why Carroll purchased some of the Mahoneys from Ashton, but as an owner of more than two hundred slaves, including a number surnamed Joice (whose freedom might also be at stake), he was intensely interested in the outcome of the case. Carroll may have judged it wise to dampen his own slaves' discontent with the court's rejection of the Mahoney's petition by purchasing some of the Mahoneys in order to *eventually grant* them freedom, six years after their final defeat in court. In a similar move, Carroll sold John Joice his freedom for two hundred dollars, immediately after the Ashton-Mahoney decision.[21]

At least one master explicitly manumitted a slave on the contingency that no petition for freedom be filed during the eight years that the slave was to serve before gaining liberty.[22] In these cases the promised freeing of an individual, rather than weakening the social fabric of slavery, may in fact have reinforced it by providing an outlet for the resistant or potentially troublesome slave. Nonetheless, freedom petitions constituted a potentially major irritant to slavery, at least in the 1790s, one that loomed larger in Baltimore than in rural areas, given the greater flow of information among city residents and the presence of the abolition society headquarters there.

The granting of selective freedom after a term of service not only functioned as a compromise to avoid freedom petitions but also harmonized with masters' desires to regard slavery as becoming progressively ameliorated in keeping with America's republican and Christian ideals. Hostility to the abolition society (which did not long survive its rebuke from the slaveholder-dominated House of Delegates) bespoke resentment toward those who failed to appreciate such progress, as well as the unwelcomeness of any interference with a master regarding the terms of releasing a chattel from bondage.[23]

The theme of granting masters more flexibility to deal with slaves also informed new manumission laws of the 1790s. Efforts to mandate gradual emancipation in Maryland, proposed in 1789, quickly foundered. Instead, one year after the failure to obtain a *post-nati* emancipation bill on the Pennsylvania model, the legislature eased a long-standing ban on manumission by will.[24] In the debate on testamentary manumission, delegate William Pinkney foreshadowed the economic analysis that would become the sheet anchor of antislavery arguments in Maryland, contending, "Never will . . . agriculture, commerce, or manufactures flourish, so long as they depend on reluctant bondsmen for their progress." Pinkney also challenged the "notion that freedmen will be instruments of usurpation" of others. He insisted that allowing slavery to continue unabated would be more likely to lead to black insurrection. Pinkney conceded that some free blacks would be lazy or criminal but noted that some whites already fit this description. Agreeing that permitting manumission by will might give a slave a motive to murder his master, Pinkney noted that the same motives also applied to whites under existing law. He ridiculed claims that manumissions by will would impoverish white families and averred that even if that were true, a diminished patrimony "honestly come by" was preferable to subsisting on the labor of slaves.[25]

Pinkney thus wrestled with the same questions that had troubled judges in the Butler case. Would having a sizable free black population increase the chances of a black revolt? Would free blacks succumb to laziness and criminality and become a public burden? Finally, should individuals be permitted to free their slaves if doing so might harm manumitters or their families? Only the last of these questions was ever answered confidently in Maryland before the Civil War. Few whites

would accept the existence of free people of color with the equanimity
displayed by the then-young Pinkney.[26]

As might be expected of Maryland's cautious and conservative
ameliorators, the repeal of the ban on testamentary manumissions was
hedged with protections for heirs, creditors, and taxpayers. Testators
could not manumit slaves if so to do would prejudice the payment of
debt. Nor could they manumit any person over the age of fifty or otherwise unable to gain his or her living. Finally, no manumissions would
be acknowledged if written up during the testator's final illness.[27] This
provision not only prevented the diminution of patrimony by
slaveholders with deathbed qualms about meeting their Maker; it also
guaranteed that few testamentary manumissions would free slaves without a significant passage of time between the promise of liberation and
its arrival, ensuring a period of preparation in which to learn the ways
of freedom.

In reality, many men and women delayed writing wills until death's
approach was evident and then promised to free slaves regardless of
the law. When heirs contested such manumissions, they generally over-
came the testimony of a decedent's intent to free slaves prior to a last
illness, as courts adhered to the letter of the law.[28] But in keeping with
the desire to safeguard masters' flexibility and credibility in promising
freedom, the legislature eliminated the "last illness" restriction in 1796.[29]

The hesitant, much-qualified expanding of masters' freedom to
manumit slaves suggests that misgivings about free black indolence
appeared almost at the outset of delayed manumission's surge in popularity. As Maryland's lawmakers moved at the close of the eighteenth
century to regulate the lives of free persons of color, they evinced concerns that had long been given voice regarding propertyless white servants, concerns that transcended racial lines. Masters must not free
people who could not sustain themselves; hence, the law required that
apprentices and indentured servants receive freedom dues, so that the
newly freed had time to find their place in the world and would not
become public charges. In the case of slaves, a surer way to minimize
such risks was to simply bar the master from emancipating the unfit in
the first place.

The Act concerning Negroes of 1796 lowered the maximum age
for manumission from fifty to forty-five. The lower age limit tempered
the increase in manumissions that might have been expected from the
simultaneous waiving of the last illness restriction on manumission by
will.[30] Manumitting masters could not free older slaves by leaving them
land or money as a means of support; courts ruled that because slaves
over forty-five could not be freed in the first place, they were legally

incapable of controlling bequests and thus still unable to meet the test of self-maintenance.[31] Courts also disparaged acts of emancipation that might impoverish a property holder, rendering him or her dependent, while creating yet another dependent propertyless laborer. Early-nineteenth-century case law specifically established a widow's right to overturn manumissions under the doctrine of refusing a husband's bequest and claiming her rights to a share of the estate.[32]

When legally challenged, the manumitting of young children also met with rebuff. Though many slave children worked from the age of ten or occasionally even younger, judges regarded them as incapable of supporting themselves until the age of majority, twenty-one for males and sixteen for females, the ages at which the binding of apprentices ended. In 1825 attorney Francis Scott Key advised George Calvert to manumit a mother and then sell the daughter to her, as "the courts . . . are very strict on the interpretation of the manumission law. . . . children of such an age as to be unable to work cannot be manumitted, even if the master makes the most ample provision for their support."[33] This entire approach to manumission helped to preserve slavery across generations of black families trying to acquire freedom and posed little or no threat to the continuation of slavery. Maryland's manumission laws did not indicate outright antislavery sentiment but rather regarded slavery's elimination equivocally and stressed selective liberation.

Although lawmakers thus reined in legal routes to freedom via petition and carefully structured the master's right to manumit, slave flight could not so readily be rendered harmless. Here, too, masters were pushed into cessions of control.[34] Blacks who ran from Maryland slaveholders were, as a group, much like their peers elsewhere in the South. About three-quarters were male, predominantly in the age range fifteen to twenty-four. The ads contain those ubiquitous but nonetheless gruesome references to twisted limbs, missing fingers and toes, burn marks, and scars, as well as poignant descriptions of people unable to look a white man in the eye or to speak to one without stuttering or trembling. Likewise, the ads sketch various runaway personalities, as seen through masters' eyes: some fugitives are described as likely to be "artful," "plausible," or "unusually well-spoken," in trying to pass as free or to claim to be at large for a legitimate purpose.

Beyond these general similarities, patterns relating to fugitives' skills, why they fled, and where they were going tell much about shifts over time in the conditions of servitude and in black ability to shape those conditions. Table 9 categorizes masters' statements about the putative destinations of male runaways.

Over time, male runaways were increasingly likely to remain in

TABLE 9

Destinations of Male Runaways from Baltimore Masters and Runaway Rates, 1773-1820

	Percent of Runaways			
Destination	1773-1790	1790-1799	1800-1809	1810-1819
Baltimore	9	17	16	29
Maryland (not Baltimore)	12	18	18	11
Pennsylvania & north	8	7	7	6
Elsewhere	7	7	4	1
No indication	64	51	55	53
No. of advertisements	177	168	109	258
Annual no. runaways per 1,000 male slaves	20	16	7	14

NOTE: Baltimore is defined as the city itself, or Baltimore Town, Old Town, and Fells Point before its 1796 incorporation. "Pennsylvania" totals include three runaways thought to be headed for points further north. "Elsewhere" includes runaways said to be going "to sea" or, in wartime, fleeing to the British or French armies. The runaway rate derives from slave population figures for Baltimore interpolated from (1) the Maryland census of 1776 (2) the first four federal censuses, as interpolated with numbers of male slaves derived from the tax lists of 1783 and 1798, and (3) the Baltimore assessment record of 1813.

Baltimore, with both the 1790s and the years from 1810 to 1819 showing major increases in the proportion of slaves who were thought to be "hiding," "lurking," or "skulking" in and around the city. In the 1770s and 1780s masters had thought that Maryland, Pennsylvania, or other more distant locations were each as likely to be the fugitive's destination as Baltimore itself. By the second decade of the nineteenth century, three to four times as many masters guessed that a slave would be "harbored" in Baltimore rather than heading for any other given place; more than half of those advising ad readers where to find runaways identified a location in or near the city as the most promising site. By contrast, no more than one-twelfth of escapees in absolute terms were thought to have headed for Pennsylvania or other free territories in any period from 1773 to 1820. Although slaveholders earlier described more men as having fled to Maryland counties outside Baltimore, such themes also gave way, especially after 1810, to the notion that Baltimore itself served as the fugitive's hiding place. The shift after 1790 toward fugitives' remaining in Baltimore coincided with a dramatic decline in advertised runaways; the proportion of advertisements fell from twenty per one thousand male slaves in the 1770s and 1780s to barely a third of that rate in the first decade of the 1800s. But the second and larger shift toward local flight in the second decade of the century occurred as escape attempts turned upward again, although at fourteen per thousand male slaves per year, the rate still failed to match those of the Revolutionary era.[35]

These fluctuations in runaway rates contrasted with a relatively stable distribution of skills among fugitives. Throughout the period, just under half of advertising masters identified a skill practiced by the men who ran from them. Tabulations of these notations confirm that slaves worked in a wide variety of crafts that played a central role in Baltimore's dynamic growth in the post-Revolutionary decades. Roughly one-fifth of skilled runaways had worked in the shipping industry, including not only sailors and watermen but also ship carpenters, rope makers, sail makers, and caulkers. Metal fabricators, such as forge and furnace hands, blacksmiths, anchor makers, nailers, and coppersmiths, composed a similar proportion of skilled and semiskilled runaways. Construction trades had been the métier of a third large group of fugitives, within which brick makers and bricklayers dominated; there were also carpenters, painters and glaziers. Finally, food and clothing production accounted for about one-seventh of skilled runaways, of whom shoemakers, bakers, tailors, and butchers were most numerous.[36] Perhaps having a craft skill gave blacks greater confidence in their ability to fend for themselves and made them more likely to run off. It is also possible that slaves brought to Baltimore to work in the crafts more commonly fit the runaway paradigm of being single young adult males. These factors may also have affected the escapees' outlook regarding where they would go.

By the early nineteenth century roughly half of the advertisers tried to alert would-be slave catchers to fugitives' likely destinations or routes of escape. Blacks fleeing Baltimore masters, like slaves everywhere, were often supposed to be seeking reunion with kinfolk or avoiding separation from them. Runaway ads routinely identified the presence of a parent, a spouse, or a sibling dwelling in a specific spot, such as "Mr. Bowen's plantation on Middle River Neck," or more vaguely, "in Calvert County, where he [the runaway] was raised." By the early nineteenth century many Maryland slaves were second, third, or fourth generation African Americans, with ties to kin scattered all over the state. Thus an 1811 ad listed "Negro George's" wife, who cooked at the Fountain Inn in Baltimore; his brother, in Frederick County; and his mother, on Kent Island, in hope of tracking down the missing George.[37] Desire to be with relatives helps explain part of Baltimore's increasing popularity for runaways. As the city's slave population swelled from less than one thousand circa 1780 to more than four thousand by 1810, slaves had a correspondingly greater chance of having a relative in the city who could help them when they ran.

The explosive growth of Baltimore's free black community, from a few hundred in 1790 to more than ten thousand by 1820, played an even greater role in the evolving pattern of runaway destinations. Constituting a majority of Baltimore's blacks after 1810, free people of color could ally with runaways, harbor them, or provide other services, even more effectively than slaves, as disgruntled but resigned masters often outlined: "He was seen at Fells' Point among the free negro houses where he is no doubt concealed" or "It is needless to describe his clothes, as by now he will have obtained a change through the management of the free negroes" or yet again, "He will probably have obtained a pass from the free negroes at the Point." Some runaways, like Maria Cooper in 1818, apparently had several options: "She is supposed to be lurking in the neighborhood of Chatham Street where her mother is hired to Mr. Robinson, or in Saratoga Street, where her grandmother lives. . . . she has also a sister living at Mrs. Bush's tavern, where it is said she was seen a few days ago."[38]

The presence of ten to fifteen thousand blacks in early-nineteenth-century Baltimore, slave and free, allowed many runaways simply to melt into anonymity, living with other blacks, huckstering, pursuing a trade, or working as day laborers.[39] Advertisers frequently expressed the fear that a runaway would seek work at the wharves and the shipyards, hoping to pass as free. Such a stratagem might be foiled by an employer who asked to see a nonexistent certificate of freedom or who was thorough-minded enough to scrutinize and detect forged freedom papers, but clearly not all hirers did so. A runaway wishing to avoid possible difficulties could, in Baltimore's labor market, adopt a slightly less devious pose, admitting to being a slave but claiming to be authorized by a master to hire his or her own time. Employers seeking an active man for a day's or a week's work often failed to ask for proof of the master's imprimatur for the slave's self-hire, if the frequent warnings of masters against such ploys are any indication. Indeed, knowingly hiring a suspected runaway gave an employer additional leverage in negotiations over wages or over the mode or timing of their payment: a fugitive would be unlikely to call attention to himself by complaining about short or late pay. So common was the practice of hiring runaways that even the master of a twelve-year-old runaway girl theorized that she might try to hire her own time as a nursemaid.[40] Thus, Baltimore's rapid growth from a town of six thousand to a city of more than sixty thousand in the forty years after the Revolution helped slaves to flee masters, at least for a time, without leaving kin, friends, or familiar surroundings.

Ultimately, many runaways did leave Baltimore to avoid recapture and fled northward.[41] But the ability to live in Baltimore undetected, while working to make money and otherwise prepare for a longer journey, must have made running away a generally more tempting option. The careful planning of the final escape journey, as described by Frederick Douglass and others, need not have preceded the initial bolt to a haven with a friend or relative.

Many runaways did not intend to decamp permanently but rather fled on the spur of the moment to escape or defer punishment or perhaps to disrupt a sale to an undesirable master. Some may simply have wanted a "vacation" from the hard work and close supervision of urban slavery. William Norris, seeking to retrieve Nicholas Everson, vexedly noted that Everson "takes a frolic of this kind about once a year, and will no doubt be found among the free negroes at Fells' Point."[42] But recalcitrants described as being "addicted to running off" may have been pursuing more proactive motives than avoidance of harm or enjoying free time.

A slave who ran away and then returned to his master, voluntarily or otherwise, could improve the chances of gaining freedom through self-purchase or delayed manumission. While at large, one could pocket earnings as an apparent free person of color or a self-hired slave, speeding up the accumulation of cash to buy one's freedom or that of kinfolk. Concomitantly, by establishing oneself as bold enough to run away, one could hope to command more serious attention from a master to the idea of self-purchase or delayed manumission. To be sure, there were risks: a master might decide to sell a runaway to the deep South, either to dissuade others from running or simply to convert a demonstrably unprofitable investment into cash. But the fact of a slave's having run away, if known to potential buyers, might diminish his value by destroying his reputation as safe property and thus actually work to reduce the attractiveness of sale. In addition, with most of Baltimore's masters holding only one to four slaves, the appeal of sale as exemplary punishment was limited.

All in all, a slaveholder otherwise reluctant to sell freedom to a slave, or to offer it in return for steadily productive labor, might well find discretion to be in order, once a black's flight and return had altered often closely balanced expectations of gain or loss from hiring, selling, or gradually manumitting him or her. The nexus between flight, sale, and manumission thus could influence any number of master-slave transactions.

For example, the ability to hide within the city changed the seasonal patterns of running away, making the slaveholder's job of surveillance of his chattels more difficult. Slaves running from rural sites had to anticipate moving across the countryside, traveling by night and perhaps sleeping in the open air over days or even weeks on the road. Under such circumstances they were more likely to flee in the warm weather from late spring to early fall than in the winter months. For masters concerned about potential runaways, the months from November to March provided something of a respite. By contrast, Baltimore masters needed to be always on guard, for even in the coldest times a slave might slip across town to a street or an alley in Fells' Point or Federal Hill and lie low among free black protectors. Just over 70 percent of rural runaways departed their masters in the six months from April through September, with less than a third doing so in the fall and winter quarters. In Baltimore these warmer months claimed only 54 percent of the runaways, little more than the remainder of the year.[43] Although difficult to quantify, the costs of preventing escape by urban slaves might thus be higher than for rural masters.

When a slave did run off, search and recapture could stretch out over days or weeks, with slave catchers' rewards and expenses eating up the profits of a year or more of the slave's labor. Typically, slaveholders offered sliding-scale cash rewards, keyed to the fugitive's distance from home when captured and returned; top rewards averaged nearly seventy-five dollars in the period 1810-20.[44] The large rewards for recovering distant fugitives may have intensified slave-catching activities on the Philadelphia road, especially where it crossed the Susquehanna some forty miles northeast of Baltimore; this in turn could have contributed to the low proportion of runaways thought to be heading for Pennsylvania. As one master opined, "if he is headed for Pennsylvania, he will avoid the scrutiny he would undergo on the Philadelphia Road."[45] And Christopher Hughes, advertising for the runaway Murry, noted that three other men had been retaken on the banks of the Susquehanna, despite the aid of a Quaker there.[46]

Even in seeking slaves hiding within Baltimore, masters had few alternatives to soliciting slave catchers, given Baltimore's tiny constabulary during the early nineteenth century. Some, like James Gunn, employed the runaway ad to encourage the slave's return on his own volition. Although pride no doubt prevented masters from speaking in print directly to a runaway, they could nonetheless declare to the public at large, presumably for conveyance to the slave, that "treatment shall be humane and liberal if he repairs his Error [and returns]." Other masters sought to dispel "misapprehensions," such as fear of being sold, that they judged might have caused the slave's flight. Ads such as these represented a master's belated concession on a point of conflict with a slave, in an effort to retrieve a fugitive without paying slave catchers.

No action produced more conflict than the sale of a slave or events that presaged sales, such as a master's death, an announcement of migration plans, or the appearance of a slave trader. Frederick Douglass's autobiography recounts the dread and sorrow that he and fellow slaves felt following their owner's death. Removed from Baltimore to the Eastern Shore, the adolescent Douglass could only wait and wonder whether the settling of his deceased master's estate would lead to his sale. Adults placed in Douglass's situation were often less resigned. Taking advantage of the confusion surrounding the inventorying of property and probating of wills, blacks fled, particularly when slave sales threatened. James Hughes, an executor, explained in an orphans' court petition seeking immediate authority to sell slaves that he was "fearfull that . . . Property will be wasted in Consequence of the plantation being advertised."[47] Other less foresighted administrators tried to obtain from the courts relief from financial responsibility to the estate for slaves who had run off.[48]

Removal to Georgia or New Orleans was widely regarded by blacks as a virtual death sentence, permanently separating one from family and friends. Blacks were accordingly highly sensitive to the prospect of distant sale, even to the point of resisting violently. When Basil and Philip, two young Frederick County slaves, learned that Haden Edwards proposed to buy them and take them with him to Kentucky, they were suspicious. After inquiries revealed that Edwards intended to resell them to New Orleans as soon as he reached Kentucky, the two young men refused to go with him. When Edwards tried to tie the men up, they struck him down and escaped. Though recaptured, Basil and Philip secured Edwards's promise to resell them to Maryland owners, and they gained his support in obtaining a pardon for their violence against him.[49]

Faced with such dangers, slaveholders increasingly sought to assuage slaves' fears by placing restrictions on the terms of sales. Table 10 illustrates these patterns.

The table lists three limits on conditions of sale that might be expected to reassure a slave who was going to be sold, assuming that blacks typically desired to obtain eventual freedom and to remain in Maryland with kin, spouses, and friends. Over time, greater proportions

TABLE 10

Conditions of Slave Sales Imposed by Baltimore Sellers, 1791-1820

Sale Requirements	Percent Frequency by Decade		
	1791-1800	1801-1810	1811-1820
Sold for term of years	19	33	36
Maryland buyer required	—	13	18[a]
Baltimore area buyer required	1	3	6
Distant buyer required	7	2	1
Total Sample	139	230	537
No. sale ads p.a. per 1,000 slaves	7	7	12

[a]After 1817, Maryland law forbade the sale of prospectively manumitted slaves to out-of-state owners; hence, sellers of such slaves had no need to stipulate a "Maryland only" sale in their advertisements. If such cases are excluded from consideration, the proportion of owners who voluntarily barred out-of-state sales rises to 25 percent.

of slaves were sold for a term of years rather than for life. Likewise, more and more sellers required that purchasers of slaves keep them in Maryland, whereas fewer openly sought to punish slaves by selling them at a distance. The advertisements leave little room to doubt that searches for Georgia, Tennessee, or Alabama buyers were intended to punish a disobedient, negligent, or runaway slave. One 1796 ad seeking to dispose of a slave "at least one hundred miles from Baltimore" noted that the woman could be seen in the Baltimore jail; another master boasted of his cook's abilities but added "frankly" that a buyer from Georgia would be preferred because of the woman's "impertinent language to her Mistress."[50] In contrast, one seller prefaced his demand for a Maryland buyer with a terse "as they are sold for no fault." Ads seeking to discourage buyers from taking slaves outside of Maryland might also cite the seller's desire to avoid separation of husband and wife or, less specifically, a desire to see the slave remain where he or she was "raised" or "bred."[51] In the same vein, sellers of slaves who had been promised eventual manumission by an earlier deed or will occasionally insisted on the prospective freed person's remaining in Maryland as a guarantee against the reimposition of lifelong bondage by a buyer who removed to the Southwest.

The willingness of many masters to refuse to sell a slave or slaves to outsiders could also represent self-denying humanitarianism, as evidenced by two-tiered pricing. That is, some sellers accepted less money from local buyers than they could hope to receive from a southwestern trader.[52] Few sellers named a specific asking price, but phrases such as "will be sold cheap to one undertaking not to remove him from Maryland" were not uncommon. Similarly, estate administrators routinely sought and obtained permission from the orphans' courts to sell slaves privately rather than at public auctions, to assure local purchase of slaves.

When sellers or administrators announced that they would sell only to Maryland buyers "to avoid trouble" or "difficulty," they also had in mind the very real possibility that a slave might run to avoid sale to a distant or otherwise unacceptable master.[53] A master might forgo a higher-priced offer from a Tennessee or Louisiana purchaser in order to gain greater assurance of consummating a slave sale without provoking costly flight either by the person to be sold or by others fearing a similar fate.

Recovering a runaway could cost perhaps one-quarter of a slave's market value, even more if the fact of having absconded reduced the amount buyers would pay for a recaptured fugitive. Securing an African American's cooperation by combining a discounted price to a local buyer with a deed of prospective manumission after a term of servitude might well generate about the same financial result for a slaveholder as having to pursue a fugitive sold at full value but against his will, and such a course would completely eliminate the chance of major loss associated with the slave's escaping altogether.

In assessing how important it was for masters to negate the threat of flight, we must also note that the prices offered by slave dealers were not dramatically higher than those obtainable for African Americans sold locally. Large-scale slave dealers, such as Austin Woolfolk, generally paid from $300 to $350 for an adult male slave in the second or third decade of the nineteenth century, prices well within normal local ranges. True, Woolfolk and his ilk could pay in full and in cash, and they stood ready to do business at the seller's pleasure; for planters seeking to dispose of large numbers of chattels, such features were extremely attractive, as slave sale records for rural counties indicate. But the typical Baltimore slaveholder, seeking to sell one or two slaves, would not receive much more money from a dealer than from a local purchaser. The advantages of selling to a dealer might thus seem small compared to the risk of loss if a slave got wind of sale plans and escaped; securing cooperation by promising sale to a local owner might well be the financially prudent action.

From the slave's perspective, threatening to flee could counterpoise if not eliminate the threat of sale. This form of contesting the conditions of slavery can be specifically linked to fluctuations in the southwestern slave trade. Escape attempts surged in years in which unusually large numbers of southwestern dealers were operating in Baltimore. In the period 1811 to 1820, advertisements to buy slaves in large numbers appeared far more frequently between 1816 and 1818 than in other years, as men like Woolfolk, a Georgian, or David Anderson of Tennessee sought to buy as many as "100 Negroes," offering cash payment and "the highest" prices to procure slaves for the cotton fields of the Southwest.[54] Slave dealers advertised infrequently before 1816 because the War of 1812 made shipment of slaves by sea risky owing to the presence of British naval raiders and privateers. Moreover, demand for slaves in the Gulf region was temporarily deranged by the war with the Creeks. In 1819 and 1820 the impact of the Panic of 1819, felt particularly severely in Baltimore, no doubt contributed to the temporary disappearance of large-scale slave traders.

Table 11 shows the relationship between overall sales of Baltimore slaves, runaway rates, and the presence or absence of slave dealers in Baltimore, as indicated by the number of advertisements in the newspapers.

Although the volume of slave sale ads remained fairly stable throughout the decade, runaway advertisements increased by 40 percent during the three peak years of slave trading activity and then declined by more than half as slave dealers' operations diminished in 1819-20.[55] Moreover, a higher than normal proportion of 1816-18 runaways came from the age group most avidly sought by dealers, males ages 15 to 24.[56] Slaves were more ready to accept a local sale, and slaveholders seeking to "avoid trouble" by selling to Maryland buyers were pursuing their own interests as well as mitigating the harshness of slave sale. Possible slave flight thus pushed masters' and slaves' interests into running in tandem.

The pursuit of profits in the slave trade also brought forth a wave of abductions of both slaves and free blacks. Consistent with the complacent view of slavery's relative mildness in Maryland, the legislature became somewhat hostile to the export of slaves from Maryland by slave traders, an issue that flared into prominence during the post-1815 cotton boom. In 1817 legislation criminalized the sale or transportation out of state of slaves who had been promised manumission after a term of years, on the presumption that term slaves would be denied freedom, once taken to Georgia or Kentucky. Earlier laws had imposed civil penalties on such sales, but the 1817 law provided for a penitentiary sentence of up to two years.[57]

TABLE 11

Slave Dealing and Runaway Rates, 1811-1820

Avg. Annual No. of Advertisements	1811-1815	1816-1818	1819-1820
To sell slaves	50	52	55
For runaways	34	48	22
To buy 10 or more slaves	1	7	2

Whites eager to ameliorate slavery thus protected the rights of blacks and the credibility of their own offers of future freedom. If term slaves could be cheated of their freedom with impunity by out-of-state sale, the reliability of prospective manumission as a device for inspiring hard work and deterring flight would wane, and the stability of slavery in Maryland, especially in Baltimore, would be disturbed. But, although the 1817 law proscribed both the act of sale and the acts of purchase and transportation, the practical effect fell almost exclusively on buyers. Court and prison records show virtually no convictions for selling a term slave to a person intending to remove him from Maryland; convictions fell rather upon the purchasers and transporters. In effect, slaveholders publicly condemned out-of-state sales but stopped short of punishing themselves for engaging in stratagems to avoid the promised freeing of a slave.[58]

As always, these efforts were couched within an overall acceptance of slavery's legitimacy. When the Baltimore County grand jury initiated public discussion of the kidnapping problem in 1816 and singled out private prisons ("houses appropriated . . . for the reception of the negroes intended to be carried to other states") as an evil, the jurymen feared that "the depraved part of our community" employed such places to effect the sale of term slaves and indentured free children. But the most damaging feature of private slave jails was that "slaves, the legal property of individuals, and, in some cases, the chief support of helpless widows, are stolen away from their owners and deposited in these cells of misery to await transportation," in conditions "abhorrent to every condition of humanity." Convinced that such nefarious practices were "increasing with enormous rapidity," the grand jury petitioned for a law barring private jails.[59]

Others campaigned against traders' holding slaves in public jails, pending transportation to Savannah, New Orleans, or Kentucky. By 1818, faced with a dramatic increase in slave flight, itself a response to the swelling activity of slave dealers, the state barred traders from lodging slaves in public jails, but it continued to allow any bonafide resident of the state to do so at his or her own cost; slaves could also be kept in private dungeons without restriction.[60] A slave dealer could comply by becoming a Maryland resident, by building his own strong house, or by arranging for would-be sellers to place slaves in a public jail pending removal. Advertisements by dealers indicate that the first two courses were followed and that the antikidnapping laws had little impact other than to foster consolidation of the trade into larger operations that could afford resident agents or private jails, or both.[61]

Another area of concern lay in the treatment of blacks seized as runaways. Maryland law presumed all blacks at large to be runaway slaves unless they produced a master's pass or a certificate of freedom. Reports of the re-enslaving of free blacks who lacked freedom papers, or whose papers were destroyed by slave catchers, led the legislature to authorize judges to use their discretion to determine a black prisoner's status. More critically, the new law declared that blacks deemed free by judges would no longer be held liable for jail fees, averting the sale into servitude of blacks proven free but unable to pay jail and court fees. This change hampered kidnappers who had captured and jailed free but poor blacks in the hopes of buying them cheaply at auction when no one could prove ownership.[62]

Jail law reforms indicate white concern regarding attacks on free blacks and term slaves, but as always, that concern was tempered by fear that assistance to such blacks might undermine slavery. When the Protection Society of Maryland was founded in 1816 to combat kidnapping, public reaction was skeptical, despite the presence of prominent commercial and professional men among its leadership. The society devoted two-thirds of an early public statement to disavowing interest in "interference with any subsisting legal tie or duty, resulting from the relation between masters and slaves," whether to "lessen the value, impair the obligation, relax the rigor, or shorten the duration of legitimate servitude." In short, the society would not intervene in disputes between masters and slaves over the carrying out of promises of delayed manumission. The Protection Society even denied any desire to "meliorate the condition" of slaves.[63] Indeed, in a memorial to the General Assembly of Maryland, it gave equal billing to the horrors attending "negroes . . . entitled to freedom after a term of years . . . [being] reduced to perpetual slavery" and "masters in many instances [being] deprived of their slaves."[64] The view that free blacks were an adjunct to the slave population remained strong in 1816.

After two turbulent years, the Protection Society reported in 1818 that it had "rescued more than sixty human beings from the grasp of lawless oppression, and restored a number of legal slaves to their proper masters." Unfortunately, the society found itself short of funds, because opponents were "leaving no means untried to paralyze the exertions of the Society," chiefly by groundlessly accusing members of abolitionist tendencies. Once again, the society categorically denied such aims.[65] But shortly thereafter, the society disbanded, as the Panic of 1819 dampened the slave-dealing boom and kidnapping with it.[66] Though ideologically much less threatening to slaveholders than the Abolition Society of the 1790s, the Protection Society fared little better in attracting sustained support. Its benevolent stance toward free blacks perhaps contributed to its speedy demise.

Humanitarian action by slaveholders both partook of and was judged by instrumental standards. Laws to check the worst abuses of kidnappers and slave traders, undertaken to reassure vulnerable term slaves of the reliability of promises of prospective freedom and thereby prevent their flight, could win public acceptance by buttressing the system of delayed manumission. Where slaves' chances to evade the master's grasp were poorer, and the master's interest in humane treatment as a prop to control was less critical, little amelioration occurred.

Consider the sale of slave women and their children. The master's interest was best served by the ability to sell women either with or without their children, with an eye to getting the best deal. Black families, however, would wish to avoid separation. Given the difficulties of fleeing slavery with children in tow, masters seeking to sell women had less reason to shape their sales strategy to counter the threat of flight. Accordingly, any increase in the tendency to keep families together over time would be strong evidence of ameliorative behavior, uncomplicated by self-interested motives.[67]

Table 12 shows the patterns of sale advertisements for women age 15 or older, by decade from 1791 to 1820, distinguishing between women offered for sale alone and those sold with children. A majority of slave women of childbearing age were offered for sale singly in each decade, with nearly three-quarters of those sold from 1811 to 1820 thus advertised, even though 55 percent of slave women resided in a household that contained one or more slave children, according to 1820 census data. Nearly two-fifths of the slave children, moreover, lived in a household with no resident black woman, slave or free. This picture suggests numerous separations of mothers and children by sale, giving little support to the idea of spontaneous humanitarianism on the part of slaveholders. This is negative evidence, of course, and it must be used cautiously. Federal census data provide no way before 1820 to

TABLE 12

Advertisements for Sales of Baltimore Slave Women of Childbearing Age, 1791-1820

	1791-1800	1801-1810	1811-1820
Percent sold alone	57	72	74
Percent sold with children	43	28	26
Sample size	53	96	234

analyze what proportion of slave women were mothers or lived with slave children.[68] The conclusion that large and perhaps increasing proportions of Baltimore slave women were sold separate from their children does not seem unwarranted, however. In short, masters made concessions over sale to those slaves who could generate pressure through plausible threats of flight or violent resistance; those unable to do so were treated worse.

Anecdotal evidence suggests that sellers anticipated that a woman sold alone might well be marketable to a wider array of potential city buyers than one with children. An eighteen-year-old girl was offered for sale in 1809 because "her being pregnant does not suit her present owner." A mother of two having "no fault but a family of children," was put up for sale in 1818, and a similar ad vouched for a woman's being sold "for no other reason than the inconvenience" of her four-year-old son and infant daughter. At least a half dozen ads offered to exchange a slave woman and her child for a childless woman of similar age and condition, and one seller urged the purchase of a woman who was "has no children, nor likely to have any." Finally, some sellers of women with children announced their willingness to part with a woman "with or without her children," according to the buyer's choice.[69]

Even in dealing with slave mothers, masters eventually began to face a small danger of runaways. Sixteen of the nineteen runaways advertised as having fled with children left their masters in the 1811-20 decade, making up 84 percent of all such cases reported between 1791 and 1820. This upsurge far exceeded that of runaways generally. None of the women were thought to have departed for Pennsylvania, and only one to an Eastern Shore county. Nine of the remainder had, in their masters' views, hidden out somewhere in Baltimore city or county with fathers, mothers, or husbands, or "at Federal Hill, where she has many acquaintances among the Shoe Blacks."[70]

Chastened by the threat of flight, masters looked for ways to smooth the transition to a new owner. Trial slave sales comprised one such device, with the seller promising to take the slave back if the buyer was not satisfied.[71] Although it aimed chiefly to influence the prospective buyer, the trial sale also created an opening for the slave to influence his fate by his behavior during the trial period. In at least one case a slave exercised something approaching a veto right over his own sale. When Gerrard Troost, manager of the Cape Sable Company, an alum-producing firm, tried to buy a laborer at an estate sale in the spring of 1816, he was temporarily rebuffed when the slave, Emanuel, refused to report for duty. Ten days passed before Troost learned from the estate administrators that "the boy Emanuel . . . is now willing to go with you," implying that the administrators had not been prepared to go forward with the sale over Emanuel's objections.

John Gibson, who sold four men to Troost later that spring, proposed deception to gain his former slaves' cooperation. "If [Troost] would buy them for the company that he would send them up the following Monday, but he requested not to mention to the Negros that they were sold, because they did not like to go [to the factory.]" Gibson hoped that the men would believe they had been hired only temporarily to the alum maker, assuming that if so, they would be less likely to run off than if they knew they had been sold.[72]

That Gibson's fears were not exaggerated may be illustrated by the complaint of Job Garretson, who sought redress in chancery court in 1802 regarding his disastrous purchase of Negro Ben from William Hollis. According to Garretson, Hollis had interested him in buying Ben by touting the black man's skill as a waterman, "knowing that I kept a small vessel in the Patapsco in carrying wood and other things to Baltimore." When Garretson lamented that he lacked cash to buy a slave, Hollis assured him that Ben could be had on a short credit. Garretson then became suspicious, asking why such a valuable man was for sale on such easy terms. Hollis invoked a variant on the "want of employment" argument, noting that his own boat had a full crew, so Ben had been employed on another boat. There, "under the care of a hired captain, with whom the aforesaid negroe could not agree, and that the skipper having whipped him the negroe complained to [Hollis] and told him that he could not bear the treatment Hollis gave him, and begged . . . Hollis to sell him, saying that if . . . Hollis would not take him from under the control of the skipper he should be obliged to run away." Garretson gibed that perhaps Ben was too used to "that business of running way and if so is not worth having[.]" Nonetheless, after seeing Ben, "who consent[ed] to live with [me]," he bought him for three hundred dollars. In fact, Garretson noted ruefully, Ben was "addicted" to running away, and did so only two months after being sold.[73]

Garretson no doubt tried to place himself in the most favorable light in pleading his case and may have pretended to a greater degree of caution than he actually exercised in buying Ben. What stands out is that Hollis virtually admitted that Ben's demand for a change of supervisor, if not legal master, coupled with a threat to run off, had pushed him into acting. Garretson, despite this knowledge, bought Ben, but only after dealing with him man-to-man and obtaining his consent for the sale. Both seller and buyer presumed that Ben's wishes had to be taken into account.

Nevertheless, Ben rejected his new master. Perhaps Garrison had flunked his trial period as master. Or perhaps Ben simply wanted to continue working on Hollis's boats, but away from the abusive hired captain who had whipped him. Garretson suspected something of this sort, alleging that Ben had returned to Hollis's service after running from his new master. Whatever we make of this case, Ben's influence over his fate, and its low-key characterization by Garretson in a claim that elsewhere crackles with animosity, permits the inference that seeking a slave's consent to a new master was not uncommon.

A similar arena in which the master formally retained full authority, but in fact conceded much to the slave's wishes, is represented by advertisements in which the slaveholder cited the slave's desires as the stimulus provoking the sale. Three ads appearing around 1810 stated that "he is sold because he is dissatisfied with his master" or "with his current place" or "at her own desire and her owner's regret."[74] Intriguingly, a number of advertisements identified the slave's wish "to live in this city" as the motive force behind the sale. Such a statement could naturally be self-serving, a clever way of stating that the goods offered for sale were "safe property" and would not run off. But it might also be quite truthful; the excitement that young Frederick Douglass felt when he learned that he would be sent to a Baltimore master and the dejection occasioned by his return to rural Talbot County were no doubt shared by many other Maryland slaves.

Thus, an advertisement such as that placed in the Baltimore *American and Commercial Daily Advertiser* by the captain of the bay schooner *Two Brothers*, regarding two slaves shipped to Baltimore from Cambridge who would "be sold only in Baltimore, as it is their wish to live in this city," can be read as evidence that slaves themselves helped fuel the rise of slavery in Baltimore.[75] Their desires to come to Baltimore justified slaveholders, buyers or sellers alike, in believing that they were maximizing gain and minimizing risk by putting slaves to work in the city. It would be perilous to presume that the female cook and male driver offered for sale on board the *Two Brothers* necessarily saw transit to Baltimore as part of a larger plan to gain freedom. They, or either of them, may have primarily esteemed the greater opportunities to earn money and enjoy free time that Baltimore's environment could provide. Or the already large relocation of blacks to Baltimore may have brought kin or friends to the city before them. In any case, such men and women were exercising control over their lives, even if they only changed the location of their servitude. Those who managed to get to Baltimore "at their own desire" must surely have eventually gained a new outlook toward a lifetime in slavery.

From the slaveholder's standpoint, granting the slave a voice in blocking or initiating a change of masters probably did not seem like a major concession of control. A more significant reduction of authority occurred when a bondman actually selected a new master, as when the executors of William Weatherly's estate advertised the sale of "two Negro men and one woman, the Negroes at private sale if they can get masters to purchase them, if not they must be sold at public sale the last day of the sale."[76] The slaves could hope to pick their new master, and presumably they gained some room thereby to discuss terms and conditions of servitude. The executors improved their chances of disposing of slave property without having to pursue runaways, and they transferred expenditures of time and effort to find buyers from themselves to the slaves. They also could hope to avoid payment of the commission fee that a public sale by an auctioneer would require. By retaining the option of sale at auction, however, the executors underlined their ultimate power. They simultaneously provided an incentive for the slaves to seek a new master and set a limit to wheedling for concessions: pushing for too much might backfire, kill a private sale, and leave the slaves on the auction block.

Explicit acknowledgments of slaves being authorized to find new masters appeared infrequently in the sale advertisements. A seller who authorized "self-sale" to save time and money would probably not have been as likely to advertise the slave for sale as a master intending to manage the transaction actively. Perhaps the more common practice would have been a unwritten understanding between master and slave that the latter was at liberty to seek a new master, subject to the current owner's approval. Surviving evidence of these arrangements comes mainly from cases in which a slave took advantage of such latitude to run off, as when Richmond Gustus of Baltimore advised newspaper readers that he had given the runaway Priscilla "a note to look for a master to buy her, but as she has not returned . . . I declare this pass to be invalid." Rural slaveholders could likewise be fooled, as may be seen from the advertisement of William Beanes of Prince George's County, whose runaway carpenter, Tom Hudson, had gone to Baltimore in the fall of 1797 "on pretence of looking for a master."[77] Samuel Pitt, the slave of William Duvall, likewise outsmarted his master, running off under color of a "certificate to hire his own time or sell himself to another master."[78]

Samuel Pitt ran away in 1817, and Priscilla in 1816, years in which slave dealers were operating in Baltimore in unprecedented numbers. Either may have looked for an alternative to sale to a dealer and then fled after efforts to find a new master in Baltimore failed. Alternatively, they may have intended to flee all along, using the pass both to facilitate movement and to gain time to disappear before the master suspected something amiss. Whatever Pitt's or Priscilla's original thinking, they transformed a slaveholder's stratagem for reducing the likelihood of escapes into a device that assisted their flight.

Other slaveholder measures to secure faithful and productive labor could also go awry, including delayed manumission itself. In 1791 Harry Dorsey Gough bitterly condemned the runaway blacksmith Will Bates as "a very ungrateful Young Rogue who was born a Slave and Manumitted by me only to serve a few years." Gough expressed his hope that "an Atrocious Ingrate may be apprehended and brought to a sense of his Duty, and that his unsuccessful Villainy will prove an example to others under similar circumstances." A prominent landowner and a convert to Methodism, Gough had complied with the church's urging not to hold slaves for life. But perhaps he was also influenced by Will Bates, who had run away before, in 1785.[79] When Bates decamped again despite what Gough saw as a generous promise of eventual freedom, Gough's rage knew no bounds.

His anger notwithstanding, Gough grounded his appeal for assistance to recover and make an example of Will in the form of a public plea to slaveholders. He implied that the failure to close ranks and enforce the completion of Will's term of servitude would increase the tendency of "others under similar circumstances" to run. In urging Will's recapture as consonant with both his own and the general interest, Gough unwittingly acknowledged the potential conflict between those interests. When he promised Will his freedom, Gough had intended to strengthen Will's desire to serve a master, albeit for less than a life term. If Will's escape succeeded, then other slaves offered delayed manumission might feel as free to run as slaves for life did, and a major justification for term slavery would disappear. Fully aware of what was at stake,

Gough underlined his seriousness by offering the staggering sum of two hundred dollars for Bates's return.[80] Whether Will Bates succeeded in advancing the date of his freedom is unknown, but Gough gauged correctly the potential for term slaves to become more, rather than less, impatient in bondage. By 1804 Will Bates had enough imitators for the Maryland legislature to authorize county courts to extend terms of servitude to cover the lost time of recaptured prospective manumittees. A generation later, in 1833, legislators took the further step of authorizing court-regulated out-of-state sales of "turbulent" term slaves, a prospect tantamount to re-enslavement for life.[81]

The legislators would perhaps have sympathized with Gough's portrayal of such runaways as "atrocious ingrates," but the fugitives had a different perspective, including the fear that the promise of eventual freedom might not come to fruition. According to the law, a master could not revoke a properly executed and registered manumission; in practice, however, if the master died or sold the slave for his remaining term of years, a new owner could find ways to abrogate the promise of his predecessor. William Green, a successful escapee of the antebellum period, had been owned by Molly Goldsbury, whose will promised him freedom at age twenty-five. But he was "handsomely cheated out of it" by Goldsbury's relative, Nicholas Singleton, whose inheritance included the right to Green's labor for the remainder of his term. Singleton, who planned to leave Maryland, hoped to sell Green out of state as a slave for life, intending (in Green's words) to "put me in his pocket." Green's mother intervened and persuaded Singleton to delay the sale for one week, in the hope of finding a person who would buy him and keep him in Maryland. When such a buyer, Edward Hamilton, appeared, Singleton sold Green with no mention of his eventual manumission, and Hamilton treated him as a slave for life until Green escaped to free territory.[82]

In this instance Singleton engaged in an unequal negotiation that temporarily secured Green's acquiescence to remaining in lifelong slavery, by granting Green and his mother a few days to find a Maryland master to buy him. Green was indeed "handsomely cheated" by Singleton, who had disposed of Green, presumably at the more lucrative price a slave for life brought, without provoking Green's immediate flight.

Both Harry Gough's and William Green's experiences illustrate the ambiguities faced by masters or slaves who attempted to finesse the rigidities of slavery through agreements aimed at giving the slave a stake in labor productivity for his master. With power so heavily concentrated in the master's hands, he could not be held accountable for keeping promises, a circumstance that tempted either party to depart from those promises when a better opportunity arose. A bondman unfairly denied freedom could go to court and file a freedom petition, but this was not a real choice for many, particularly when a term slave was sold out of the state.[83] Precisely because the master's promise of freedom could be withdrawn, some term slaves still ran when they could.

To assure that manumission bargains were honored, a white patron might offer to protect a slave's interest, but here, too, the slave's legal incapacity could create difficulties. When Gibson Readle sued Ninian Willett over Willett's failure to honor a self-purchase agreement with his slave John, he alleged that John was "hard working and industrious" and had "long since . . . earned for Willett more than double the sum of the payment of which he was to have been set free." But Readle had not witnessed John actually paying Willett the sums in question, and John, as a black, could not testify against Willett, so the suit failed. Even with a white intermediary, John could not compel Willett to live up to their self-purchase agreement.[84]

Looked at coldly in terms of maximizing one's short-term interest, self-purchase agreements were an ideal strategy for masters seeking to extract the most from a slave. Not only did the self-purchaser provide funds to buy a replacement, but his payments toward the purchase of freedom represented a form of insurance for the master. If the slave died before gaining his freedom, the master's loss would be mitigated by keeping what the slave had already paid over, those monies being legally the master's property. Also, the master selling a slave his liberty could reconsider the price, insisting on more than had initially been agreed upon if slave prices had risen since the bargain had been struck.[85]

These advantages for the master constituted obstacles to self-purchase that might be overcome by having free black kin or whites buy a slave and then immediately manumit him. But no matter how the transaction was managed, things could go wrong. When Joseph Hart advertised Moses Lemmon as a runaway, he noted that Lemmon had over three hundred dollars in his possession, earned as a hostler at a Baltimore hotel. It is tempting to speculate that Lemmon ran after failing to convince Hart to sell him his freedom, or after Hart reneged on a price.[86]

Whatever may have induced Lemmon's flight, tension could build up in all the arrangements designed to assure the provision of reliable slave labor. In conceding eventual freedom or the choice of a new master, the slaveholder inevitably refocused his own interests, shortening his perspective to the near term. Doing so increased the pull of prospects for short-term gain, which might impel a master not to abide by promised concessions. When individual masters gave in to this impulse, they undermined slaves' willingness to trust those very mechanisms, such as delayed manumission, that had been employed in the first instance to maintain slaveholders' own longer-term interests.

Running away, slave sale, self-sale, and gradual manumission thus functioned as arenas in which masters and slaves commonly negotiated and contested the terms of their relationship. Additional complexities entered the picture when power relations became triangular through the hiring of slaves to another master. Historians have established that slaves could play on the resulting division of authority to achieve their own goals.[87] Complaining to the master about unreasonable treatment by the hirer, in order to avoid an unpleasant job, could give a slave more influence over his work life than might normally be available. To recall the case of Job Garretson and Negro Ben, the scene opened with Ben's complaint to his master about harsh treatment by his surrogate master and a demand for a change of supervisor.

Hired-out slaves had other opportunities to derive advantage from having two masters. Journeys between master and hirer could become springboards for escape attempts. Maryland masters often described a missing slave as last seen on his way to a job in or around the city. Or a runaway could pretend to be a slave hiring his own time. Here too, the ability to avoid recapture simply by blending into the ever-growing free black population of the city presented an opportunity uncommon elsewhere: a runaway posing as a slave hiring his own time could earn money without even leaving familiar territory. So, at least, feared William Dorsey, as he made a far-from-unique announcement: "All persons are forwarn'd from hiring or employing Molatto Man DANIEL, bred to the Anchor Business, without [my] permission." The brevity of Dorsey's ad makes it difficult to be certain whether Daniel had absconded altogether or was merely suspected of underreporting his income to Dorsey.[88] Other advertisers expressed similar warnings about workers who might try to hire themselves out as sailors, ironworkers, chimney sweeps, sawyers, axmen, or domestics.

These warnings were, on the one hand, aimed at white employers who might unwittingly offer work to a runaway; on the other hand, such advertisements also threatened prosecution of those who knowingly "harbored" such workers. Baltimore employers presumably found runaways potentially appealing for many of the reasons that today drive the hiring of undocumented alien workers. With the threat of exposure always available as a disciplinary instrument, the in-town runaway had virtually no leverage in any disputes that might arise over pay or working conditions, other than to run off yet again. So long as he escaped detection, a fugitive's employer could not be held financially responsible to a slaveholder for property loss, as a legitimate hirer could be, if a slave was injured, died on the job, or ran off.[89] Virtual freedom from such responsibility in turn reduced the employer's need for close supervision of such workers, further trimming their cost. In short, all the advantageous features of slave hiring, such as smaller initial outlay to purchase labor power, a supply of labor tailored to short-term demand shifts, and lessened risk of property loss through death or disappearance applied even more strongly to the employment of slaves hiring their own time, legitimately or otherwise.

For many African Americans, gaining more autonomy must have outweighed other considerations, particularly when self-hire meant "living out," in a household free of slaveholders.[90] Estimating the number of black people who lived in what has been called quasi-freedom must be a treacherous business; those so situated had good reason to avoid census marshals or tax assessors. It is therefore all the more surprising to discover that 238 of Baltimore's slaves were identified in the 1820 census as living in households containing no white person, a ratio of about one in every eighteen of the city's slaves. More than two-thirds of these persons were adults, so the phenomenon does not represent prospectively manumitted children living with their freed parents. The proportion of slaves in all-black households more than quadrupled between 1810 and 1820; none of the first three censuses had found as much as 2 percent of the slave population so situated.[91] This shift toward "living out" in the second decade of the nineteenth century coincides with other patterns that show greater concessions of authority exacted from masters by slaves; masters were inclined to cooperate because they hoped to blunt the multiplying threats to control posed by the changing environment for blacks in Baltimore.

Not all slaves who lived on their own negotiated self-hire agreements or seized their status through local flight to quasi-freedom. Some older slaves were allowed to go at large by masters blocked from emancipating them. The stricture against manumission of a slave over forty-five could be circumvented by a master's ceasing either to demand labor from or provide maintenance for the slave.[92] Permitting a slave to "go at large" occurred frequently enough for the state to enact its prohibition several times. The 1796 Act concerning Negroes had authorized county courts to prosecute complaints regarding slaves who "begged" or were "burthensome." Significantly, the law was toughened and fines to masters increased in 1817, as part of new legislation penalizing employers dealing with self-hired slaves.[93] But masters and slaves continued to ignore the law.

A review of Baltimore County wills turned up twenty cases in which a master specifically authorized a slave to go at large; presumably many more such actions occurred informally.[94] In a typical case John Battee stated simply enough that "Old Will may go where he pleases at my decease and when he cannot maintain himself then he is to return to the family for a subsistence."[95] Perhaps Will benefited from Battee's action; perhaps he found that he had been "turned out to die," as Frederick Douglass bitterly characterized his aged grandmother's fate when she could no longer work for her master.[96] In all likelihood Will found work in Baltimore, joining the growing ranks of quasi-free casual laborers there. At least one prominent Baltimorean found such cases altogether too common. Newspaper editor Hezekiah Niles, an antislavery Quaker, complained in 1815 that a "large proportion" of the city's paupers were "worn out negroes" sent to Baltimore by their masters to "beg or starve."[97] Exemplifying Niles's assessment, Negro Rachel, a sixty-year-old black woman, asked the orphans' court in 1820 to support her in her old age from the estate of a former master whose heirs had left Maryland and left Rachel to her own devices.[98]

Relationships in which slaves gained autonomy by playing owner against hirer or by convincing owners to allow "living out" as an alternative to such manipulation, or yet again by going "at large" with the master's acquiescence, no doubt became familiar to urban whites employing slave labor, as instances in which white and black short-term interests could coincide. Rarer, but more threateningly, blacks and whites conspired to play on a hirer's interest to part him from his money. Job Garretson concluded his catalog of woes by insinuating that Hollis and Ben had set out from the beginning to dupe him. Garretson complained that Ben had run from a previous owner and that Hollis had employed Ben as a runaway and then purchased him for "some small sum of money in the situation of a runaway" from his then owner in Calvert County. Garretson claimed that Hollis was trying to repeat this coup when he offered to buy Ben back for half of what Garretson had paid for him.

Nor was Garretson alone in his fears of potential cooperation between unscrupulous whites and runaways. Joshua Barney, seeking the return of Harry Harrison, a runaway shoemaker, advertised that he believed Harrison to be in the vicinity of Port Deposit, on the Susquehanna, and implied that the Woodland family of that locale had connived at Harrison's flight. Barney had bought Harrison only weeks before his run "on the recommendation of Major Woodland" and was now in receipt of an offer by the major's brother to "buy Harry Harrison running." Barney clearly intended to shame the Woodlands through his advertisement and perhaps to corroborate his suspicions.[99] Similar aims probably motivated Richard Anson, a Virginian, to advertise in

the *Baltimore American and Commercial Daily Advertiser* for his runaway Tom. Anson's ad unfolded a picaresque tale featuring Mistress
Elizabeth Marks as the central character. According to Anson, Marks
had sought out Anson in order to hire out Tom, a sawyer, for a short
stint of work. She and Tom had promptly disappeared, and Anson was
forced to conclude that he had been cheated of his slave. Swathing his
anger in public spirit, Anson advised Baltimoreans that Marks was
rumored to have sailed from Norfolk to Baltimore, where he expected
that she would switch roles, offering to hire Tom out as a preliminary
to yet another disappearance.[100]

Machinations on this order of duplicity appeared infrequently in
newspapers and court records; Marks, Hollis, and the Woodlands, even
if guilty of conspiring with slaves to defraud "honorable" masters, behaved most abnormally. But for a slaveholder, especially a small to
middling artisan, for whom purchasing or hiring a black laborer meant
risking much if not all of his liquid capital, even marginal threats to the
profitability of slaveholding might loom large. To such men and women
the attractions of slave buying or hiring may have been significantly
tempered by the dangers of fraud stemming from the very flexibility in
labor control that made such arrangements appealing. Finally, precau-
tions taken to control slaves and free blacks could be turned to advantage by African Americans. Passes, permits to go at large or to hire
one's time, apprentice discharges, freedom papers, and sailors' protections could be and were forged, sold, and stolen to facilitate free movement and employment.

Slaveholders' efforts to make servitude more secure by palliating
strains on the master-slave relationship through concessions of autonomy
temporarily succeeded in blunting slaves' northward flights. But the
accompanying growth in Baltimore's free black population called into
being a graver threat to the slave owner: the ability of slaves to flee and
be sheltered within the city itself. For masters a prime attraction of
gradually manumitting slaves had lain in its reducing the risk, uncertainty, and contentiousness associated with slaveholding. As slaves
learned to seize the opportunities associated with gradual manumission to advance their own interests more swiftly and certainly, masters
found holding slaves an increasingly uncertain proposition, in terms
both of maintaining control and ensuring return on their investments.
They drifted to a safer, though often less convenient course: they hired
free workers, drawn in no small measure from the ranks of recently
freed slaves. The story turns now to a closer examination of how African Americans and their families became free via manumission.

4

MANUMISSION AND THE
TRANSFORMATION OF SLAVERY

Manumission in many societies coexisted with perpetual bondage, frequently in the shape of self-purchase by slave artisans and sometimes monitored through recognition of the slave's legal personality as a contracting party.[1] But manumission played a comparatively minor role in North American slavery, with debatable exceptions in the mid-Atlantic region; historians of slavery there have portrayed manumitters as individuals of conscience or economic maximizers, or both at the same time, seeking profitable exits from a locally declining labor institution.[2] This contrast was first noted by Frank Tannenbaum, who cited slaves' greater access to freedom in Spanish- and Portuguese-speaking America as a factor distinguishing those systems of slavery from that which prevailed in British America. Tannenbaum targeted differences in religion and in the European history of slavery of each society to explain the differences.[3]

Although early national Maryland hardly fit the cultural mold Tannenbaum described for Brazil or Latin America, the state did develop a large population of free people of color and did have many manumitters who did not abandon slaveholding. Masters instead employed offers of delayed manumission in the ongoing management of slave workers, countered by slaves' attempts to negotiate the conditions of servitude. Viewed thus, manumission became yet another arena in which masters and slaves contended, conspired, and sometimes cooperated in shaping their respective worlds. This relatively rare North American juxtaposition of frequent manumission with continued reliance on slave labor helped expand slavery in Baltimore until about 1815 and stabilized it for a while longer. Only in the late antebellum years did manumission there operate solely as a slaveholder's exit from slavery.

Baltimore's declining position in foreign trade after 1815, coupled with the financial crunch of the Panic of 1819, disrupted the city's economy well into the 1820s and may have contributed significantly to the loss of its status as a magnet for slaves. While slave numbers dropped, free black population soared at a rate in excess of natural increase and manumissions combined.[4] Voluntary relocation of free persons of color to Baltimore thus replaced an earlier wave of involuntary migration by slaves.

By 1830 the extensive in-migration of both free blacks and subsequently manumitted slaves created the paradox of an essentially free labor city largely surrounded by a slave labor region. Though Baltimore merchants, craftsmen, and entrepreneurs could still buy or hire slaves from planters seeking to trim the ranks of their bound workers, they all but ceased to do so. So long as slaves had formed the dominant element in the influx of black workers, masters could develop and manipulate delayed manumission to maintain control of their chattels in an urban setting. But the very dynamism of Baltimore's growth, especially as compared to the torpor of the surrounding slave labor economies, upset this balance.

As free blacks came to outnumber slaves in the city, lifelong slavery tempered by occasional manumission evolved toward a system of slavery as a stage of life, ended by testamentary manumission, self-purchase, or flight. In this regard, delayed manumission, whatever its short-term utility for securing reliable labor, served to increase the attractiveness of Baltimore for would-be black migrants. The presence of mounting numbers of blacks, in turn, eventually increased the level of pressure on lifelong slavery as a system and accelerated its marginalization in the city.

To a degree, we can say that slavery's sickness in Baltimore was contracted in the countryside. Relatively low rates of manumission in most of Maryland's rural counties sufficed to keep slavery viable there; but as Baltimore became the prime destination for the exodus of free blacks from everywhere else in the state, slavery in the city became all but unsustainable, despite its previous compatibility with relatively high rates of manumission.[5] Marylanders manumitted thousands of slaves by individual voluntary acts recorded in deeds or wills. Here, Maryland's path diverged from that of neighboring states. The northern states ended slavery through legislative or judicial action, typically through the delayed emancipation of all slave children born after a fixed date. Some southern states liberalized private manumission laws in the 1780s or 1790s but then clamped down on the practice in the early 1800s, to contain increases in the number of free blacks.[6] In Maryland, despite repeated efforts to limit private manumissions, the practice remained legal and popular, although not equally so throughout the state.

Maryland's manumitters granted freedom to men and women in virtually equal numbers from the 1770s through the 1820s, contrary to the general tendency in Atlantic slave societies for about two-thirds of those liberated to be women.[7] This pattern fits neither with the assumption that slavery's unprofitability led masters to sell black men to the Southwest, while more frequently retaining or manumitting less valuable women, nor with the supposition that women were more often freed as a consequence of sexual liaisons with masters. Given the skew elsewhere to manumitting women, the Maryland ratio provides strong inferential evidence that slaves there, not just masters, were helping to determine who gained freedom.

The attempt to determine what motivated masters to manumit their slaves has led researchers to consider also whether persons of mixed racial descent were more likely to become free. In Maryland this approach yields similarly negative evidence, which may also suggest that white motivations did not alone decide who was manumitted. Left to their own devices, masters might have preferred to free slaves of mixed race, either to liberate their own children by slave mothers or in the belief that mulatto or "yellow" persons would be more intelligent and thus better fitted to be free than "Negroes" or "blacks." Even a master with no intentions of freeing slaves might have been more likely to select someone of mixed race for craft training, thus giving that slave a better opportunity to work or buy himself free.[8]

In fact, little in the public record suggests that free people of color or prospectively manumitted slaves in Maryland were disproportionately of mixed race. Manumissions generally did not provide a physical description of the slave being freed, nor did masters acknowledge kin ties. Where it is possible to compare the color labels applied to slaves with those of free people of color, the proportions of each group described as mulatto or yellow are about the same.[9] Although Maryland law offered slaves the hope of freeing themselves by proving descent from a free woman, typically a white indentured servant, only a few hundred freed men and women, a tiny fragment of those liberated, could thus capitalize on their mixed-race ancestry, and they did so over the objections of their masters. Working with this admittedly sketchy evidence, it would appear that Maryland whites did not see mixed-race appearance as a key factor inclining them toward freeing a slave. Or if they did, such leanings failed to influence overall patterns of manumission, suggesting that the desires and actions of slaves, independent of coloration, were critical in shaping who became free.

Whoever was being liberated, the deeds that did so timed the bestowal of freedom with considerable diversity. Masters could emancipate a slave "from this day forward," but often they established a future date on which freedom would occur. In rural counties about two-thirds of deeded manumissions had delayed effect.[10] In Baltimore the tendency to grant delayed freedom decreased during the post-1815 decline of slavery. Before 1815 half of Baltimore manumissions were conditioned on a further term of service; after 1815 that proportion fell to a third.[11] By looking at individual manumissions, changes in law and court precedent touching manumission, and discussions of the subject in the press, we can discern the motivations of masters and slaves that informed these patterns.

A master considering manumission might be moved by benevolence, egalitarian principles, fear for his soul, desire for gain, or all of the above. Some deeds state a belief that slavery is against God's will or inconsistent with the principles of American society. But such unequivocal statements are generally quite rare, even in manumissions of the 1780s and early 1790s, and become virtually nonexistent in nineteenth-century deeds.[12]

Of course, failure to record humanitarian sentiments does not prove their absence. It was easy for manumitters to leave their motives unrecorded because court clerks, attorneys, and conveyancers who drew up legal documents had quickly developed a formulaic code for manumissions that satisfied the law's requirements but said little else. As early as 1789 Baltimore printers sold forms for manumission that provided all the boilerplate to give the deed legal effect, with blank spaces left for the name, the age, and the date of freedom.[13] The statement of intent, with slight variations, indicated that "diverse good causes and considerations" had caused the manumitter to act.

Baltimore's notable Quaker and Methodist presence invites further investigation into the role of faith and benevolence in manumission practices in the city. But matching manumitters' names with congregation membership lists reveals that less than one-tenth of Baltimore manumissions could be identified as having been granted by masters identified with either discipline.[14]

The Friends in Maryland had largely divorced themselves from slavery before Baltimore's post-Revolutionary expansion. The Baltimore Yearly Meeting had agreed as early as 1768 to disown members who bought and sold slaves and was considering disowning slaveholders by 1773. By 1778 the practice of hiring slaves was being discouraged, and slaveholders were barred from conducting any church affairs. Baltimore Quakers regarded themselves as largely free of the toils of slavery by the 1790s and were turning their attention outward, to petitioning the Maryland General Assembly and the U.S. Congress for laws to restrain the slave trade.[15]

Baltimore's Quakers ultimately succeeded in distancing themselves from slavery, but Methodism's encounter with the institution yielded far less clear-cut results. As early as the 1780s, the Methodist church in America had denounced slaveholding in all forms among its itinerant preachers and was moving to ban both slave dealing and the holding of slaves for life among its lay members. But hostility to these measures in Virginia and the Carolinas began a long retreat on the issue, culminating in an uneasy "local option" approach that allowed regional conferences to determine church discipline on slaveholding.[16]

The Baltimore conference long adhered to the policy that Methodist elders and preachers should not own slaves for life and should manumit those acquired by marriage or inheritance, after terms of service approved by the elders, under penalty of expulsion.[17] But compliance was far from perfect. Methodists initially had few slaveholders in their ranks; as church members amassed wealth, however, their tendency to hold slaves increased: the 1820 census showed 145 Methodist slaveholders in the city, a number more than double that of 1810 and in excess of the documented manumissions of slaves by Methodists for the entire preceding thirty-year period.[18] Whatever their degree of faithfulness to church dictates, manumission by Methodists accounts for about 140 of the more than 2,000 manumissions by deed that survive from early-nineteenth-century Baltimore.[19]

Both Methodists and Quakers may have slowed the growth of slavery in Baltimore, to the extent that church members with the means to do so bought slaves less often than similarly situated individuals outside those sects. Certainly some noteworthy examples of the exclusion of slave labor can be attributed to such influences, as in the construction of the Baltimore and Ohio Railroad or among the laborers in the mills and foundries owned by a prominent Quaker family, the Ellicotts.[20] But neither Quakers nor Methodists were responsible for the large and continuing volume of manumissions in the city.

The most common explanation offered by manumitters, appearing in about one-quarter of the deeds, was the "further consideration" stirred by receipt of a sum of money "paid to me in my hand this day," ranging from a token dollar to as much as five hundred dollars. Denwood Jones, in his 1821 manumission of "my negro man Kit" justified his action "in consideration of the love and affection I have for [him] from his good behavior, as well as the sum of one hundred dollars."[21] Only a handful of the hundreds of manumissions specifying payment identify the source of the cash; in these cases "manumission" almost invariably featured the purchasing a husband, a wife, a son, a daughter, a mother, or a brother by free black kin. The vast majority of payments have no attribution; in all likelihood these represented slaves buying their own freedom.

Buying and selling of freedom occurred commonly enough to warrant legal recognition, even during Maryland's attempts to restrict manumission in the aftermath of Nat Turner's Rebellion. In 1832, when the legislature sought to limit future manumissions by requiring the newly freed to leave the state, it nonetheless stipulated that "if any slave or any person, for or in behalf of such slave, shall, previously to the passage of [this] act have entered into an agreement . . . for the purchase . . . of the freedom of the said slave, . . . and there shall have been paid or performed all or any portion of the stipulated price or consideration for such freedom," then that person could remain in Maryland.[22] Since Maryland law did not otherwise acknowledge a slave's legal personality in manumissions, most were in law deeds of gift and not contracts.[23] However, the master manumitting prospectively could not revoke his or her action without challenge once the deed was filed with the county court; a slave thus denied liberty could file a petition of freedom.

But the slave could not formally participate in establishing the terms of manumission or insist on their being recorded. This explains why a transaction as critically important to slaves as manumission, which might be expected to occur in many different modes and terms, takes on such a bland and uniform aspect in the deeds actually filed: masters were required only to identify the slave being freed, testify to his or her ability to earn a living, set the date of freedom, and have the deed signed by two witnesses.[24]

Nevertheless, we can occasionally glimpse a hint, a shadowy outline, of negotiations between master and slave preceding manumission and occasionally continuing during and after the filing of a deed. We have already seen that manumissions could be acts of self-purchase; some of the deeds speak to the question of how slaves amassed the sums needed to buy freedom. In 1820 Dianna Howard, a free black woman, manumitted Augustus Howard, "whom I purchased from William Brown" as well as Samuel and Emanuel Howard, "purchased" from John Chauncey of Harford County. The ages of the freedmen make it quite likely that Dianna Howard had freed her husband and two sons, possibly purchasing them with sums earned by the entire family.[25] Deeds of this sort, often found with the bills of sale from the white master to the black kinfolk, compose the most common variation on unadorned self-purchase.

White philanthropy also came into play on occasion. Isaac Tyson, a wealthy Quaker who owned merchant flour mills on the Jones Falls in Baltimore, manumitted James Davis in 1817, noting that he had purchased Davis eight months earlier, in August 1816, "of a certain John Williamson of South Carolina." Williamson in turn had just acquired Davis from Peter Carnes of Baltimore. Tyson stepped in to prevent Davis's separation from his family, "fully believing he will be able so to refund the money paid for him," some $412. It is worthy of note that Tyson did expect to be repaid and did hold Davis as a slave some months before freeing him, perhaps to ensure himself that Davis possessed the industry and self-discipline necessary to pay back his purchase price. Tyson appears not to have insisted on security for the funds advanced on Davis's behalf.[26]

Other freed men and women, who faced more demanding lenders, often had no security to offer but the promise of their labor power. In 1813 Negro Cato Mink indentured himself for a year, in return for maintenance plus thirty dollars. Mink, a former slave, may have thus made up a part of his purchase price. Edward and Elizabeth Brown were obliged to take a far bigger risk when, in 1819, they mortgaged "all the right, title, Interest and claim . . . to their freedom" to James Blair as security for a one-year loan of four hundred dollars. If they defaulted, they would regain their freedom only if "they serve[d] faithfully for 5 years." No mortgage release was filed in 1820 when the debt fell due, so the Browns probably slipped back into slavery, at least for five years, possibly forever.[27]

The Browns may have gained their freedom and subsequently acquired the debt that dragged them down; in other cases bondmen who could not pay their full purchase price bought freedom on the installment plan. William Carroll's master agreed to manumit him "when and so soon as [he] pays . . . five hundred dollars and not sooner, provided that not less than eighty dollars is paid in any one year and the whole sum is paid within five years." If Carroll could not keep to the payment schedule, he would stand to lose all that he paid in the interim, and his freedom would be foreclosed on.[28] Thomas Perry arranged to buy his freedom from Michael Lucas for two $120 payments and then borrowed money, presumably to prevent default on his obligation. Lucas moved ahead with the agreement on January 2, 1801, noting that he had received $60 from Mr. Henry Rhodes "for the use of Thomas Perry," this being the residue of the first payment still due Lucas.[29]

Manumission deeds that say nothing of money can also uncover some of the give and take that informed the institution. Numerous deeds offered freedom after a term of years, "provided that the said negroes shall serve faithful and in all things remain faithful and obedient servants until" the freedom date.[30] Manumitting masters could thus offer the reward of freedom but demand steady work and no running off in exchange.

Slaves could seek to reduce the amount of uncompensated labor they rendered in other ways too, though. Edward Wrotten specified that his slave David would be freed in six years, provided that "all sick time from this time forward be made up at the end of the six years before he is absolute free."[31] Wrotten may simply have been unusually meticulous in protecting himself from reduced worker output once he promised to free David; nonetheless, by insisting on full makeup of illness he virtually ensured more labor from David in the next six years than he would otherwise have obtained. Wrotten thus mixed the positive incentive of eventual freedom with the threat of delaying that freedom if David "malingered"; Wrotten, needless to say, would be the one to determine whether or not David had measured up.

Other manumitters also manipulated freedom dates, but they relied more on the positive incentive of freedom granted sooner than promised. In 1808 former governor Richard Mackall drew up a deed of manumission promising eventual freedom to some thirty-two slaves. Diverging from a common pattern in multiple manumissions, Mackall set no uniform age of freedom, such as freeing all males at twenty-eight or all females at twenty-five. Mackall freed two slaves who were over forty immediately and set up terms ranging from eighteen months to twenty-one years for the others, with anticipated ages at freedom varying from twenty-two to forty-two. But Mackall later shortened the terms of several slaves, on individual bases. Mackall may have filed the original document, with its generally long terms, as a benchmark, hoping to spur his workers to greater efforts in return for freedom more speedily obtained, either by an agreed commutation of the term or by self-purchase of their remaining time.[32]

Linkages between slaves' behavior during their term of years and a potential speedup of emancipation could be quite explicit: Edward Griffith promised Jack and seven other adolescent slaves freedom at the age of thirty but allowed in the manumission deed that, "provided that the said negroes shall serve faithful and . . . remain . . . obedient servants until they come to the age of 25 years I do hereby agree and determine that they shall be free at the age of 25 years." Griffith's straightforward language vividly illustrates what many more circumspect manumission deeds no doubt concealed. As master, he "determined" when Jack and the others would become free, but only after

44, "upon condition that [he] shall immediately after the execution of the deed of manumission except from me a bill of sale for his mother, an aged negro woman named Hannah, and shall . . . support his said mother during her life."[39] But as noted above, most manumissions occurred only after the slave had labored five to twenty years as an adult.

However manumission was granted, the basic unit of exchange in bargaining over freedom was the black worker's labor or, more specifically, the promise of more work, more production, and fewer interruptions to work than could be compelled from a slave for life. The starting point for a delayed manumission might thus have been a verbal agreement to allow a slave to purchase freedom for himself or herself or a family member with labor, or cash equaling a putative sale price, or a combination of the two. Both in shaping such an agreement and in bringing it to fruition, the competing interests of slaveholders and the would-be freed persons might be subject to further negotiation or manipulation at every stage of the process.

Masters discussing delayed manumission with a slave might, for example, seek to maintain maximum control by keeping the promise of eventual manumission informal. In that way a master could ensure flexibility regarding the length of a slave's term of service or price of self-purchase. Slaves benefited most from a clearly worded commitment to freedom, recorded at the county court house, which was legally binding on the master or his heirs or assignees. Accordingly, the act of recording the promise of freedom could itself become a bone of contention.

Problems surrounding the formalizing of manumission deeds imply that "immediate" acts were not impulsive gestures by humanitarian masters but rather represented a slave's final satisfaction of the master's long-spun-out demands. Occasionally, a manumitter testified directly to this point. Henry Darden's grant of immediate freedom to Benjamin took effect when Darden and two co-owners pronounced themselves "fully satisfied by his faithful services and monies paid"; they had "purchased [him] for a valuable consideration with a promise he should be free on his good behaviour by a limited time."[40]

Should a master be induced to put the promise of eventual manumission in writing, he or she could still seek to retain room to maneuver by delaying the recording of the deed at the county courthouse. A good many masters yielded to the temptation to thus deprive their slaves—at least for a time—of the right to petition against them, in case they defaulted on their promise of freedom. As early as 1796, the state legislature felt compelled to regulate the recording of manumissions by means of a statute requiring their registration within six months of

having "agreed," presumably with the young slaves or their parents, on a potential early release date. An 1823 manumission revealed another negotiation: Job's master, James Chaplain, promised to free him on January 1, 1837, "provided . . . that if the said boy Job . . . or any other person . . . shall petition any legal authority for his freedom then this deed of manumission shall be null and void . . . and Job . . . shall remain a slave for life." It does not seem unreasonable to regard Job's eventual manumission as an out-of-court settlement of a claim in law to his freedom.[33]

Regardless of the slaveholder's rationale, gradual manumission had an obvious potential for extending slavery across generations in the name of compensatory service rendered to manumitters or creditors, or both, of free blacks. Immediate grants of freedom, however, appear to have been no less strongly motivated by the same desire. A survey of manumission deeds filed in the Baltimore County Court reveals that men and women manumitted with immediate effect tended to be older at the moment of freedom than counterparts liberated after a further term of service. A majority of women manumitted immediately were over thirty, an age reached by only two-fifths of female gradual manumittees. Nearly two-thirds of the men manumitted immediately were over thirty, as compared to about half of the men granted delayed manumissions. In fact, the modal age for immediately freed blacks of both sexes was forty, suggesting that a good many manumitters extracted virtually all the labor they could before releasing their slaves.[34] Female slaves thus manumitted typically already had borne children, who were already slaves, and masters and freed people could and did go through the same permutations of granting, denying, and buying freedom as surfaced in gradual manumission. Masters granting "immediate" manumissions were thus, as a group, no less moved by self-interest and no more influenced by humanitarian or egalitarian motives than their gradualist counterparts.

In fact, masters who formally granted delayed manumission actually conceded some control over their chattels' lives during their term of service: a master could not legally revoke a prospective gradual manumission for which a deed had been filed at the county courthouse, nor, after 1817, could a term slave be sold out of state.[35] The master who confined freedom overtures to oral promises could renege on those offers more readily. Of course, the passage of a law barring out-of-state sales of term slaves suggests the existence of a practice that could negate a prospective manumission by removing the slave from access to Maryland's courts via a freedom petition, in the event of the master's refusal to liberate the slave at the expiration of his or her term.[36]

Nonetheless, the prospective freedman whose master attempted to backtrack on a written promise of liberty had legal recourse, and as judged by the law of 1817, he had some measure of public sympathy to draw on. It may not be coincidental that a higher proportion of manumission deeds granted freedom immediately in the 1820s than in earlier decades. Given the strictures of the 1817 law, an 1820s master seeking to wheedle more work or cash from a slave or his kin in return for eventual manumission was well advised to keep his promises unwritten, to eventually grant immediate liberty, as it were. Had such a master reflected on the growth of the domestic slave trade to the southwest during the same time period, he or she might have been tempted to retain the financial option—and threat to the slave—of sale to Georgia or Louisiana, by filing no manumission deed until the actual day of emancipation.

The slave whose master made no written promises was much more vulnerable to the loss of prospective freedom through changes in the master's outlook, or for that matter, a change of masters through sale, death, or gift. For slaves so situated, attempts to gain freedom through manumission may well have involved a ceaseless round of pleas, bargains, negotiations, and reconsiderations with a master who could not be bound to his or her word. Many "immediate" manumissions must have been the outcome of lengthy and contested interactions between master and slave.

Further evidence for this view may be derived from examining the age distributions of slaves freed by immediate manumission. Despite the existence of an eighteenth-century statutory "model" age of thirty-one at which to manumit slaves, masters in fact chose every conceivable age up to the legal limit of forty-five, as we might expect of decisions governed more by personal interaction than resort to customary procedures.[37] There was no particular age that defined the moment of freedom for even as much as one-tenth of either male or female ex-slaves who were manumitted immediately; no five-year age grouping captured more than two-fifths of such manumissions.

Gradual manumitters were not necessarily more liberal in their promises than immediate ones: when Sarah Turnbull filed manumission deeds in 1804 for twenty slaves, each was to gain freedom on his or her forty-fifth birthday. Turnbull also stipulated that any children born to the women or girls while serving their terms would serve as slaves until their forty-fifth birthdays, thus guaranteeing that Turnbull and her heirs would have slave labor at their disposal for as much as eighty years into the future.[38] In fact, an unusually determined master could successfully evade the age limit on manumissions, as Charles Goldsborough demonstrated by manumitting Benjamin Jackson, age

being signed and witnessed. The frequency with which the six-month rule was violated, as evidenced by the reregistration of "defective" manumissions, not to mention the large number of deeds registered in the sixth month after their creation, suggests that many masters may have sought to extract more from their term slaves by deferring deed registration as long as possible.[41]

What did masters hope to gain from such a strategy? If masters saw delayed manumission as an incentive for their slaves to give steady and productive labor, an incentive so valuable as to make eventual manumission an economically desirable outcome, why would they undermine this incentive by introducing elements of uncertainty over making good on their promises of freedom? Slaveholders perhaps behaved inconsistently or erratically because they harbored doubts about the path on which they had embarked and wanted tangible evidence of "good behaviour" or "faithful service" from a term slave before making an irrevocable commitment to liberation. Thus, when William Browne manumitted Phill in 1800, he specified a seven-year term of service to be backdated from January of 1797. Browne was honoring his original bargain with Phill, but only after Phill had performed nearly half of the agreed-upon service.[42]

In another revealing case, Joseph Blackiston, manumitting Negro John in 1805 with immediate effect, noted that he had sold John in 1797 to Thomas Granger for a term of seven years, with an expiration date of December 25, 1804, "at which time I was a going to manumit the said negro man, but Thomas Granger requested me not to [do so], for fear he should know he was to be free at the end of seven years and cause him to behave amiss." Blackiston deferred to Granger and refrained from filing a manumission deed, but he did tell John of his intentions, inasmuch as "the term has expired and [John] has since complained to me that Thomas Granger will not let him go from him." Significantly, Granger had himself granted delayed manumission to eight of his slaves in the 1780s and 1790s but had become disenchanted with the device. His attitude was revealed not only by his objection to John's knowing he was to be free, but also by his two subsequent manumissions, in 1814, which were "immediate."[43]

What could be done to thwart such delaying tactics or to deal with slaveholders who—even worse—disavowed verbal commitments and refused, like Granger, to let their slaves go at the end of their terms? The greatest security could be gained by purchasing freedom in a cash transaction, thus avoiding prolonged negotiation while still in slavery, but the costs of immediate self-purchase could be prohibitive. Adult male slaves for life typically sold for $300 to $350 in late-eighteenth-

or early-nineteenth-century Maryland, a sum equal to fifteen or sixteen months' wages for day laborers in Baltimore; in the rural areas it would take even longer to earn such a sum. Nevertheless, hundreds of manumission deeds record substantial cash payments by slaves and free people of color, to free themselves or relatives. Where did the money come from?

Dealing with this question means uncovering complex meanings behind the language of those deeds. Many manumission documents entailed both the sale of a slave to a purchaser identified as a spouse, a sibling, or a parent and the purchaser's immediate manumission of that slave. With a self-purchase the manumitter acknowledged the receipt of cash and then granted immediate freedom. But in fact, many such deeds effectively describe not a single transaction occurring at a discrete moment in time, but rather the completion of an installment purchase that may have been negotiated three, five, or ten years previously. Blacks generally gained formal recognition of such agreements only when the final payment was made or when performance of the installment "contract" was interrupted either by the death of one of the parties or by the master's transfer of his or her interest in the would-be self-purchaser.

Struggles over manumission could extend beyond the master's life, as revealed in testamentary manumissions, crafted to avoid slave flight at a master's death. In Maryland most slaveholders held small numbers of chattels, at least compared to the large plantation standards of the deep South. In fact, in Baltimore four-fifths of the slaveholders had fewer than five slaves. In both rural and urban settings, slaves nonetheless typically comprised significant shares of a decedent's wealth. A master's death therefore frequently compelled the division of slaves into inheritance shares, as described by Frederick Douglass in his autobiography, or the conversion of slaves into cash by sale to settle the estate.[44]

The prospect of being sold soon after a master's decease caused some blacks to flee rather than to submit to a new and unknown master. Anticipating such problems, many slaveholders in their wills promised eventual manumission. They hoped that would induce their slaves to continue to give them reliable service and later provide years of income-generating labor for their heirs. As a form of endowment for the support of minor children, slaves represented a potentially high-yield, middle-term investment. An adult man, worth perhaps three to four hundred dollars at sale, might readily generate sixty dollars of income each year, clear of expenses, if hired out.[45] A property earning 12 to 20 percent of its value in yearly income was not to be spurned; by comparison, city lots usually rented at 6 percent of their presumed value.

50 Dollars Reward.

ABSCONDED from on board the Sloop *Jolly Miller*, in Baltimore, on the 28th inst. a Negro Man, named JACK, sometimes calls himself JACK ALEXANDER; about 5 feet 8 or 9 inches high, not very black, with a small scar on his forehead, round face and talks fast when first spoken to; he is a very active and a good countenanced fellow. It is supposed he will obtain a pass as a free man: his object is to go to sea, and will be trying to ship on board some vessel bound out. He had on and took with him a brown jacket with pearl buttons, and waistcoat of the same; his trowsers coarse white country cloth, with a variety of other clothes that he has with him. Whoever takes up and secures said Negro in any jail, shall receive, if taken in the city, 20 dollars; if 30 miles from Baltimore, 30 dollars; if 40 miles, 40 dollars; and if out of the state, the above reward, and all reasonable charges, if brought home to

Ananias Divers,

Near WM. PATTERSON, Esq'rs. Mills, Gunpowder Falls.
MARCH 30th, 1810.

N. B. All Masters of vessels and others are forewarned harboring or taking off said Negro, at their peril.

BALTIMORE—Printed by W. PECHIN, Office of the *American.*

Runaway slaves such as Jack Alexander often sought to pass as free men to obtain employment. Masters offered sliding scale rewards keyed to the fugitive's distance from Baltimore when captured. Advertisement of Ananias Divers, 1810. From the broadside collection of the Maryland Historical Society

Most mortgages and commercial loans were also pegged at 6 percent interest.[46] Of course, land might appreciate in value, whereas a slave's aging would eventually lower both income-producing capacity and re-sale value. Nevertheless, leaving slaves in trust to one's children might well generate a high yield of income over spans of ten to fifteen or even twenty years.

Children's guardians filed numerous accounts with the orphans' court detailing earnings accrued to an estate by hired-out slaves. Thus

$50 Reward.

Ranaway on Saturday the 17th inst. a coloured woman by the name of

EASTER,

Who was formerly the property of Arthur Hill, near Reisterstown;—the said Easter is rather between a mulatto and black, short chunky, with thick lips and somewhat freckled in her face; she is about 22 years of age; she had on a light calico frock when she went away, and a cloth over coat, olive colour. She has some relations living in Baltimore at Fell's Point, where she is expected to be lurking at this time. If she is taken in Baltimore County and secured so that I get her again I will give 25 dollars, and if out of the State 50 dollars.

JACOB WOOLERY,

Within four miles of Winchester.

Dec. 24, 1825.

Baltimore became the destination of many runaway slaves seeking help from kin in eluding pursuit. Advertisement of Jacob Woolery, 1825. From the broadside collection of the Maryland Historical Society

John Wooden managed the estate of Joseph Bowen for his three children, Rebecca, Pitt, and Wilkes. The principal income of the estate derived from the hire of Lee, Allen, Milly, and Betty, who together brought in around $250 a year. Edward Pannell, administering his brother John's estate from 1801 to 1810, hired out a skilled shipwright, Peoly, for as much as $242 a year to shipbuilders James Biays and Dixon Brown.[47]

Promises of eventual manumission were included in Lewis DeRochebrune's will, presumably as a way of averting slave flight and the resulting loss to the estate. DeRochebrune, a shipbuilder and the owner of seven adult male slaves at his death in 1802, manumitted each man but staggered their freedom dates at intervals of from three to fifteen years. He named fellow shipwright William Price as one of his executors, and Price hired out all seven men. All of this suggests strongly that DeRochebrune was attempting to provide a long-term flow of cash support for his heirs; he may have spaced the manumission dates with this in mind.[48]

Caleb Hewitt, a tobacco manufacturer, left slaves in trust to his daughter, Mary, in his 1805 will and promised manumission to two of them, Saul and Charles. The two men apparently obtained their freedom in 1811 or 1812, when Francis Hopkinson, Mary's guardian, noted in his annual account to the court a revaluation of the estate "due to slaves who have become free."[49] In a third case, James Piper, rope maker and merchant, directed in his will, "All my indented apprentices, male servants and male slaves shall be continued in the rope walk for the remainder of their time of servitude after my decease, . . . that the profits arising from their services shall be received by my Executors to the use of all my children." Piper, a Methodist who took seriously the church discipline's ban on holding slaves for life, had previously granted deeds of delayed manumission to his slaves, and having placed them on a par with his other bound laborers, expected all to serve out their time for the benefit of his heirs.[50]

The wills of craftsmen/manufacturers DeRochebrune, Hewitt, and Piper and the accounts filed by their heirs' guardians reveal that slaves' craft skills could continue to generate profits even after their master's death. Foresighted masters could thus use offers of gradual manumission quite successfully to conserve wealth and income for their posterity.

In comparing manumission by deed with manumission by will, it is noteworthy that slaves freed by will were significantly more likely to be compelled to endure a further term of service than those manumitted by deed: less than one-fifth of testamentary manumissions were immediate, versus nearly three-fifths of deeds granting freedom.[51] A promise of delayed manumission by deed registered the master's offer of future freedom; slaves with such deeds in hand had wrung a more secure prospect of emancipation from their masters than those working without guarantees toward an eventual "immediate" manumission. In contrast, a master promising freedom directly after his or her death was indeed emancipating a slave more quickly than one delaying that event until after a further period of service to an heir. The relative disinclination of testators to free slaves immediately fits with the view of manumission as the product of a contested negotiation between master and slave. In deeded manumission, which most likely signified either the execution of a self-purchase agreement or the master's formal recognition of service rendered following an initially unwritten or unrecorded promise of eventual freedom, "immediate" emancipations were common. Where the master acted more unilaterally, as a testator, and immediate manumission entailed an unrecompensed sacrifice of property, delayed manumissions were the rule.

It might also be noted that in the city of Baltimore manumissions by will were a smaller proportion of all grants of freedom than they were in the rural counties of Prince George's and Dorchester.[52] In rural areas, where threatened flight or the ability to purchase freedom were perhaps less viable options, weakening slaves' ability to negotiate for freedom, masters who did manumit were more likely to hold on to slaves until death and less likely to concede freedom by a deed in their own lifetime. In one respect manumitters by deed and by will acted similarly. Very few of them cited religious sentiments or beliefs in liberty as justification for freeing a slave; most testators simply identified the name, age, and freedom date of the prospective freed person and moved on to the next bequest.

In sum, manumissions appearing in the wills of Baltimoreans provide surprisingly little support for the view of testamentary manumission as a convenient marriage of self-interested exploitation of slaves during life with benevolence after death. Rather, they suggest that slaveholders sought to extract continued profit from their chattels even after death, for the benefit of their heirs, and that such manumissions may well have been motivated in large part, like deeded manumissions, by the desire to forestall flight and secure further uninterrupted service.[53]

Although negotiated manumission might flow from a wide variety of situations, its appeal as a strategy for securing bound labor was unquestionably greatest among small slaveholders, for whom the resistance or flight of individual slaves posed a greater proportional threat to economic well-being. In Baltimore holders of three or fewer slaves were much more likely to engage in manumission than masters who held seven or more slaves. The latter group comprised 277 households listed one or more times in one of the first four federal censuses of the town or city of Baltimore. The ownership of seven slaves would have placed a rural slaveholder at or just below the mean holding for a Maryland master, but a Baltimorean so circumstanced had more slaves than all but 5 percent of city slaveholders. These "large" slaveholders of the early nineteenth century manumitted their chattels at the rate of only three slaves per thousand per year, barely a third of the overall rate for city slaveholders.[54]

This disparity makes good sense if we regard negotiating delayed manumission or self-purchase as a form of insurance against slave flight or death. Risks of loss were hedged, but chances for maximum exploitation of a slave's labor were compromised. Such strategies appealed less to holders of many slaves, who could better afford to "self-insure" by hiring slave catchers to retrieve fugitives, and more to small slaveholders, to whom the successful defection of even one slave might spell financial disaster.

The distinction between large and small slaveholder propensity to manumit also helps to account for the disproportionately large number of manumissions granted by women: roughly one-tenth of Baltimore's slaveholders were women; they held a corresponding share of the city's slaves, but they liberated between 20 and 25 percent of all persons manumitted.[55] Such behavior might reflect a higher level of discontent with slavery on the part of women than men. But in addition women slaveholders were much less wealthy than men and thus more reliant on their slaves for the production of income; women were therefore prime candidates for the risk-avoidance tactics of gradual manumission, regardless of their views on slavery's propriety. Slaves made up 35 percent of the wealth of the female slaveholder of median wealth versus 24 percent for her male counterpart.[56] The average male slaveholder had assessed property valued at over $1,400, slightly more than twice the average for women on the tax rolls.[57] Thus, although women slaveholders typically owned the same number of slaves as men, they had far less other wealth, and like men with small holdings, they may have been inclined to trade eventual freedom for secure income in the interim.

Those few women who did fit the definition of "large slaveholder" were, like men, far less likely to manumit slaves than were owners of one, two, or three chattels.[58] They manumitted slaves at the rate of about five per year per thousand slaves owned, a rate well below the general average for Baltimore and less than one-half that of a sample of women owning one, two, or three slaves.[59]

Perhaps the greatest economic significance of gradual manumission, whether practiced by men or women, or by large or small slaveholders, lay in its creation of a new form of labor power that could be purchased by employers: the term slave. The combination of large numbers of gradual manumissions and long terms of service brought into being a market in which substantial numbers of slaves could be bought and sold at prices well below those prevailing for slaves for life. That buyers and sellers were active in this sector of the market for slaves is beyond doubt: surviving court papers for Baltimore record more than four hundred sales of term slaves in the first thirty years of the nineteenth century. It can also be confidently stated that many unrecorded sales occurred; again, the requirement of the law of 1817 that sales for a term of years be registered implies that many buyers and sellers had failed to do so. Indeed, many of the surviving bills of sale record—through notes scrawled on the back sides of the bills—repeated transfers of a slave from master to master.[60]

Allusive anecdotal evidence appears elsewhere. Frederick Douglass, describing a chance encounter with two Irishmen in Baltimore, noted that one of the men quickly asked him if he were a slave for life or for a term of years, suggesting that either status was fairly common for a young Baltimore black around 1830.[61] Estate appraisers appointed by the orphans' courts frequently valued slaves on two different premises: as slaves for life or to be sold for a term of years.[62] David McKim, purchasing slaves for the Maryland Chemical Works in 1826-27, bought eleven slaves for life and four slaves for terms of six to ten years.[63]

Although term slavery thus appears to have been driven mainly by masters' calculations of self-interest, the institution nonetheless appealed strongly to slaves, who associated it with service in Baltimore. As an 1802 advertiser selling a slave put it, "She wants to go to Baltimore so she can get free." Another announced that two slaves from Cambridge would be sold "only in Baltimore, as it is their wish to live in this city." What these slaves perhaps knew was that Baltimore masters were interested not only in buying term slaves, but also in selling freedom to those same persons, payable by earnings as craft workers or day laborers.[64]

Baltimore could also be a place of concealment for urban and rural runaways aided by free people of color, according to pursuing masters, as discussed in chapter 3. The presence of a growing and increasingly free African American population in Baltimore allowed many runaways to melt into anonymity, living with other blacks, pursuing a trade or working as day laborers, passing as free or as slaves hiring their time with a master's approval.[65] Thus Baltimore's rapid influx of people of color helped slaves to flee masters without leaving kin or familiar surroundings and exacerbated underlying tensions in measures designed to assure the reliability of slave labor. Not only was slaves' willingness to trust informal offers of self-purchase or gradual manumission undermined by the inability to hold masters accountable, but also the option of flight became more feasible.[66]

By the 1820s the uncertainties and anomalies of term slavery elicited a negative comment, nonetheless suggestive of the institution's ubiquity, from Nicholas Brice, chief judge of the criminal court of Baltimore County. In an 1827 public letter to the governor, Brice contended that "the manumission of slaves . . . at certain ages, or after a term of years, appears to be peculiarly injurious . . . and renders [Negroes] wholly unfit." Brice argued that "the state should make a law for the gradual emancipation of these people at proper ages, or establish some tribunal to decide . . . and not leave a matter of such importance to the community . . . to individuals who in general consult only their own interest."[67] Brice believed that freed term slaves constituted a potentially significant threat to the institutional stability of slavery. For him, the benefits that individual masters secured through gradual manumission, in the form of more productive workers, added up not to a social benefit but to a threat that needed to be curbed by imposition of sterner control over manumission.

In effect, Brice was proposing to limit slaveholders' decision-making power over the granting of manumission and to shield them, whether they liked it or not, from the pleas, importunings, and offers of self-purchase of their slaves. Brice may thus have sought to establish a new balance between positive and negative mechanisms of controlling term slaves, who in his view "were a sort of middle class, neither slave nor free; exempted from many of the motives for obedience which influence slaves."[68] Thus, while Brice did not object in principle to gradual emancipation, he strenuously denounced the undermining of the master's ability to maintain control of a prospective free black through negative incentives. Brice aimed to create such mechanisms anew and to hold out the threat of denial of manumission to term slaves who absconded, shirked, or otherwise failed to hold up their end of the manumission bargain. Simultaneously, he would rein in masters whose manumissions on "contingencies" or other "injudicious" acts tended to set bad precedents and weaken the ability of masters generally to control their bondmen.

Brice's thoughts bore no immediate fruit, but in the early 1830s Maryland legislators surpassed what he had urged. The 1833 "act relating to persons of Colour, who are to be free after the expiration of a term of years" authorized county courts to sell out of the state any slave whose conduct was "notoriously vicious or turbulent." An absconding term slave could be sold "within or without the state" upon application of any master or mistress. The incentive of future freedom could now, for the unruly, be counterbalanced by its threatened denial, by selling them south. To be sure, the law dictated that the county clerk supply Negroes thus sold with a copy of their deed of manumission, but as opponents of the law pointed out, southwestern slave traders, the likely buyers of such slaves, would not let such a document long remain in the slave's possession.[69]

The 1833 law did enshrine some additional protections for the term slave, however, thus furthering the tendency Brice had disparaged to treat them as "possessed of some rights in common with free men." The courts could only act if satisfied on "the testimony of disinterested witnesses" that the master had "notified such servants of the existence and effect of this law, and that this information had failed to correct his or her habits."[70]

Thus, slaveholders constructed an elaborate series of graduated sanctions for the disobedient or unproductive term slave: putting him or her on notice, threatening adjudgment by a court as vicious, and ultimately, sale back into possibly perpetual bondage. But enforcing these penalties consumed the master's time and money—court expenses had to be paid from the purchase price of the slave sold out of state— and the outcome, given the court's interpretive role, could not be certain. Even this effort to curb the term slave's seizure of autonomy left such men and women more room for further negotiation with their masters than that afforded the slave for life. So, by their continued resistance, term slaves slowly reshaped the terms and conditions of gradual manumission to win greater autonomy and to become in Brice's words "a sort of middle class," entitled to legal notice and protection, however precarious, before masters could change their status.

The evolution of term slavery into a quasi-regulated institution governing manumission and self-purchase invites comparison with mechanisms performing the same function in other slave societies, notably *coartación* in contemporary Spanish colonies and slaves' use of the *peculium* to purchase freedom in ancient Rome. In all three societies, manumission by self-purchase served to stabilize master-slave relations, especially in urban and craft settings, by allowing slaves to acquire wealth of their own with which they could purchase freedom, by providing public recognition of their new status, and by regulating future relations between former masters and freedmen.

Coartación, meaning to limit or cut off, was the right of a slave to demand that his price be set by a court of law and that he be permitted to pay this price in several installments. Originating as a customary procedure in seventeenth-century Cuba, it was codified in the eighteenth century; in that form it later spread to Louisiana after Louisiana was transferred to Spanish control in 1763.[71] *Coartación* relied on the idea, derived from Roman law, of the *peculium,* property accumulated, managed, and disposed of by the slave. In both colonial Cuba and imperial Rome, slaves might hope to amass enough wealth to buy themselves free, either by payments in cash or kind or by the purchase of a replacement slave. In neither society was a master compelled by law to allow a slave to accumulate such wealth; rather, the voluntary concession of that privilege, accompanied by respect for slaves' claims to property thus acquired, served as an incentive to hard work that stood to benefit the master as well as the slave. Here, the behavior of Cuban, Roman, and North American slaveholders converged.[72] Likewise, masters allowing a slave to hold his or her own property might also expect the slave to provide some or all of his maintenance from that property. Slaves who had provision grounds placed at their disposal might be expected to provide some or all of their own food; urban workers allowed to hire their own time might also be required to maintain themselves from sums left over after the master received a portion of the slave's earnings.

Neither Romans nor Americans emulated *coartación*'s formalizing of the slave's right to self-purchase through court intervention, but all three societies did tolerate, and even provided some legal protection for, installment payment contracts for freedom. And although neither Roman nor American courts would impose manumission of a slave on an unwilling master, slaveholders in those societies could go to court and bind themselves to manumit, both to legitimize their actions and to make their promises credible to slaves, in the hope that slaves would enter wholeheartedly into the self-purchase bargain. Likewise, all of these societies regulated the ages and conditions of those to be set free, to prevent masters from "dumping" slaves unable to support themselves and to prevent the too-rapid growth of a population of freed people.[73]

In all three societies the slave who had been promised freedom was, in Brice's terms, a member of a "third class," not wholly a slave but certainly not possessed of all the rights or duties of a freeborn person. *Coartados*, as black Cubans who had partly purchased their freedom were often called, could not be held responsible for debts nor made to serve in the militia. In imperial Rome, most ex-slaves were classified as "Junian Latins," a status short of full citizenship in the empire that nonetheless gave them some important property rights, such as the right to make a will.[74] As we have seen, in Maryland term slaves could still be bought and sold, but they could not legally be transported out of state, beyond court supervision of their right to eventual freedom.

Perhaps the greatest difference in the treatment of the freedman lay in how Rome, Cuba, and Maryland dealt with the question of the freeman's obligations to his ex-master. On the surface a sharp divide appears: Roman or Cuban slaveholders could use legal process to re-enslave former chattels who were "ungrateful" or "negligent," that is, freedmen who failed to show appropriate deference to former masters or who did not perform ongoing duties that had been stipulated as part of the freedom bargain. Marylanders who felt insulted or ignored by their onetime slaves had no such right. This important distinction goes far to help explain their making prospective manumissions contingent on faithful service in the interim before freedom arrived, as well as the desire to punish the ungrateful with extended terms or even the reimposition of slavery for life: Maryland masters could exact deference and service with the force of law only while the would-be freeman was yet a slave.

The "problem" of the term slave, if not peculiar to Baltimore, at least attained there its greatest dimension. In Baltimore city and Baltimore County, according to the fragmentary surviving court papers, just over 20 percent of all surviving bills of sale are for a term of years. For the compared rural counties, we find in Dorchester about 5 percent of all sales, and in Prince George's County only 2 percent of total slave sales, were for a limited term.[75]

Would-be employers of bound labor, including those in the crafts and in industry, could thus choose from alternatives less costly than annual hiring of slaves, alternatives that tied up capital less permanently than purchasing a slave for life. Under such circumstances slaveholders employed gradual manumission, not merely as a profitable exit from slavery, but also as a low-risk way of continuing to enjoy the advantages of owning human chattel.

One way for a master to gain from gradual manumission would be to buy term slaves in succession, replacing those who gained their freedom with new time-limited slaves. Such an owner might have reasoned that people with a promise of eventual freedom were less likely to run away than perpetual bondmen. They might also work harder, out of motivation to acquire a good reputation on which to build a life as a freedman or to continue employment with the ex-master after freedom arrived. Moreover, the owner of term slaves avoided the expense of maintaining old, worn-out slaves, although owners of slaves for life could offer delayed emancipation to deal with this problem as well.

A cross-referencing of slave bills of sale and deeds of manumission reveals that many slaveholders purchased one or more slaves after emancipating others; such a comparison provides potent evidence to regard manumission as part and parcel of strategies to employ slave labor successfully in an increasingly hostile environment in Baltimore. Of 757 manumitters filing deeds of manumission before 1825, 68 (about

9 percent) later purchased one or more slaves.[76] The prevalence of re-purchase among employers of craft or manufacturing labor may have been considerably more widespread, as nearly one-third of the manumitters were free blacks, Quakers, or women who had no intention of using slave labor in shops or factories.[77] If these groups are discounted, about one in eight white males who manumitted slaves would later buy a slave or slaves. But the incompleteness of the surviving Baltimore manumission and sale records means that the actual repurchase rate was probably still higher. Because it is necessary to find two transactions to identify a repurchaser, incomplete sales or manumission records will result in undercounting the repurchasing proportion of manumitters.[78] Thus, if only half of all Baltimore sales are to be found among surviving records, repurchase by manumitters might take in not an eighth but a quarter of all manumitters.[79]

Failure to record slave sales could further artificially depress the repurchase rate. After the 1817 ban on out-of-state sales of term slaves, which also imposed more stringent requirements for recording such sales, registrations of slave sales in Baltimore increased 55 percent the next year, and more sales for a term of years were recorded then in any other single year from 1789 to 1830.[80] In view of these facts, a plausible estimate is that from 20 percent to as high as 40 percent of Baltimore manumitters acquired new slaves in the two generations between Baltimore's post-Revolutionary War rise and 1830.

This estimate reinforces a modified view of the usage of manumission by city-dwelling craftsmen, emphasizing its character as a tool in managing slave workers and as yet another contested ground in master-slave relations. Indeed, the existence of sequential or serial slaveholding helps to make sense out of the petty contingencies and sanctions with which masters hedged their grants of eventual freedom. More was at stake than the extra few dollars of labor that might be garnered by requiring makeup of lost sick time from a given slave: masters were attempting to set or maintain standards that could apply in the future to prospective freed men and women of similar circumstances.

In sequential slavery's most fully developed form, we find masters buying slaves for life, commuting their servitude to a term of years, and then buying a replacement when that slave's term expired. John Kelso, a butcher and merchant of Baltimore, thus bought Thomas Cook, age twenty-three, for $300 in 1802. About nine months later, presumably satisfied that Cook was earning his keep, Kelso manumitted him, effective in 1811, after a further eight years of service. Apparently, Kelso found the experiment of offering delayed freedom to be a useful work incentive, for in late 1810 Kelso purchased Romulus, a sixteen-year-old who had fifteen years to serve, paying $300 for him likewise. In 1820, with Romulus still having a few years to serve, Kelso bought a thirteen-year-old boy named Jacob for the remaining eight years of his servitude.[81] Although Romulus's eventual fate is unknown, it is conceivable that he was sold with a few years left on his term, so that Kelso could recoup some of his $300 investment. An adult male with five years to serve might have brought $150 in 1820, allowing Kelso to have enjoyed ten years' worth of labor for a net outlay of $150 plus maintenance. As a Methodist, Kelso was also complying with the letter, if not the spirit, of church discipline banning the ownership of slaves for life.[82]

That at least some manumitters transacted business in this manner is graphically and depressingly illustrated by another of Kelso's hands, a man named Jerry. In 1807 John Woodard of Prince George's County sold Jerry, then "about 50" to Frederick Eislen, a Baltimore butcher, for $115. Perhaps Eislen overestimated his need for hands, for in 1808 a hand-scrawled note on the back of the 1807 bill of sale indicated that Eislen had "assigned" Jerry to John Kelso for $75. Two years later, Kelso passed Jerry on to Stephen Hill, yet another butcher, for $60. Hill, perhaps finding the aging Jerry an ineffective worker, hired him out to Nicholas Jackson for $25 and then manumitted Jerry with a term expiring at the end of his hire with Jackson in 1811, declaring in the deed that Jerry was "about 45."[83] In this case Jerry dealt with five masters in four years, as each sought to obtain a year or so of low-cost labor followed by a resale at or near the last purchase price.

But some masters had no wish to retain the services of term slaves, preferring instead to schedule a slave's future manumission and then sell him or her to a new owner, often recording both transactions in the same document.[84] Methodist scruples regarding selling slaves for life may have helped generate some such transactions.[85] But more tangible appeals to self-interest may have informed other actions. When Samuel Davis manumitted Harriet and sold her to John Fisher for a term of eight years and six months, Davis promised to "be answerable for any damages that may be sustained by the said Negro Woman being pressed to be free at a shorter period than the time she is sold for." Because Harriet's age was not given, there is no way to tell whether the $150 Davis received was a "below market" price. But the inference that Davis was disposing of troublesome property and attempting to wangle compliance from Harriet by promising eventual freedom is strengthened by the fact that Davis had originally intended to sell her to another buyer: Fisher's name appears throughout the bill interlined in place of one

John Vernon. Harriet may have threatened to run off to dissuade Vernon from buying her or, for that matter, to induce Davis to sell and manumit her in the first place. Or her agitating the question of gradual emancipation might have driven Davis to sell her and Fisher to seek security for her good behavior during her term.

The goal of securing reliable labor from term slaves could even override customary slaveholder approval of slave women bearing children and thereby increasing the master's wealth: when Lucy Soper bought Margaret for a term of six years, she required that Margaret "make . . . ample compensation, for all lost time that may arise in consequence of such Issue or Issues which might so happen."[86]

These examples show how gradual manumission could be at once a vehicle for resolving disputes between masters and slaves and a mechanism for transferring the problem to a new master, within its more general use as a device for securing dependable and productive labor from slaves. Looking at the operations of manumission as a regulator or modifier of the terms of slave labor in Baltimore, we see an institution driven by complex and shifting forces. Masters' reliance on gradual manumission helped spread slavery among craftsmen and at first strengthened slavery in Baltimore, as masters evoked such strategies as sequential slaveholding to maximize gains and minimize the risks entailed in capitalizing their workforce. But, as we have seen, African Americans were much more active in that process than to tamely take the bait of long-delayed freedom and self-purchase.

5

FREE BLACK FAMILY STRATEGIES FOR
GAINING FREEDOM

In early America families worked together to maintain themselves. By pooling their labor, fathers, mothers, sons, and daughters could hope to gain a "competency," that is, enough wealth to live comfortably and to stake the children to a start in life through inheritance of land, tools, livestock, fishing boats, or money with which to acquire craft training or attract a suitor. Although this view of family economics derives primarily from whites in New England or the mid-Atlantic region, blacks, too, strove to unite their families' productive capacities.[1]

In order to do so, people of color had first to create the family as a legal entity, by securing freedom and the right to own their labor power. Some might be fortunate enough to be manumitted en bloc by a Quaker or Methodist master, but most blacks had to struggle to free themselves. Manumission as a "gift" from a master, whatever the legitimacy of such a construction, represented one route to autonomy, but far more often freedom had to be purchased with labor and money.

The process might be envisioned as a kind of bootstrapping, beginning with obtaining the freedom of one family member, possibly by pooling resources accumulated by others. Over time, the freed person could hope to save or borrow more money, eventually "buying out" spouse, children, or other kin. Ideally, an entire family could together leave slavery behind, but that could occur only with the agreement of the master or masters who owned the family's members.

Slaveholders, who wished to maintain predictable, flexible, and cheap labor, knew that an unvaried reliance on slavery might not meet these objectives. At the same time the emerging but imperfect market for free labor could not yet be trusted to produce enough surplus workers for seasonal peak periods of work or steady and compliant workers on a year-round basis.

Manumitting slaves presented attractive possibilities for meeting these challenges. If a master could dictate the cost and term length of a gradual manumission, he or she could reshape the institution of slavery to emphasize its advantages, such as the legal ability to compel labor from the worker, and to minimize its disadvantages, notably lifelong commitment to providing for the worker and the resulting costs of capitalizing one's labor force. The story of term slavery in Maryland thus often centers on clashes and accommodations between powerful whites and dependent blacks, driven by blacks' search for autonomy for their families and whites' attempts to manipulate that impulse.

Finding out how blacks freed family members again entails burrowing beneath the language of manumission deeds to uncover underlying activities and contingencies. Anna Emory, for example, had agreed in 1803 with "negro Samuel, commonly called Middleton's Sam" to make Sam's wife Chloe and their children his property "as soon as he . . . shall pay or cause to be paid unto Anna Emory . . . seventy five pounds." Sam sealed the bargain by paying Emory fifteen pounds on January 7, 1803, and made five subsequent payments over the next two years, including, in November of 1804, "One Dutch Oven, price 15 s." By January of 1806 Sam, now having taken the name Sam Stewart, had "settled . . . the full consideration" and obtained an immediate manumission of Chloe, though not of her children, from Robert Goldsborough, the administrator of Anna Emory's estate.[2] Had Emory survived to that point, she would almost certainly have issued a manumission deed for Chloe, but she would have had no compelling reason to record the financial details. Goldsborough did so to account for his handling of the estate and to protect himself against possible charges by Emory's heirs of wasting or looting it.

Sam Stewart's ability to raise seventy-five pounds in Maryland money (about two hundred dollars) within three years distinguished him as being uncommonly quick to accumulate wealth. Far more typical was the lot of William Chambers, who needed nine years to scrape together $120 to buy freedom for his wife Hannah and their five children, or Isaac Bellows, who freed his wife eight years after contracting to purchase her.[3] At that, Chambers was fortunate that his wife's master did not insist on further compensation to free William and Hannah's children, four of whom were born after the price of freedom for Hannah and their eldest child had been set.

Many masters demanded "expences" or "consideration" for the maintenance of young children born while a mother's self-purchase was pending. They might indenture such children as servants, denominate them as term slaves, or regard them as slaves for life, requiring a separate purchase agreement from their parents. When Jesse Higgins sold Coffee Gibbs his wife Jane's liberty, they resolved the fate of the Gibbs's seven children by Higgins's agreeing "to take two girls and one boy for terms specified in their manumission and indentures" as full satisfaction for freeing Jane and her four younger children. Gibbs succeeded in obtaining legal freedom for his entire family, but Higgins retained control of three valuable workers, the eldest children. In a similar transaction, Phill Howard in 1817 paid one hundred dollars to Mary and Isaac Paul as a down payment on the freedom of his wife and their three children and registered a deed manumitting his wife Mary and daughter Mary Ann. A year later, perhaps unable to produce the remainder of the purchase price, he indentured his two grown children, George, twenty-four years old, and Rachel, eighteen years old, to the Pauls for five-year terms.[4]

Even infants commanded a price, as Peter and Cassey Porter discovered. Peter had bought Cassey from James Troth, a Talbot County tavern keeper, in 1795, promising to pay Troth thirty pounds in Maryland money, or about eighty dollars. Porter paid Troth fairly quickly, but the latter procrastinated over having Cassey's bill of sale drawn up by the county clerk. When Cassey gave birth to a son before she had formally become a free woman, Troth seized on the opportunity to squeeze a further five pounds from the Porters for manumitting one-year old Harry in 1797.[5]

Matters could become particularly complicated when masters insisted on shaving the terms of manumissions involving spouses and children. A deposition in an 1815 Baltimore case described a "bargain" between George Stevenson and Negro David, a free man, respecting David's wife, Jane, and sons. Stevenson had agreed to manumit Jane and two boys, Aron and Ben, upon payment of one hundred dollars, an unusually low price for such a transaction. Perhaps one reason for the low price was that Stevenson retained legal title to Aron and Ben, stipulating nonetheless that David was to bear the expense of maintaining the boys. Thus, Stevenson avoided the expense of providing for two boys too young to generate a positive cash flow as workers, while also holding back on manumitting the children as a form of security for David's payment of the one hundred dollars. Moreover, he declined to issue manumission papers for the ostensibly free Jane, stating that "when David paid the . . . one hundred dollars, he would Emancipate the whole of them together, . . . at one cost and trouble."[6] When Stevenson died before the debt was cleared, the whole matter was thrown before the courts.

Although Troth and Stevenson may have been petty connivers, their interest in using children to control their parents was far from rare.

After 1809 Maryland law specified that children born during a prospectively manumitted slave mother's term of servitude were slaves for life unless the mother's manumission set other terms.[7] Manumitters could declare future children of a term-slave woman free at birth, or they could categorize such offspring as term slaves themselves. Most chose to remain silent, and even among those who did specify the condition of future children, only a handful granted immediate freedom. More than 90 percent of those who spoke to the subject declared prospective children to be slaves for terms of eighteen to as many as forty-five years. Indeed, the number of manumitters who prescribed term slavery for unborn *grandchildren* of women granted delayed manumission exceeded the number freeing such women's unborn children at birth. A few emancipators even stated expressly that "all future generations" of term slave descent would themselves be term slaves "until the end of time."[8]

Under these circumstances, women who served a stint as term slaves would commonly find that their children were slaves with long terms to serve. Slaveholders could seek to derive advantage from this anomaly, by choosing either to take possession of the children or to leave them with their parents, as their need for child labor dictated. To keep families together, some free people of color agreed to bear the cost of raising their own children, rather than claiming support from the legal master. Such bargains might well be nested within the question of a woman's obtaining freedom in the first place. When John Jones manumitted Dafney, with immediate effect, he required her to keep her three children "until I call for them." Jones could thus bank on the future labor of two boys and one girl whenever, in his judgment, he could extract more from them than their maintenance would cost. In the meantime Dafney would raise her children at no expense to Jones.[9]

Both large and small slaveholders had to deal with thorny questions surrounding the manumission of black children. Many white Marylanders believed that manumitting small children contravened the law by setting at large individuals who could not support themselves and who might become public charges, but manumissions by deed of parents and children occurred frequently and generally went unchallenged.[10] As the examples cited above suggest, however, most manumitters freed young slaves only after they had worked some years as adults to "pay" for their rearing. Nearly half of all male freedmen were over thirty when manumitted; nearly three-quarters were over twenty-five. Black women tended to be freed a bit younger, but about two-fifths had passed thirty when manumitted, and a little more than three-fifths were over twenty-five.[11]

The prevalence of long terms of servitude for prospectively emancipated children played a critical part in perpetuating slavery in spite of widespread manumission. A majority of slave girls promised eventual enfranchisement would live through five to fifteen, or more, of their childbearing years while still legally slaves. Any children born to them during this period would be slaves for life, unless specified otherwise in their own prospective manumissions. The thrust of this practice was not to terminate slavery, immediately or gradually, but rather to extend it to new generations of blacks, while transmuting it: the institution was sustained, but individuals could, eventually, escape its oppressions. Slaves and masters maneuvered for advantage over which members of black families became free and when. Blacks knew that the purchase of a young man's freedom might create an extra wage earner in the family, thereby speeding up the buying of other family members still enslaved. But doing so in preference to liberating a young woman could lead to her bearing children and passing the curse of bondage on to another generation.[12] The agony of dealing with such choices can only have been increased by the knowledge that children or siblings might be sold out of the state, never to be seen again, even as free members of the family struggled to generate cash to buy them out.

Buying out family members must always have been onerous when the value of an adult slave routinely equaled twelve to twenty months' earnings for a laborer, but difficulties could become insuperable when fate conspired against a black family. In an 1829 case a Maryland freedman who had married a slave was compelled to buy his wife and infant child at a public estate sale following the sudden death of her master. Having only recently acquired his own freedom, he was obliged to seek credit for almost all of the purchase price, with the patronage of two white guarantors of his debt. They took title to his wife and baby as security and, when he proved unable to clear his debt, seized his family and sold them to Georgia.[13]

This tragic case also illustrates the intertwined operations of manumission and the laws of property and debt. For the freed person, the very effort to keep a family together devoured any slender stock of capital he or she might have accumulated, forcing an overextension of resources and acquisition of heavy debt under terms of repayment that could not be controlled. In the case set forth above, a man who had risen to become a captain of a Chesapeake Bay schooner lost not only his family but in addition all the liquid capital he had paid to the administrator of his wife's master's estate. There is no way to know how frequently free blacks suffered such doubly crushing setbacks, but the heavy financial drain of self-purchase, whether successfully consummated or not, must have played its part in preventing free blacks from attaining tangible property other than themselves. It thus surely contributed to the white perception of free blacks as improvident and unsuited to life in a competitive society.

For the "white gentlemen" who beneficently lent their names as security to the freedman's debt, the transaction held much promise of gain and relatively little risk. If not called upon to act, they could congratulate themselves on having assisted a worthy black in uniting his family in freedom. If compelled to claim their collateral property, they could console themselves with the thought that here lay proof of blacks' unreadiness for freedom and of the likelihood that they were better off under the care of a master. Moreover, they might realize a tidy profit if the sale price of the woman and child exceeded their exposure for the remaining portion of the freedman's debt. For men who sought profit from private lending, few collateral properties can have been as reliably negotiable as slaves. Thus could self-purchase and debt combine to transfer wealth from some of the poorest members of society, the newly freed, to well-off whites.

In at least one documented case, parents who were both still slaves, perhaps seeking to avoid this cycle of debt and reimposed dependency, purchased freedom for their son but not for themselves. Fielder Dorsett, in manumitting a twelve-year-old boy named Jones, noted that Jones's father, John, "the slave of Mrs. Martha Roundell" had put up the money to buy Jones, on "Conditions that I should set him free from Bondage." Dorsett then dictated that Jones was freed on "Condition that he serve John and Henrietta, his Father and Mother, . . . during their natural lives, . . . to be released from such Service when they . . . shall think proper."[14] In this case the anomalous outcome made Jones, a prospective freedman, the lifelong servant of his slave parents.

Entanglement in such situations presented blacks with unenviable choices. Children born while the mother was still enslaved added to the costs of buying freedom for a family already under financial strain. But couples who deferred having children until the woman was free also ran risks. Given the many years needed to buy freedom, a woman might have passed her prime childbearing years before such a date arrived. Moreover, a couple who delayed having children also delayed reaching the point at which children could begin contributing to the household economy.

Many men and women sought to avoid this dilemma by shortening the term of installment purchases or by obtaining money on credit with which to bargain for liberation. Borrowing to buy freedom could also satisfy a master unwilling to engage in manumission paid by installments. Finally, borrowing could generate cash quickly and allow a free person of color to avert the sale and dispersal of his or her loved ones following upon a slaveholder's relocation or after the death of the slaveholder and the ensuing division of the estate. Thus, John Joice, identified by Charles Carroll of Carrollton as "Old Shoemaker John," became free immediately in 1802 upon payment of two hundred dollars by a third party, Samuel Hopkins.[15] Carroll's manumission of Joice said nothing about Joice's obligation to Hopkins, but other deeds speak more plainly. Buying freedom on credit did not erase the possibility of separation from one's kin but rather postponed it. Not all families were able to clear their debts and free their children.

In a Kent County case, Isaac Hackett freed Delia, her son Jake, and a daughter in 1793, "upon receipt of thirty pounds . . . by William Sluby," and set Delia's freedom date as "when the said Negro woman's husband, Negro Chester Bowes, who is a free man, pays to Sluby . . . the aforesaid sum of thirty pounds and the Interest thereon." Two years later, Sluby duly filed another manumission deed, freeing Delia but not mentioning either of her children.[16] From Chester and Delia Bowes's standpoint, an effort to "refinance" their debt to Isaac Hackett proved only partially successful, because their children most likely remained in slavery.

Given the difficulties faced by free blacks hoping to borrow and repay freedom loans, the question arises, What inherent attractions did such measures hold, as distinct from desperation-induced borrowing to avoid forced migration or sale of kin south or westward? The impetus for buying oneself out could come from several sources. Moses Stevenson, agreeing to purchase himself from James Carey for fifty pounds in 1789, secured Carey's promise *not* to demand service from him. Stevenson thereby gained immediate freedom of action to sell his labor as he saw fit, in order to meet his obligation to Carey, rather than serving Carey for a term of years. Along the same lines, one of the provisions of Sam Stewart's purchase of Chloe from Anna Emory was that Chloe would be able to work for Sam during the time he paid for her freedom. Emory did extract a hiring fee of five pounds a year, and Sam became responsible for Chloe's maintenance as well, but in this case their joint action no doubt facilitated Sam's fairly speedy repayment of Chloe's purchase price.

For William Berry, a master's borrowing led to an opening for his manumission from Morgan Brown. Berry had been owned by Brown's brother-in-law, who offered him to Brown as collateral for a debt. By subsequently assembling the twenty-six pounds and ten shillings owed Brown, after his master failed to do so, Berry gained his liberty in 1783.[17]

Slaves and free people of color, then, had ample reason to venture into the world of credit and borrowing in order to leave slavery behind. But what motivated white lenders?

In the case of Morgan Brown, the manumission documents provide little clue as to his motivation. He may have had scruples about owning slaves for life (he did manumit other slaves on terms), or he may simply have sized up William Berry as the best available bet for recovering the money owed him. But Brown's case was not an isolated one. In several instances merchants and private lenders functioned repeatedly as go-betweens or brokers of manumissions by self-purchase. Men like Philip Fiddeman of Queen Anne's County, Joseph Court of Anne Arundel County, Thomas Sluby of Kent County, and David Stewart of Baltimore County engaged in a series of individual manumissions for cash, repaid with interest by the beneficiaries, in transactions stretched out over their life spans in business. Let us examine the story of Philip Fiddeman.

Between 1790 and 1816 Philip Fiddeman recorded eleven deeds of manumission in Queen Anne's County, freeing twelve women and seven men. Fiddeman was not slowly downsizing his holdings; he never owned more than six slaves at any one time. But neither did he cease to own human chattel, at least as measured by the first three federal censuses. Indeed, most of his manumissions noted a former owner from whom he had bought the slave about to be freed. In two-thirds of the cases Fiddeman had received money, ranging from token amounts to sixty pounds, or $160, for his 1801 grant of freedom to Adam. Where no payment was mentioned, Fiddeman stipulated terms of service, ranging from seven years for adults like George Garnet to twenty years for nine-year old Hetty.

In at least two instances, Fiddeman adjusted terms of servitude, possibly to recognize loans repaid faster or slower than scheduled. George Garnet became free in 1809, one year sooner than promised in his original 1803 manumission, but his son Henry, promised freedom in 1813 in return for service until January 1, 1823, saw his term lengthened in 1816, with a new date of freedom set for July 1, 1824. The first deed filed respecting Henry had not included any language stipulating that Henry make up for time lost by illness or running away; how then could Fiddeman extract an extra eighteen months of service from him?

By law, Fiddeman's original deed would bind him to freeing Henry on the promised date, unless he went to court to have Henry's term lengthened for absconding. There is no evidence—either in court records, or in the language of the second manumission, or in runaway ads— that Henry did abscond.

Fiddeman could have justified lengthening Henry's term, however, if Henry's freedom was conditional on a combination of service rendered and cash paid and if Henry or someone acting in his interest had failed to make a stipulated payment. Failure on Henry's part to perform contractual obligations fully and punctually would have released Fiddeman from his corresponding duty to manumit, allowing him to dictate a new release date or even to cancel the manumission altogether. Although this inference is admittedly speculative, it is not an unreasonable one. If a contract, even a written one, defined Fiddeman and Henry's manumission agreement, its absence from the public record is hardly surprising; rather, this reflects normal practice. Neither contracts nor their supporting documents, such as penal bonds or other transfers of property incident upon failure to perform, were recorded with county courts. Even if such had been the practice in Maryland, no recognizable or binding contract could exist between a slave and a free person. To return to Fiddeman's and Henry's dealings, the extension of Henry's term of servitude via the registration of a new deed of manumission might best be compared with the extension of the term of payment for a loan. Just as renegotiating the repayment of a loan might lead to redefining its terms regarding collateral or interest rates, Henry's need to renegotiate the terms of obtaining his freedom may have led to his new and longer term of service.[18]

The picture of Fiddeman that emerges is that of a rural entrepreneur ranging widely to seek opportunities for profit on the economically stagnant Eastern Shore. He might have relocated to Baltimore, as many other merchants or artisans did, but Fiddeman and Thomas Sluby chose to remain where they were, in Queen Anne's County and Kent County, respectively, and try to reap a return on investments in private lending. Lending to slaves seeking to purchase freedom may well have presented itself as a simple, secure, and risk-free type of loan. A brief comparison may illustrate.

When Fiddeman lent to a free white person, he no doubt sought to secure his loan by having the borrower assign collateral to him in the event of default, such as land, work animals, or slaves. He would also have demanded that the loan be guaranteed by cosigners. As we have seen in the case of Morgan Brown and William Berry, manumission by self-purchase on credit could be triggered by a defaulting borrower's loss of assigned property to his lender: Fiddeman may well have undertaken some of his manumissions for the same reason. Fiddeman probably preferred slaves as collateral, because they represented a commodity of stable value that could be either converted to liquid capital by sale or held as a short- to medium-term income-producing asset by hiring out.

But actually gaining control of one's collateral from a nonpaying borrower could be time-consuming and uncertain. Debtors or their guarantors could attempt to evade their responsibilities through legal action; lengthy and expensive court battles might ensue before Fiddeman could actually obtain seizure of property and execution of a debt. Even then, he might find that the proceeds of a sheriff's sale failed to recoup his outlays or that he had to compete with other creditors, perhaps entailing further litigation.

By contrast, lending to slaves or free people of color allowed Fiddeman to short-circuit most of the uncertainties imposed by the law for recovering unpaid debts. When Fiddeman lent to an African American, he literally took legal possession of his "collateral," by purchasing the slave whose freedom he intended to sell. If the slave or his free black kin failed to repay Fiddeman, he could proceed directly to "execution" by reselling his human property. Even if a free person of color felt that Fiddeman was cheating him in such a transaction, his or her testimony would be inadmissible in a court, effectively barring any legal recourse.

Not only did Fiddeman have virtually impregnable legal guarantees of recovery; he could also be reasonably sure that his black borrowers would do their utmost to repay him, because they were seeking to reunite families in freedom or to obtain that freedom for themselves. Should they falter, he also had the option of compounding with them by manumitting a slave in tandem with selling that person for a term of service. The price of the sale would be dictated by what Fiddeman deemed a suitable return on his loan, and a term of service would be set accordingly.

We can get a glimpse of how such transactions worked by looking at the story of Henry Toomey. According to his former owner, Tristram Thomas, "Harry Toomey fell into [his] possession in right of his wife, . . . served him a few months as a slave, after which [he] sold Harry to William Thelery, . . . the object of the sale . . . being to enable the said Harry to obtain his freedom after fulfilling a certain contract of service." Thomas thus commuted his investment in Henry Toomey into cash, while Toomey worked out his time with a new owner.[19] It is worth noting that these details about Henry Toomey's acquisition of freedom did not appear in his manumission deed; their existence was recorded only by chance when Thomas penned a letter supporting Toomey's request for pardon from a larceny conviction.

In addition to the option of selling a freedom-seeking black, a manumission broker could secure profits by transferring his interests to other slaves, such as the would-be freed person's children. As mentioned above, George Garnet obtained his freedom from Philip Fiddeman in 1809, a year ahead of his scheduled manumission date. But in 1810 Garnet mortgaged his two daughters, Phillis and Netter, to Joseph Blake and Richard Rochester for $160. He entered into this grim bargain in the same year that Phillis and Netter's mother, and George's wife, Jenny, was to be freed by yet another slaveholder, Thomas Burgess, at the expiration of a two-year term.

George Garnet may have needed money to complete the purchase of Jenny's freedom. Although no payments were mentioned in Burgess's delayed manumission of Jenny in 1808, the very short two-year term of service he stipulated renders the imposition of further required payment, either in George's labor or in cash, quite likely. Alternatively, George may still have owed Philip Fiddeman for his own manumission. In any case he could get the cash he needed to liberate his entire family only by offering up Phillis, age twelve, and Netter, age two, as hostages to a new set of white lenders. As Phillis and Netter had themselves been prospectively manumitted by Thomas Burgess upon reaching their twenty-sixth birthday, they ran less risk of remaining trapped in life-long slavery than George's sons. In Henry's case, no manumission of any kind had as yet been arranged with Fiddeman; a younger son, named George after his father, had been promised freedom by Burgess, but it would occur only after a twenty-seven-year term, at the age of thirty-four.[20]

Shedding the yoke of bondage all too often meant shouldering the burden of debt, with the threat of permanent enslavement hanging over one's head. When Rosalia, a woman freed by Thomas Mordieu, sought to buy her son from Mordieu's estate, executor John Dubernat set a price of seventy-five dollars on the boy and required Rosalia to obtain security for the credit purchase. After she failed to do so, Dubernat petitioned the orphans' court for the right to sell the boy and protect the estate from loss, because he feared that "she would make for Santo Domingo and carry her child thither."[21]

In short, the sale of freedom from master to slave was fraught with uncertainties, ambiguities, and unstable agreements, like every other aspect of master-slave relations. Whites like Philip Fiddeman could envision the brokering of manumission as an income-generating device and perhaps see themselves as humanitarians at the same time. Nonetheless, despite the advantages they enjoyed, they could not be certain of black compliance with the terms of mortgaged freedom. One could minimize the risk of loss presented by black flight, by freeing parents but not children, or husbands but not wives, but risks remained.

Moreover, like other businessmen, Fiddeman faced subtle restraints not fully encompassed by the legalities. If he pressed his legal advantages relentlessly and sold or repossessed people of color who failed to meet their obligations, would he find subsequent "customers" willing to borrow from him to buy themselves out? That Fiddeman engaged in as many sales of freedom as he did, with only the Garnet family case coming to light as a "problem case" suggests that he and his black counterparts judged each other well. The power relations between them were no doubt far from equal, but Fiddeman apparently forbore extreme pressure on his black clients in Queen Anne's County enough to generate repeated manumission business over a twenty-six-year period.

For blacks hoping to unshackle themselves or their family members, men like Fiddeman may have represented a last resort, to be turned to when one's master exhibited recalcitrance or when an executor could not free one from the dead hand of an estate. Such a hypothesis helps explain why manumission brokering would be relatively more visible in rural counties like Queen Anne's or Kent than in urban settings. In Baltimore free blacks or slaves hiring their own time enjoyed extensive opportunities to earn wages and thereby deal directly with a master willing to consider the sale of freedom. Similarly, the spread of slavery in Baltimore's craft shops created a network of employers who might be willing to buy a term slave, thereby helping a slave to complete a mixed cash-and-service self-purchase bargain. Accordingly, the need to resort to a lender to acquire lump sums for buyouts would be less pressing. Those blacks who did seek to borrow in this fashion might find more prospective lenders to choose from and might be less likely to deal with any given merchant. People with liquid capital not tied up in land or slaves already were far more numerous in the city; a few of them might even be blacks, with whom one might hope to deal on less onerous terms.

It is also possible, to return to a white lender's perspective, that loans for the purchase of freedom might have appealed less to a Baltimorean, who could invest in bank stock or manufacturing companies or could speculate in urban lots and rents. Furthermore, the single young black males who made up a notable proportion of Baltimore's hired-out slave workforce, although they may have been prime wage earners and thus likely risks for loans, also fit the profile of the high runaway risk, perhaps discouraging the buyout option. In addition they were less likely to have wives or children assignable as collateral security. All of these factors would make a would-be manumission broker in Baltimore cautious about carrying too much risk by engaging in more than an occasional loan of this type. On the rural, isolated Eastern Shore, merchants like Fiddeman could make brokering of freedom into a profitable sideline. In Baltimore, with far more masters to choose from, blacks gained a far larger proportion of manumissions in return for loyal service but without the encumbrance of debt.

On the Eastern Shore there were more laborers, black or white, free or enslaved, than employment opportunities, other than at seasonal peak moments of demand, such as during the wheat harvest. In this setting manumission could be attractive to a master, if accompanied by cash payment. A slave attempting to obtain freedom on these terms might well migrate across the bay to Baltimore to find wage work or turn to someone like Fiddeman.

In Baltimore the labor shortage could cause artisans, merchants, and professionals to compete for the workers and servants they wanted, offering delayed manumission in return. Thus, the contiguity of two rather differently structured labor markets generated a flow of black workers from rural seats to the town of Baltimore and concomitantly encouraged a partial transition from slave to wage labor in each setting. But regardless of locale, employers wished to retain power over their workers and sought to use indebtedness, linked to continuing control of workers' family members, as their hold. Free blacks, fully aware of this strategy, endeavored to wrest their children from the slaveholders' grip at the earliest opportunity.

We can gain insight into how these struggles played out by examining manumissions to see which family members blacks tried to free first, and correspondingly, which persons slaveholders clung to most determinedly. Freeing boys, for example, might have seemed financially more advantageous to black families, because they could earn more than young girls, but obtaining freedom for boys might be more costly than buying out girls. Slaveholders could employ the same rationales to arrive at somewhat different conclusions, of course. Holding onto boys and letting girls go might maximize a slaveholder's income from enslaved children, so long as they could be employed profitably. By the same token, maintaining control of girls might be preferable to a slaveholder who wished to combine manumission with the continued reproduction of new generations of slaves.

Both black parents and slaveholders might be expected to display considerable variation in their strategies for freeing or retaining children in slavery, to the extent that decisions were tailored to short-term labor needs within the slaveholder's or the black family head's respective business enterprise or household. In other words, patterns of slave retention or freedom acquisition may have responded to the same kinds of forces that drove the hiring of servants in economies based on family labor, such as colonial New England. Small slaveholders in particular might be expected to space out manumissions of a group of children in order to assure a continued supply of farm or domestic labor.

One further complexity has to be worked into the equation of manumitting family members, and that is the timing of delayed manumissions and their impact on the family's life cycle. Were black parents, for instance, more desirous of manumitting their eldest or their youngest children? Again, whatever the quality of emotional attachments among family members, older children could earn more and might be more valuable as free workers. Alternatively, younger children, particularly infants, might be easier to set free, precisely because they had less short-term economic value and might the more readily be sold to a parent by a white master. In addition, parents might well fear that their youngest children were the most vulnerable to remaining forever in slavery, as they were most likely to be orphaned while still in childhood. With so many competing factors impinging on the desires both of African Americans and manumitting slaveholders, it might be expected that few clear patterns of child manumission would emerge. But two things do seem to have made a difference for an enslaved child's prospects of becoming free: gender and place of residence.

Girls and boys had fairly equal chances of being manumitted prospectively after a term of service; however, girls were much more likely to benefit from immediate manumission during their infancy or childhood, as shown in table 13.

Of approximately 2,500 children whose manumissions indicated their sex and age at freedom, 53 percent were girls and 47 percent were boys. Four-fifths of these manumissions promised freedom after a term of servitude, with boys and girls being equally likely recipients: 991 girls and 990 boys received delayed manumissions. But girls composed almost two-thirds of the children manumitted with immediate effect, outnumbering boys by 304 to 177.[22]

It is difficult to account for a skew toward immediate manumission of female children that is not replicated in delayed manumissions. The hypothesis that masters were more reluctant to free male slaves because of their higher value is appealing, but it fails to explain the even sex distribution of delayed manumissions. The theory that black parents might have leaned toward manumitting daughters to avoid their reaching maturity and bearing children while still enslaved falls afoul of the data as well. But if we imagine these two sets of attitudes converging, the patterns begin to make sense.

In economic terms, slaveholders saw slave children as assets that would appreciate over time, boys yielding a greater eventual return through their labor or by bringing a higher price if sold. Although chil-

TABLE 13

Manumission of Children, 1770-1830			
	Boys	Girls	Total
Immediate Manumissions	177 (37%)	304 (63%)	481
Delayed Manumissions	990 (50%)	991 (50%)	1981
Total	1167 (47%)	1295 (53%)	2462

dren under five commanded little value, because they were too young to work and might well die before paying for their upbringing, even infants could be sold for a positive price, with boys fetching somewhat more than girls.[23] Boys and girls five or older, the dangers of child mortality largely behind them, became increasingly valuable with each passing year; boys of all age groups sold at higher prices than girls of a like age. This sex-based disparity increased as children approached adulthood. Left to their own devices, slaveholders disposed to manumit slave children might then have consistently favored the manumission of less valuable girls.

Free black parents whose children had been born as slaves would have known that buying out their sons and daughters would become more costly as they grew older and that girls, even infant girls, could be freed more cheaply than boys. In fact, the skew toward freeing girls immediately may reflect that free blacks generally found it difficult to amass money to purchase any of their male children, or indeed girls beyond their earliest years. Age distributions of immediately freed children lend support to this proposition, as table 14 shows.

Nearly twice as many children were freed before their fifth birthday as between ages five and nine, and more than twice as many were freed before age five as were liberated between the ages of ten and fourteen. In all three age groups, girls significantly outnumbered boys. This suggests that parents found it easiest to purchase infant or very young children, perhaps because slaveholders were more willing to avoid risks of mortality and pocket small profits by selling this subset of slave children.

When, for whatever reason, immediate manumission of children yielded to term slavery, the concomitant shift in the price mechanism, from cash to future service, worked to equalize the number of boys and girls prospectively freed. Slaveholders still demanded more for liberating males, but those demands could be met by fixing longer terms of

TABLE 14

Immediate Manumission of Children by Sex and Age at Freedom

Age Group	Boys	Girls	Total
0-4	73	111	184 (38%)
5-9	46	62	108 (22%)
10-14	33	44	77 (16%)
15-19	25	87	112 (23%)
Totals	177	304	481

service for boys than for comparably aged girls. Two-thirds of the boys promised future freedom had to serve terms of more than fifteen years, compared to just half of the girls; more than a third of the boys would be term slaves for more than twenty years, compared to barely one-fifth of the girls. See table 15.

In short, prevailing prices for slave children significantly shaped which African American children were manumitted and the timing of those acts. Further support for this view derives from comparing child manumission patterns in Baltimore with those of nearby rural counties. A much higher proportion of manumitted children gained their freedom immediately in Baltimore than in the hinterlands. Of 551 manumissions by white masters of city-dwelling slave children, 197 (36 percent) took effect immediately, compared to just 284 of 1,911 manumissions (15 percent) of children in rural counties. The market value of slave children did not vary significantly between city and countryside, but costs of food and shelter were decidedly higher in Baltimore, and opportunities to employ children were certainly no greater. Accordingly, urban slaveholders may have been more disposed to sell slave children to their parents and less interested in retaining control of them until early adulthood than their rural counterparts. Also, urban black parents almost certainly had more access to cash than rural ones, both through wage work in Baltimore's craft shops and shipyards, and from entrepreneurial activities such as huckstering, carting, or doing laundry. The result was that city folk were better placed to purchase children outright and could thus free more of their children immediately, settling less frequently for the uncertainties of delayed manumission.

But other obstacles, besides accumulating the funds needed to purchase freedom for one's kin, had to be overcome. Slaveholders could refuse to part with their chattels or could seek to extract exorbitant

TABLE 15

Delayed Manumission of Children: Sex and Length of Service

Years of Service	Boys	Girls	Total
1-5	4 (<1%)	47 (5%)	51
6-10	98 (10%)	153 (16%)	251
11-15	209 (22%)	280 (29%)	489
16-20	315 (32%)	278 (28%)	593
>20	351 (36%)	216 (22%)	567
Totals	977	974	1,951

NOTE: These data exclude thirty delayed manumissions of indeterminate length, i.e., until the death of the manumitter or his spouse.

prices, given their position as "monopoly sellers" of the human beings parents most wished to rescue from slavery. Faced with intractable masters, free people of color sometimes persisted for many years in their attempts to free their families, even pursuing the matter beyond their own deaths through instructions in their wills. Thomas Pitt, a black Baltimorean and a great-grandfather, was still struggling at the end of his life to free his son George and George's children by his late wife Dinah, as his will, recorded in 1819, reveals. George and his children were the slaves of Parker Lee of Harford County. Pitt ordered his executors to "purchase and set at liberty" all three, but "if difficulties occur . . . endeavor particularly to purchase the father, but if he cannot be purchased . . . and it be practicable to purchase the two Children . . . that they be purchased accordingly." Perhaps anticipating trouble with this plan, Pitt asked that one hundred dollars be set aside as a trust for the "comfort of each one or all of them who cannot be purchased and set free." If neither George nor either of his children could be freed, Pitt directed that fifty-dollar trust funds be set up for three sons of a daughter who had predeceased him. In this case the three boys were prospectively manumitted term slaves, whose legacies were to be turned over them when they attained their freedom. The balance of Pitt's estate was to be divided among three sons already free. Despite these elaborate contingencies, Pitt's priorities were clear. Above all else, he wanted all of his descendants to be free: children and grandchildren already freed or promised freedom would receive bequests only after the executors had made every exertion to free George and his children.[24]

Pitt's case was not unique. Carlos Hall was perhaps the richest free black in Baltimore in the 1820s, having amassed a small fortune by devising, manufacturing, and selling an improved boot-blacking substance. But Hall himself had only gained his freedom in 1817; in the meantime his enslaved daughter had been sold or taken to New Orleans by her master. When Hall died in 1823, he had not given up hope of freeing her: he left "one thousand dollars plus the interest on a six thousand dollar trust to liberate my daughter Mary Ann Hall." Frank Armstrong's will offered nine hundred dollars of wages due him from George Grundy "for the purchase of freedom of my Daughters Rosetta and Angelina, by Leah, Slave of Christopher Hughes, provided he will take such a sum as I may leave after my funeral expences and Physician are paid." And Amy Scoggins left all of her tiny estate, "two horses, one waggon, one cart, one bed, bedding and bedstead, curtain, six chairs and three tables" and a few other household effects, "for the sole use and benefit of my beloved husband Isaac Scoggins . . . to be applied towards obtaining his Freedom."[25]

Blacks displayed a settled determination to enfranchise their spouses and children, combined with a desire to minimize terms of servitude incident upon such manumissions by purchase. Nonetheless, even when they were free of dealing through whites, freedom was not always granted immediately. Nearly a quarter of deeds of manumission granted by a free person of color promised the beneficiary only eventual freedom, after a term of servitude.[26] In a few cases these black masters used manumission to ensure their own support and maintenance in old age. David Polk, "advanced in years and . . . soon . . . unable to support and maintain himself," felt he had "not only a natural claim to the . . . assistance of his . . . son . . . and grandson," but "a peculiarly strong claim . . . having purchased them at great expense . . . and having at a still greater expense brought them up and educated them." Seeking to "insure to himself the certainty of not being left helpless and destitute in his old age," Polk set his son David and grandson Benjamin Handy free only at his death. Much as a patriarchal father in colonial America might have retained control of his land in life to assure continued loyalty, obedience, and service from sons, David Polk reserved the grant of freedom to his descendants until his death.[27] Polk's desire to protect his own interests may have been widely shared: fully half of the boys manumitted by free black men were required to perform a term of service.[28]

Other blacks delayed liberating their children and employed the broad legal powers of the slaveholder to guard those children from white depredations in the guise of indentureship. Maryland courts could and did bind out as indentured servants poor children whose parents could not support them. First envisaged in the seventeenth century as a means of providing for the welfare and maintenance of orphans, by the early nineteenth century the binding of children, with or without the consent of living parents, often assumed the characteristics of an institution for supplying child labor to landowners and the well-to-do generally. Although free black children were not exclusively the target of such court actions, they were, particularly in many Eastern Shore counties, disproportionately likely to be taken from their parents and bound to serve a farmer or a tradesman. One way for a black parent to avoid losing a child through such indentures would be to own the child as a slave; the courts had no authority to remove a slave from a master's household. Indeed, the possession of a slave, even if that slave were one's own child, might undercut the presumption of being propertyless and thus a suitable target for the binding out of one's other children.

The hypothesis that ownership of one's children might represent a conscious defensive strategy to avoid white control fits well with regional data regarding the frequency with which black parents chose to delay to adulthood the manumission of their children. In Baltimore city, where the involuntary indenturing of free black children was rare, only 10 percent of black-granted manumissions of children were delayed. In rural Maryland, where court bindings of "indigent" free blacks constituted a much higher proportion of indentures, 23 percent of black-granted manumissions stipulated a term of servitude preceding a child's freedom. In fact, in Kent County, where indentureship had become virtually an all-black institution by the early nineteenth century, 31 percent of black-granted manumissions were delayed until adulthood.[29]

The case of Ben Copper, a free black sailor, illustrates how manipulating children's status could protect against white exploitation. Copper, the father of two boys, had arranged for his sons to be employed as hired hands by Patrick Gallagher, a white lime kiln operator. Worried that Gallagher might try to gain legal control of his sons during his absence on a voyage to the West Indies, Copper made out bills of sale for his two sons and presented them to his friend Thomas Winston, shortly before his departure. When Gallagher in fact obtained "fraudulent" indentures for Copper's sons, by claiming that they were indigent free blacks, Winston petitioned the orphans' court to have the indentures voided.

In the ensuing hearing, the white Gallagher asserted that the boys were free, to back up his claim to them through articles of indenture, but the black Winston triumphantly produced the bills of sale to prove that Copper's sons were his slaves and hence beyond Gallagher's grasp. As a black man, Winston could not testify directly against Gallagher's claims regarding the boys. But he could successfully pray that the court recognize a documented transaction between himself and Copper that effectively negated Gallagher's strategy.[30]

Taken together, the black manumission data and the Copper case suggest some new lines of thought concerning the vexed question of how and why some blacks became slaveholders. One line of thinking, espoused by scholars since the time of Carter Woodson, views black slaveholding as primarily a beneficent enterprise, typified by the ownership of kin, and as a product of antebellum laws restricting manumission. For these writers, black slaveholders were people whose children could not legally be freed or whose children's emancipation would have required them to leave the state in which they resided.

Recently, Michael Johnson and James Roark have challenged this interpretation, working with extensive census data on black slaveholding as well as family papers of prominent free people of color who owned large numbers of slaves. In their view free people of color, pressured by white hostility to their very existence, and perceiving this pressure to be on the rise in the antebellum South, turned to slaveholding as a way of demonstrating their acceptance of and solidarity with core values of white southern society. For Johnson and Roark, black slaveholding thus represents a gesture of accommodation to the dominant forces of their world, which may have had relatively little to do with protecting kin or keeping families together.[31]

The Maryland data regarding black manumissions cannot be fully comprehended by either of these two streams of thought. Most black manumitters freed relatives, but the law and practice of Maryland did not require that black children be held as slaves until attaining their majority. The Maryland legislature tinkered fairly often with the legalities of private manumission but never banned it outright or required that manumissions be granted only by acts of the legislature, as did several deep South states. Likewise, although the state did enact statutes in the aftermath of the Gabriel and Nat Turner insurrections to prevent the migration of free people of color into Maryland, every indication is that these laws were all but universally ignored. In short, free black parents in Maryland had little reason to think that freeing their children would ensnare them in legal difficulties with the public law. The view of black slaveholding as a device forced on black parents by white social policy does not explain why significant minorities of Maryland blacks chose to keep their children in term slavery.

The Johnson-Roark thesis also runs into difficulties in explaining slave ownership by blacks in Maryland, at least for the period before 1830. Census data show few if any free people of color whose households contained more than one or two slaves. Bills of sale recording the purchase or sale of a slave by an unrelated black are likewise virtually nonexistent.[32] Of course, it could be argued that Maryland's relatively less inhospitable reception of free people of color, at least as compared to South Carolina or the Gulf states, rendered the strategies described by Johnson and Roark unnecessary, making Maryland's exceptional case compatible with their underlying arguments about black masters.

But perhaps the behavior of Maryland's black slaveholders suggests areas of overlap between these two strands of interpretation. Most black masters in Maryland did own kin, rather than strangers, as Woodson and his continuators argued. However, those masters chose their status for instrumental reasons, rather than having it forced upon them by restrictions on manumission. The rationale behind the choice to become a slaveholder, as Johnson and Roark suggest, derived from a need to assume the role, status, and legal rights of the slaveholder. Ben Copper's slaves were his sons, but he was not forced to own them; he seized on the prerogatives of the slaveholder and even delegated them to someone outside his own family, his friend Thomas Winston, as a way to protect the boys from a predatory white employer.

Even though Copper's maneuvers were undoubtedly atypical, they represent no more than an unusual variation on the central theme of the operations of slavery and manumission in Maryland: the contest over the terms of labor and its projection into the future via struggles to control black children. Slaveholders' interest in delayed manumission and in selling freedom to slaves sprang from the oversupply of African American workers in the countryside. Selective manumission offered a way to streamline while retaining the flexibility to "gear up" by hanging on to claims to the next generation of African American workers. For their part, African Americans made the most of the combination of economic and social factors that rendered gradual manumission a sound strategy for masters; they did their best to counteract the transmission of slavery to their children. Chapter 6 reviews these on-the-ground struggles from the standpoint of ideology and examines the significance or lack thereof of white antislavery thought in shaping the world of free people of color in early national Maryland.

6

POLITICAL-ECONOMIC THOUGHT
AND FREE BLACKS

By 1830 some fourteen thousand free African Americans made up almost one-fifth of Baltimore's residents, outnumbering slaves nearly four to one. The commercial outlook of Marylanders had strongly shaped the emergence of this black community over the preceding forty years. Self-purchase or delayed manumission contingent on hard work were the modes by which people of color became free; migration to Baltimore was often part of the process of liberation.

In this setting discussions of emancipation shifted away from the abstract antislavery of the Revolutionary era and slavery's moral impact on whites, to pragmatic estimates of the capacities of freed people and their effects on the American economy. By the second decade of the nineteenth century, appeals to religious or republican sentiment were giving way to political-economic assessments of blacks as workers, savers, and consumers. The workings of delayed manumission critically affected perceptions of free people of color as economic actors and ultimately buttressed intellectual justifications for race-based exclusion of blacks from full participation in society. This new, more virulent form of racism contributed to squeezing blacks out of the crafts and to the increased concentration of blacks in lower-paid, unskilled work. The resulting loss of income made it harder for blacks to come up with a purchase price in cash or future work to buy themselves or family members out of slavery. These difficulties, coupled with an expanding market and rising prices for slaves sold to the cotton states, slowed the pace of self-emancipation of Maryland's blacks in the decades after 1830 and thus help account for the state's far advanced but incomplete transition from slavery to freedom by 1860.

The central question whites posed about former slaves was whether freedmen would work without compulsion.[1] In postemancipation plantation societies, the perceived withdrawal of former slave women and children from field labor would often feed doubts on this point; in Baltimore the idea of the "lazy" freedman drew strength from the outcomes of delayed manumission. To be sure, blacks saved for years and accumulated impressive amounts to buy themselves or family members out of slavery or to pay debts incurred in self-purchase: an adult male slave's price matched the median taxable wealth of urban property holders.[2] But these expenditures on the invisible asset of personal liberty left little capital with which to obtain the tangible property that signified a worker's industry, thrift, and accumulative mentality. In the same vein manumissions negotiated by commuting slavery for life into a term of service generally did not take effect until the freed person had passed the age of thirty, denying that person the benefit of many of his or her peak earning years. However freedom was attained, after the long struggle to pay its price was over, an African American family could maintain a given level of subsistence with lower earnings than before. Such a choice might have been quite tempting to people who had often won freedom through extremely heavy and prolonged physical labor, as the work record of Scipio Freeman at the Maryland Chemical Works suggests. But any diminution of labor that might flow from that circumstance could be observed and adduced as "proof" of free black sloth.

Maryland commentators were not slow to conclude that freed blacks were "lazy" or "improvident." Antislaveryite Daniel Raymond complained that, "in regard to manumitted slaves . . . nine out of ten . . . industrious and moral before, become vagabonds, and one half of them perhaps, get into the penitentiary." Editor Hezekiah Niles found in 1819 that "free blacks among us are less honest and correct, less industrious and not so much to be depended upon . . . as the well-treated slaves," and he argued that "worn out slaves," manumitted by their masters to avoid supporting them in old age, were one cause of the problem.[3]

The negative comments about blacks of antislavery sympathizers like Niles and Raymond underline the point that intellectual support for emancipation, as a device to preserve and protect whites' republican virtue, failed to evoke any corresponding enthusiasm for freed blacks. It is not much of an overstatement to say that Revolutionary-era antislavery was a program intended to benefit whites, whereas the actual emancipation of blacks was seen as the price to be paid. Throughout the decades from 1780 to 1830, proponents of antislavery stressed the gains of ending slavery; opponents dwelt on the unacceptable social and economic costs of freeing blacks. What changed over time was the increasing presence of free people of color, with the concomitant opportunity or burden, depending on one's position, of assessing their successes and failures in free society.

An exchange in the *Maryland Gazette* in late 1790, occurring as the legislators debated legalizing manumission by will, illustrates ideas in play early in the period. "A Freeman" opened the debate with the argument that Americans' claims to cherish liberty were inconsistent with the continuation of Negro slavery. He then smeared slavery by pointing to the "impious" Algerine practice of enslaving Europeans, disposed of historical precedents for slavery's legitimacy with reference to the historical ubiquity of monarchy, and rested his case with an invocation for slaveholders to free their chattels in obedience to the Golden Rule.[4] Antislavery was republican, Christian, and moral; slaveholding was the obverse of these virtues.

Two weeks later "A True Friend to the Union" responded that although slavery "ha[d] been a curse to the southern states," it seemed likely to be "entailed" on them for some time to come. This writer insisted that, "As the evil came among us slowly . . . so must it be done away, almost as gradually as it came on." His principal justifications bespoke fear of free blacks ("You could not with propriety, let all loose among us at once") and concern that financial "ruin to white inhabitants would ensue." Citing the "convenience" to propertied men of being able to leave slaves to their daughters, whose "hire, with the industry of their mistresses, yields a competency for the support of all," the defender of slavery embodied a patriarchal inclusion of white women and black slaves in the same dependent category and an assertion that slavery would foster labor and industry. Whatever the virtues of antislavery as a theoretical construct, actual emancipation was to be weighed for its economic and political consequences.[5]

In a rejoinder the Freeman conceded that many free blacks "would abuse their freedom and render themselves more miserable than they are in bondage" and quickly passed on to a restatement of the moral necessity for whites of liberating their slaves. True Friend's rebuttal of December 16 hammered away at the point that "a general manumission" would be dangerous without "exportation. . . . It would not do to keep them among us."[6] Eventually, the Freeman entered a carefully qualified class-oriented defense of free blacks, claiming that their "industry and honesty" would equal that of whites "of a similar station" in life.[7] The debate between True Friend and Freeman thus turned chiefly on the criteria for evaluating the desirability of emancipation for white society. Freeman advanced no independent counterargument for the potential gains of liberating slaves; he contended mainly that free blacks would implicitly be no more harmful to society than propertyless whites.

In so doing Freeman was scarcely unique; at least one contemporary combined advocacy of immediate abolition with a demand for colonization of all freed blacks. "Othello," in a pair of letters to the *American Museum* in 1788, insisted that slavery was "inconsistent with the declared principles of the American revolution" and urged that "we should set all our slaves at liberty, immediately, and colonize them in the western territory." Othello then linked emancipation and the encouragement of industry among whites, claiming that abolition would make America "a richer and more happy country" because "our lands would not then be cut down for the support of a train of useless inhabitants," whose existence inspired only "sloth and voluptuousness among our young farmers and planters."[8] In common with many opponents of emancipation, Othello apparently held no great expectations for the future of blacks in America.

Othello, Freeman, and True Friend positioned themselves along a spectrum of views ranging from ambivalence through pessimism to a negative certainty regarding the prospects of free blacks. They all drew on the idea, still prevalent in the late eighteenth century, that work was a divinely ordained curse on sinful man that most persons naturally sought to avoid. This perception originally contained no racial overtones; many late- eighteenth-century thinkers feared that white Americans could sink into indolence because of the supposed ease of satisfying basic wants and needs in a well-endowed country. James Madison worried that western settlers would succumb to the temptation to enjoy the produce of rich new lands without having to labor extensively. Their resulting indolence and torpor would unfit them for the responsibilities of citizenship, threatening the stability of the republic. Madison favored the encouragement of commercial agriculture to induce Americans to work hard to sell surplus crops and accumulate wealth.[9]

To some who worried about white industriousness, the "sloth and voluptuousness" encouraged by slavery were equally threatening to republican virtue, making the extinction of slavery desirable. But however beneficial emancipation might prove in preserving a sturdily working white citizenry, the resulting creation of a free black populace presented problems. To men who metaphorically associated change with decay, who feared that white Americans would yield to the temptation to live rudely to avoid work, the notion that ex-slaves could be self-reliant and industrious was alien. Blacks had lived without the ability to accumulate property, and the urge to do so would not automatically come with striking off their chains. Free blacks would become a propertyless class of dependent laborers, constituting another problem for the maintenance of the commonweal.

Observations, accurate or otherwise, of "shirking" by slaves do
not appear to have played a central role in this line of thought. Theoretical concerns dominated the formation of the belief that the benefits
of industry and labor, deemed so essential to the progress of white
American society, were unlikely to be earned or enjoyed by free blacks.
The near uniformity of these late-eighteenth-century stereotypes of
"lazy" free blacks as a "useless" caste predated the presence of any
substantial population of free people of color.[10] But the weight given to
such stereotypes increased as free blacks became a more visible and
numerous element of society.

In 1805 the Maryland General Assembly expanded efforts to manage free blacks, cracking down especially to ensure that they not dis-
turb the security of slave property. A law requiring free blacks to obtain court-registered certificates of freedom cited as its chief object the
prevention of "slaves coming into possession of the certificates of free
negroes . . . running away and passing as free." In order to obtain
convictions in crimes involving blacks, the legislature also broadened
the state's rules of evidence to admit the testimony of slaves and free
blacks against each other.[11] At this stage free blacks were still seen as
an anomalous adjunct to the slave population. Acts more frankly designed to create mechanisms for controlling free blacks per se received
less emphatic support. A prohibition on free black emigration to Maryland and bans on "tumultuous meetings" or carrying guns were en-
acted, but all had loopholes granting wide discretion in enforcement.
Moreover, these laws failed to provide monetary rewards to private
citizens who prosecuted violations, a sign that their enforcement was
not of central importance to Marylanders.[12] Free blacks thus did not
bulk large in the concerns of whites, but nonetheless they were regarded
with suspicion.

More broadly based evidence of perceptions of free blacks appears
in petitions to Maryland's governors seeking pardons for convicted criminals. Petitions on behalf of whites routinely averred that the proposed
beneficiary had led a life of "industry, honesty, and sobriety" before his
unfortunate misstep, while those for free black felons, whether drafted
in 1790 or 1820, made such claims far less frequently and attracted
relatively few signers when they did so. In fact, pardon petitions on
behalf of slaves more commonly attested to the subject's work ethic
than those for free blacks.[13]

Ex-slaves in Baltimore frequently sought self-employment as carters, hucksters, washerwomen, or chimney sweeps; whites could mis-
read such desire for autonomy as unwillingness to work steadily over
long periods, that is, to become wage workers. Similarly, seasonal un-

In capacity for freedom

employment at the port or in craft work, or layoffs due to hard times, provided further "evidence" of incapacity for freedom.[14] The prudent and foresighted laborer, aware of the vicissitudes of the local labor market, would save up to get through lean times, but a free black who did "follow some regular course of industry" would still be mired in the "habits of thoughtless improvidence . . . contracted while a slave" and would inevitably become a public charge.[15] Even those who were an "ornament to the ranks of day laborers" were prone to "indolence" stemming from "an understandable lack of familiarity with the mystery of property," a mentality difficult to erase.[16]

The supposed shortcomings of slaves and free people of color as savers and accumulators were ironically complemented by the suspicion that they were inadequate consumers. Niles, a proponent of developing the "home market" for American manufactures, worried about the presence of people too poor to purchase such goods. Daniel Raymond also advocated a high-production, high-consumption economy and explicitly identified African Americans as an impediment to that goal. Slaves did not "labor to increase the product" because they did not "derive the benefit of the increase," but more critically, the bare subsistence level at which most slaves lived focused them strictly on obtaining the "necessaries" of life. In contrast, the free white worker's "wants always exceed his power of supplying them, as artificial wants spring up" as soon as necessaries were met.

economic theories + impact of black + stereotypes of blacks

Freeing blacks would not increase their demand for "comforts," as habits of enforced frugality acquired in bondage would be retained and even transmitted to their children. Overlooking the impact of self-purchase on freed peoples' disposable income and consumption patterns, or perhaps drawing the right conclusion for the wrong reason, Niles and Raymond held that the problem of the parsimonious ex-slave underlined the importance of free birth as a prerequisite for satisfactory membership in society. They looked for outward signs of prosperity as a way of ascertaining the freedman's character and, seeing instead an absence of household goods, they equated the absence of those symbols of respectability with a supposedly irredeemable poverty.[17]

free birth

These hard-eyed assessments of free blacks against standards of political economy that valued high consumption were reinforced by older, environmentalist pessimism about the capacity of freed blacks to overcome the degradation of slavery and reorient their behavior. Blacks' status as propertyless laborers thus served both as evidence of innate immorality and of unfitness for life in a competitive society, threatening a consequent slowdown of the engines that propelled American growth.

economy valued high consumption

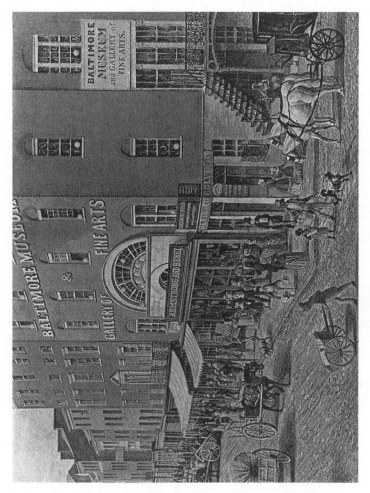

Detail of commercial street scene in early national Baltimore, where black workers and families were able to unite in freedom. Lithograph printed by E. Sachse and Company, c. 1850. Maryland Historical Society

never given the opportunity to be equal!

The charge against freed people of economic shortcomings drew strength from other, more axiomatic objections. Raymond asked, rhetorically, "In a political, a moral, an intellectual, and a religious point of view, is not a white population better than a black one?" Likewise, Hezekiah Niles prized a "uniformity of habits and manners" in America and found its development impeded by the presence of blacks and slavery. Convinced that blacks would continue to pose a "problem" for white America, and immersed in a city with a swelling population of free people of color, both pro- and antislavery thinkers turned to the analysis of demographic trends to determine whether America could purge itself of blacks to white advantage.

In 1819 Niles projected a slave population of three million by 1835 and feared that such numbers would "prove a serious incumbrance on the white population. . . . it will be difficult to employ and maintain them to advantage."[18] Raymond, while caught up in the Missouri controversy, went beyond linear projections of slave population growth and analyzed free and slave state census data to construct a demographic argument for manumission and against "diffusion,"—allowing slaves to be taken into the territories of the Louisiana Purchase. He found that slave population grew at a faster rate than white population in a slaveholding state, that white population grew faster in free states than in slave states, and that free black population grew less than half as fast as the white population in free states. To Raymond, these patterns proved that diffusion would encourage growth of slave population and retard that of whites, whereas more extensive manumission would reduce the ratio of blacks to whites.[19] If freed slaves did "become a nuisance to society," were they not as slaves "an infinitely greater nuisance?" Besides, the "idle, vagabond blacks do not raise families, or comparatively none." Those who exhibited industry would raise children, and manumission must thus either promote the extinction of unworthy blacks or aid the development of a reliable black citizenry. Freedmen "would . . . acquire the habits of free men . . . or dwindle to nothing."[20]

Raymond's patronizing tone notwithstanding, his observations accurately captured some aspects of manumission and self-purchase. Free black parents would be raising children, as opposed to having them languish in slavery, to the extent that their hard work allowed them to buy out their sons and daughters (unless good fortune or industry had permitted them to become free early in life, before having children). In that sense free blacks might well "dwindle" if they could not break their families out of the transgenerational cycle of term slavery.

diffusion

Raymond's pamphlet did not long go unchallenged. Proslavery Baltimore attorney Joseph D. Learned countered that diffusion would enrich both masters who went west and those who stayed behind, allowing improved slave maintenance and reducing the dangers of a slave insurrection arising from ill-fed, ill-clad chattels.[21] Learned also debunked Raymond's data on free blacks, insisting that "seven-eighths" of them had been born in slavery and that freeborn people of color would raise larger families. In a telling comment showing his familiarity with gradual manumission, Learned observed that "much the greatest portion [of manumitted slaves] have not acquired their freedom until the natural period for increase is past." This would artificially depress the growth rates of free blacks, whose "numerous offspring, perhaps, are held in slavery," falsely inflating the slave population growth rates that so alarmed Raymond.

Likewise, northern experience with free blacks might not be a valid predictor for the South: the harsher climate and more competitive labor market rendered free black subsistence there more "scanty and precarious," so free blacks in the South would grow at a faster rate than Raymond expected. Finally, if slaves actually did increase faster than free blacks, that merely proved the "degraded" state of free people of color and argued against their liberation, for "only the most worthless [were] freed, and that for the purpose of being relieved of them."[22] Proponents and opponents of diffusing slaves to Missouri thus both forecast that blacks might not succeed in freedom, but they differed over whether manumission would accentuate or alleviate the demographic threat to white prosperity. Exporting slaves to Missouri and deporting freed blacks to Africa in the guise of colonization both had their adherents in Maryland, where a state chapter of the American Colonization Society had been founded in 1817.

Robert Goodloe Harper laid out the case for colonization in a lengthy public letter developing themes that were already hardening into conventional wisdom.[23] Harper neatly combined the conceits of white-oriented antislavery and black unworthiness, asserting that colonization would "confer a benefit on ourselves, by ridding us of a population for the most part idle and useless, and too often vicious and mischievous." Freely admitting that white "prejudices" influenced these perceptions, Harper nonetheless saw free blacks as "condemned to . . . hopeless inferiority and degradation" by their skin color. He discounted the significance of the transition to free status for blacks and embraced the equally conservative notion that public opinion would immutably reject black participation in republican society.[24]

Harper insisted that this "impassible barrier" to social equality

meant that for the African American "the incitement to good conduct
. . . which arises from the hoping of raising himself . . . is a stranger to
his breast." Self-discipline would never take root, and even the rare
freedman who discarded habits "contracted while a slave" might be
reinfected by "the slaves among whom he is forced to live," leading to
the inexorable outcome of "liv[ing] as a pauper, at the expense of the
community." Imbued with the idea that desirable changes could only
occur over imperceptibly long periods of time, Harper despaired equally
of whites accepting blacks and of blacks meriting such acceptance.[25]

Harper brought his argument full circle by objecting to free blacks'
tendency toward "corruption of the slaves . . . by rendering them idle,
discontented and disobedient." Painting a gloomy picture of free black
disorder provoking otherwise hard-working and loyal slaves into flight,
theft, and resistance to masters, he opined that free blacks would be to
blame if future slave misdeeds provoked masters "to a severity, which
would not otherwise be thought necessary."[26]

Harper's sometimes tortuous reasoning bespoke a fundamental
objection to the anomalous status of emancipated blacks in a society
with race-based slavery. That objection nonetheless had some ground-
ing in real experience. Free blacks were aiding discontented slaves in
escaping their masters, for example. Because they could not be sub-
sumed satisfactorily under preexisting social categories, they threatened to blur the definition of other groups, including whites. Black
workers, slave or free, also inspired a contempt for hard work among
"the class of free whites who ought to labour" and who instead, "saw
labour as a badge of slavery," so Harper concluded that free blacks
were "injurious to all."[27]

Colonization would allow free blacks to escape white prejudice,
lessening the corruption of slaves and encouraging white immigration
into slave states. Harper closed with an adjuration against sending colo-
nists to British-established Sierra Leone, as "our colony . . . ought to be
republican."[28] Far from a mere rhetorical flourish, Harper's uncharac-
teristic optimism about black potential in Africa represented another
salute to social homogeneity. Although their indeterminate status could
only disrupt America, free blacks might erect their own republican society in Africa, contributing by subtraction to the purification of the
United States. These views resonated with the political community of
Maryland; in its 1817-18 session the legislature unanimously endorsed
the colonization principle.[29]

Harper's privileging of homogeneity as a way of reading free blacks
out of the polity melded with other invocations of republican equality
advanced for the same purposes. An anonymous contributor to Hezekiah

Niles's *Weekly Register* decried treatment of free blacks: denying them equality tended to "aggravate their feelings of inferiority"; however, giving blacks full equality would lead to "a war of complete extermination (as was the case in St. Domingo)." Seeking to bolster his view of free blacks as inveterately vengeful, and reading manumissions as acts of white benevolence, the writer observed the lack of black "testimony of gratitude for this boon [of freedom]." Citing the experience of the "most sensible, informed and discreet members of the Methodist society," who had freed slaves, the author found a unanimous sentiment that those freed were "unhappy, abject, and miserable, and to society its greatest evil." Freely conceding that slaveholding was "politically wrong," this commentator characterized emancipation as a hypocritical sop to white conscience, of "no benefit to [blacks], unless we raise them to the enjoyment of equal privileges, and . . . amalgamate with them on the most liberal and reciprocal terms."[30]

Both procolonization writers dwelt on the benefits or social costs of emancipation for broad "classes" of whites and blacks but displayed little interest in evidence of individual African Americans' success in freedom. Harper mentioned Paul Cuffe, a wealthy free black ship captain and merchant from Massachusetts, to recapitulate his argument on the alleged social incompatibility of the races: whatever Cuffe's attainments, he would not be invited to dinner by any white merchant of Boston.[31]

By the period of 1815-19, the view of "mere" emancipation as a dangerous half-measure that might corrode white Americans' moral fiber or cheat them of economic opportunity, while bringing little happiness to former slaves, had gained wide currency: far-reaching action would be needed to attain the desideratum of a uniracial, white society. Avowed antislaveryites, limited in the upper South by this time to Quakers, a few Methodists, and emigrants from northern states, could deride the impracticality of colonization, but their own conservative environmentalism generated equally improbable and ponderously gradual remedies, informed by many of the same doubts about black capacity to survive in an increasingly competitive society.

In 1819 Hezekiah Niles's editorials on the "mitigation" of slavery vetoed colonization, advocating the gradual extirpation of domestic slavery, preceded by education in self-denial and love of property while the prospective freed person was still enslaved.[32] Like Harper, he feared the mingling of free negroes and slaves, contending that "mixture is fatal to the improvement of both." In gauging the time needed for the transformation of slaves to free men, Niles alluded to "our ancestors of England," who when "first known to the Romans" were "as much the objects of scorn . . . as the negroes are to us." Freedom had come far too quickly for Niles's virtually geologic sense of progress; in Baltimore's uncontrolled atmosphere, freedmen were doomed by contaminating contact with those still enslaved.

Such corruption of nominally free citizens was a critical problem, for Niles, like Harper, stressed social uniformity as essential to America's realizing its destiny as a chosen land for a chosen people. In a teleological account of American origins, Niles avoided the construction of slavery as "entailed" on America by England, but he still laid the blame for its introduction squarely on the monarchical British. Noting with approval the "growing disposition to ameliorate" the institution, he nevertheless warned of the dangers of inaction. Taking his text from Jefferson's *Notes on Virginia,* Niles lamented "industry destroyed" by slavery's degradation of honorable labor and alluded to a possible race war if slavery continued.[33]

This anxious review of the history of slavery, like Niles's plans for its extirpation, bestrode new and old attitudes toward the flow of human affairs. In his introductory paean to a rising American republic, the lineaments of a nineteenth-century progressive view of change may be discerned. But in thinking about blacks, Niles operated with eighteenth-century categories, seeing freed people as a subset of slaves, unlikely to be swept up in America's advance.

Like Raymond, Niles studied black and white demographics, viewing with alarm the doubling of the slave population between 1790 and 1810 and extrapolating further growth that would cramp opportunities for white workers. Here Niles was tapping into strains of thought about employment and wealth loosely derived from the classical economists, a harbinger of things to come in slavery debates. Although whites would gain from ending slavery and the attendant competition for jobs, to give slaves freedom at once would be "worse than 'throwing pearls before swine.'" Only a few free blacks could grudgingly be conceded to be industrious; most had few dreams of attaining independence and the accompanying willingness to work hard. Instead, "they will make a thousand shifts rather than seek employment," including theft or receiving goods stolen by slaves. Concluding this vilification, Niles found that free blacks had no one but themselves to blame for the "slacken[ing] . . . zeal of the friends of emancipation."[34]

Niles's preoccupation with free black crime derived in part from the influx of free blacks to the newly erected state penitentiary. Black property crime, less visible when privately punished by slaves' masters, had become a "new" phenomenon in the public eye. Prejudice against free blacks may have contributed to higher conviction rates and fewer pardons; in turn, perceptions of free blacks as a criminal class added to their ill-repute and stirred up early reservations about the wisdom of the penitentiary concept.[35] Responding to charges that the penitentiary was failing to reform criminals or deter crime, the Maryland legislature targeted blacks as the problem. Stopping short of proposals to re-enslave free black criminals, an 1818 law allowed courts to whip or banish free blacks in lieu of a penitentiary sentence; the statute barred the penitentiary to criminal slaves. The reauthorizing of corporal punishment for free African Americans symbolized their affinity with slaves in white minds and registered the political community's reluctance to pursue the presumably hopeless task of reforming free blacks by subjecting them to closely supervised hard labor in the penitentiary.[36]

The antislavery political economist Daniel Raymond elaborated on the theoretical difficulties in devising systems of crime and punishment for blacks, linking inadequacies of manumission and public misperception of the dignity of labor to the failure of the penitentiary "both to prevent crimes and to reform criminals."[37] Hard labor was "wholly ineffectual in reforming the convict," because laborious employment was not, as outmoded notions held, a punishment. Rather, Raymond pictured the "fatigued laborer" in the penitentiary "eat[ing] heartily and sleep[ing] soundly, the two greatest comforts and blessings an uneducated man can hope to enjoy." Moreover, the close control and the formation of "habits suited to a penitentiary" left a man "entirely unsuited to the world, or to personal liberty."[38] Then, linking ex-convicts and ex-slaves, Raymond stated, "We see this same principle . . . producing the same effect in regard to manumitted slaves."

The problems symptomized by black convicts could be attributed to lack of suitable education, according to Niles. Brought up in slavery and surrounded by slave companions after winning freedom, blacks could not be expected to emulate honest white freemen, "but by the exertion of virtues that would exalt a white man to a high rank in society." Only schemes for gradual emancipation that inculcated self-denial and a love of property in the prospective freedman while still a slave could make the transition to freedom successful.[39]

Attempting to overcome the contradiction between slow-paced emancipation and the manumittee's clean break with slavery, Niles made a startling proposal to remove twelve thousand slave girls a year to northern households, where they would serve a term of years and then become free. These children, "isolated from their former companions . . . immersed in a moral atmosphere . . . and educated to a virtuous life," would become useful citizens; moreover, they and their children would acquire whiter skins. Denying any veiled approval of race mix-

who is Niles - newspaper editor freedom to press ideas overdone

ing, Niles argued that skin color was governed by climate and environment and that "a family of colored people, insulated by white people, and having no communication with others of a darker race . . . would in time lose . . . their darkness."[40]

Although white tutelage might improve blacks, Niles also advocated his plan as "the proper means of checking the propagation of the slave species." Only thus could Americans hope to "eradicat[e] the offensive colour and the distinctions it causes." Emigration and etiolation would together lead to "the final accomplishment of . . . the desire of every man's heart in America—the final abolition of slavery and the extinction of the slave species, as we designate the people of color—for such they are in the United States." For Niles, changing color was the key preparation for freedom, without which African Americans could not escape mutually reinforcing white prejudice and black improvidence.[41]

Niles also projected more direct benefits from his plan: Slave owners could profitably sell female slave children at prices that would appeal to Northern householders seeking domestic help, and slave mothers would gladly relinquish their daughters to future freedom and respectability. Any public subsidy needed would be far smaller than that projected for African colonization. Niles stressed relocating only women, in a statement striking for its interpenetration of patriarchal views with those of an emerging model of female governance of a domestic realm. He contended that "women are more tractable than men" and that therefore the "transferred female negro . . . would sooner fit herself for freedom," as her "communication with the females of the family, would daily and hourly impress upon her mind a sense of right and wrong."[42] Although the free black man at large in society could not hope to improve, the black woman, shielded in the bosom of a proper white home, could make the transition to life as a free person. White women, themselves secluded from direct participation in the affairs of the republic, would teach virtue to young black women, who would absorb the habits needed for success. Black men were simply not included in this child-focused plan for creating self-reliant but safely subordinate members of a republican society.[43] Niles was not alone in demanding segregation of freed people from slaves. Daniel Raymond also felt that "Blacks . . . who have been born free, and educated with the expectation of being free, . . . make as industrious, sober, good citizens, as any." Like Niles, Raymond favored placing black children with "some good master, who should instruct them."[44]

Aversion to immediate liberation bespoke a deep commitment to closely monitored change as essential to improving black moral char-

is this same as other states?

joke

acter. Others were even less sanguine than Niles and Raymond about
the feasibility of black improvement. John Pendleton Kennedy, like
Harper, regarded prejudice against blacks as insuperable, making freed
people a "proscribed and a forbidden class," unable to "compete for
work with . . . whites." In his view the free blacks generally became
profligate and contaminated the slaves with their vices.[45] "A Colored
Baltimorean" pleaded vainly for whites to "Give us the same stimulus
to honesty, industry, and virtue. . . . And if we fail . . . then brand us
with the epithets of thieves, vagrants, &c."[46] But in general, only whole-
sale relocation, whether to the west, the east, or the north, was deemed
likely by most whites to secure the environmental purity needed to
nurture the habits of freedom.

However implausible these assessments of free black character and
their proposed remedies, the workings of manumission did foster a
world in which slaves for life, slaves serving a term of years, and freedmen were commingled within and across family lines. Slavery as a stage-
of-life institution could be perpetuated for generations as women promised freedom at twenty-five, thirty, or older gave birth to children who
became slaves for life or until well into their adult years, according to
the provisions of the mother's manumission. It is not surprising, then,
that those at least marginally sympathetic to black liberation, like Niles
and Raymond, sought either to get black women out of Maryland or
to wish the "problem" of newly freed blacks away by predicting their
disappearance or deracination.

An unabashed conservative like Robert Harper could call for colonization without internal contradiction, but those like Niles, who had
a foot in each camp, could only strain to bridge the conceptual gaps in
their mental universe by indulging in fanciful hopes, such as turning
black servant girls white by moving them to northern homes. In turn,
although Daniel Raymond sympathized with humane proposals to su-
pervise the black transition to freedom, his focus on self-interested economic action allowed him to define the "problem" of the fate of blacks
out of existence, by proclaiming that they would either thrive or disappear. It was all too easy, however, for conservative opponents like Joseph Learned to appropriate Raymond's methodology and mount a
defense of the status quo, by arguing that self-interest should indeed
reign supreme, both in manumission decisions and respecting the diffusion of slavery.

By 1824 even unqualified adherents of antislavery had become
tinged by negative estimates of free black capabilities. Elisha Tyson, a
leader of the early abolition society, a challenger of kidnappers, and the
bane of slaveholders generally from the 1780s onward, chided an audi-

ence of free people of color: "How lamentable is the reflection that the misconduct of some amongst you . . . should afford ground for the assertion that you are unworthy of liberty." Tyson urged greater attention to religion and more sobriety among his hearers and argued that more decorous free black behavior would "lead [slaves] to be faithful servants."[47]

Only one Baltimore commentator sought straightforwardly to reform delayed manumission in a Maryland setting. The peripatetic Benjamin Lundy, newly arrived in Baltimore in 1825, believed that black labor could be linked to the desired modes of acquisitive and accumulative behavior by public regulation of delayed manumission terms. He enthusiastically endorsed self-purchase on an installment plan in his antislavery weekly, the *Genius of Universal Emancipation*. Apparently unaware of gradual manumission's long history in Maryland, Lundy produced precise calculations to the effect that a slave allowed initially to work for himself just one day of the week could buy successive increments of his work week and become free in seven and one-half years. Masters could "ensure . . . punctual performance" of tasks during the buying-out period, and blacks would learn "habits of industry and temperance." Perhaps unconsciously mirroring the sentiments of many slaveholders, Lundy concluded that "any slave who failed to save enough" to buy himself out "is scarcely entitled to the enjoyment of civil liberty."[48]

Whereas Raymond objected to the supposed suddenness of manumission by will, Lundy criticized deeded manumission and the shifting, unenforceable bargains that masters and slaves struck; he returned repeatedly to the theme of validating free black worth by contractual self-purchase, urging that slave earnings be protected by law and that self-purchase agreements be enforceable by law.[49] In 1827 Lundy enthused over the *coartación* laws of the former Spanish colonies and government-mediated pricing of self-purchase. The regularity and predictability of the process would "incite [slaves] to industry and economy, and prevent those from gaining their freedom who are unworthy of it."[50]

Lundy also strove to show the bankruptcy of bound labor both at the microeconomic and at the macroeconomic level. He claimed on the one hand that free labor was cheaper than slave labor, because of the lower productivity of the latter, and on the other hand that both employers of labor and workers would find a free labor economy more generally prosperous and progressive, because of the higher levels of consumer demand that free replacements for slave workers would generate. Like Harper, Niles, and Raymond, the editor of the *Genius* concerned himself

delayed manumission

only tangentially with the fate of blacks once they attained freedom, and he, too, framed his discussion in terms of whether, and under what white-managed plans, they could become reliable wage workers.

For Lundy the visibly structured acquisition of freedom would both mold free blacks into promise-keeping actors in a market economy and validate their worth in white eyes. But slaveholders had already constructed an elaborate array of positive and negative incentives within the framework of delayed manumission in order to obtain greater production from term slaves. Varying the term of servitude, with reductions for "faithful and obedient" service or additions for illness or running away, was a key device in this realm. Lundy's desire to eliminate the uncertainty surrounding the promise of prospective freedom would have vitiated a cherished management tool. Slaveholders' views on reforming manumission were reflected in the 1833 law allowing the out-of-state sale of refractory term slaves who had failed to respond to lengthened terms. Lundy's proposed hobbling of slaveholders' freewheeling and open-ended transactions with slaves, and of the powerful advantages they enjoyed in negotiating manumission, found little public support.[51]

In this uncertain environment, term slaves used all the options available to dissuade slaveholders from retaining them for their full term, or to seize freedom from masters who reneged on promised manumission: they withheld their earnings as hirelings, they threatened and assaulted their masters, and sometimes they ran away. The program of slaveholders to maximize the exploitation of term slaves by tightening discipline through the threat of sale thus generated resistance that further fueled perceptions of blacks as unwilling or unable to conform to the canons of the work ethic.

The rejection of Lundy's reform proposals and a concomitant weak showing for Daniel Raymond's antislavery candidacies for the legislature in 1825 and 1826 further registered white indifference to or distaste for African Americans in Baltimore. These events were soon followed by the Baltimore carters' petition of 1828, to bar free blacks and slaves from working as draymen, one of the first legislative efforts by white workingmen in Maryland to ban black competitors. Intellectualized reservations toward free black workers were now succeeded by overt hostility; the carters decried free blacks as "more easily influenced by temptations to steal, less influenced by the desire of maintaining an honest reputation, and . . . less fear[ful] of the operations of the law than the white people." Opposition from Baltimore merchants alarmed by prospective increases in drayage costs stymied the petition, but by the 1830s public opinion had settled into regarding free blacks as an ineradicable nuisance with a consequent retelling of the Revolutionary-era myth of the "entailment" of slavery's curse on America to apply to unwelcome freed people.[52]

The modes of thought and life that allowed whites to profit from a slavery they described as evil had been adjusted to encompass exploiting free blacks seen as unworthy of enjoying the advantages of free society. Along the way contests between masters and slaves over the terms of manumission may well have contributed to white resentment of free African Americans; many former slaveholders would have shared Hezekiah Niles's sense that manumission had proceeded too rapidly, at least compared to their desires. The partial effacing of the "stain" of slavery in Maryland, a consequence of African American pressure and narrowing profitability, occurred without a significant diminution of white revulsion toward blacks. Rather, in the transition to free labor, assessments of freed people as inadequate workers, savers, and consumers augmented earlier, more visceral fears of blacks and thus contributed to the elaboration and strengthening of racism.

CONCLUSIONS

On July 4, 1828, an "immense throng of spectators . . . filled every window . . . and the pavement below . . . on Baltimore Street . . . for a distance of about two miles." A crowd of seventy thousand, "placed as closely as they could be stowed," assembled to view an enormous parade celebrating the groundbreaking of the Baltimore and Ohio Railroad. The city's drive for western markets in place of its stagnating oceanic trade was symbolized by a float bearing a fully rigged ship, *The Union,* which led a lengthy procession of artisans with floats displaying their crafts. Crewed by leading merchants and manufacturers, the ship responded to hailing calls from parade officials, its captain bellowing that he was "bound for the Ohio over the mountains, by the railroad." Recalling the frigates that Baltimore's shipyards had constructed, *The Union* also evoked the spirit of Independence Day. Commercial and patriotic themes were further tied together by the frail flesh of Charles Carroll of Carrollton, a major backer of the railroad, who at age ninety-one was the last living signer of the Declaration of Independence and hence an inevitable choice as icon of the festivities.[1]

Although the association of Carroll with the Revolution made him an ideal person to preside over the inauguration of the railroad, his activities as investor, landowner, slaveholder, and occasional manumitter serve equally well to represent the shifts in economic activity and patterns of labor use in Maryland over the course of his long life. Heir to a huge estate, including more than two hundred slaves, Carroll had been part owner of an ironworks that relied on slave labor drawn from underemployed workers on his plantations.[2] A sponsor in the 1790s of a measure to bring about *post-nati* emancipation in Maryland, Carroll nonetheless freed only a small fraction of his chattels and continued to use slave labor in industrial ventures into the 1820s.[3] But now his commitment to the railroad, an enterprise that would rely exclusively on

rail road

free labor, fell in line with the growing shift of Baltimore and Maryland's northern counties away from bound labor.

Carroll's status as the chief person honored at the railroad's dedication offered craftsmen working on floats a chance to show off their skill by making presentation items for Carroll en route. Hatters finished a beaver hat for him, and cordwainers produced a pair of green morocco slippers. Not to be outdone, weavers turned out a bolt of "shambray" that tailors then made up into a coat. The bookbinders obtained copies of dedicatory speeches, bound them, and produced a finished volume for Carroll as they rolled along. Dozens of other groups took part in the march, with special interest attaching to two cars from the Union Manufacturing Company that bore over a hundred female mill hands. These were placed near the head of the procession on its return to the city, a rare public recognition of women workers.

Efforts to embrace dignitaries, craftsmen, political activists, military veterans, and women in the railroad's dedication did not extend to people of color. If free black workers or slaves were among those marchers representing the seamen, rope makers, bakers, bricklayers, or carters and draymen, which were all trades with many African American workers, no mention of them appeared in the press. In this regard the absence of blacks in the July 4 parade exemplified the theory that ceremonies show society as their participants would like it to be: white Baltimoreans acknowledged no role for black workers in the prosperous future that the railroad's construction was designed to foster.

The parade's implicit message of yearning for an all-white society in Baltimore more nearly predicted the future than its frankly stated desire for the railroad to bring back the booming growth of the years before 1815. Construction delays, financial setbacks, and political struggles with backers of the rival Chesapeake and Ohio Canal over right-of-way slowed the westward progress of track-laying gangs; the road did not reach the Ohio River for twenty years and more. Difficulties with laborers also brought work to a halt, most notably when an Irish track-laying crew working near New Market, Maryland, in 1831 destroyed extensive sections of track after a contractor absconded with their payroll. Company efforts to end the trouble failed; eventually, the local militia company was called out to restore order. At least in this instance, reliance on supposedly more productive white workers backfired.[4]

But as the Baltimore and Ohio crept westward from Baltimore, black workers, free and slave alike, became less significant in the city's labor force. African Americans had composed about one-quarter of the city's eighty thousand residents in 1830; that proportion would decline to about one-seventh of the more than two hundred thousand residents of 1860. By then white wage workers had increasingly replaced free blacks, even in the ranks of unskilled laborers, just as freed people had supplanted slaves a generation earlier.

In assessments of these longer-range developments from a late-twentieth-century perspective, two themes about workers and American cities have predominated. Under the subject heading of white workers, treatments tend to focus on working-class formation, with a heavy emphasis on origins of class consciousness. Recent variations on this theme either substitute an examination of artisan republicanism for that of class consciousness or attempt to link the two. In these stories black workers, slave or free, are largely irrelevant or even nonexistent, or are employed as a static background, a "before" picture from which discussions of white labor's working-class development commences.[5] Alternatively, studies of urban blacks before the Civil War typically pass fairly quickly over slavery and the process of emancipation and expend most of their effort in depicting the struggles attending the building of free black communities and culture.[6] The impact of these thematic choices has been to relegate the study of urban slavery and emancipation to a minor role, as if the absence of blacks from the Baltimore and Ohio dedication ceremony of 1828 had in fact mirrored the makeup of the urban craft workforce and society for the entire early national period.

This present work has operated from the premise that bound labor's eclipse by wage labor was not an inevitable product of historical forces somehow embodied in the "rise of capitalism" but rather a contingent outcome flowing from a particular interaction of local, regional, and international economic and social events and processes. Understanding how Baltimore's transition from bound to free labor came about is important precisely because the transition did not occur in all nineteenth-century cities embedded in slave society.

During the city's first period of vigorous growth, from the 1770s to around 1815, urban businesspeople in the crafts and manufacturing owned or employed slaves and bound white laborers to perform large and increasing shares of the city's work. Indeed, it is difficult to imagine how Baltimore's rise to prominence could have occurred without the ability to meet labor needs by uprooting rural slaves, bringing them to the city, and exploiting their labor in shipbuilding, rope making, ironworking, brick making, and a host of other trades.

Dislocating African Americans from the rural communities that they had begun to construct in late-eighteenth-century Maryland was not without consequences for slaveholders, as the high runaway rates of the 1780s and 1790s suggest. In the short to medium term, individual slaveholders mitigated this problem by grudgingly conceding, under pressure from their slaves, measures of present or future autonomy. Thus, slaves sometimes had a choice among new masters when sold, or the chance to win freedom through hard work or self-purchase (or both) over long years of service. The spread of industrial and craft slavery after 1790 beyond its initial base in ironworking and shipbuilding testifies to the success initially achieved by slaveholding craftsmen in buying peace and exploiting the labor of slaves uprooted from the countryside. By the close of the first decade of the nineteenth century, significant numbers of entrepreneurs in occupations dominated by smaller operators, including tobacco manufacture, the leather trades, and some aspects of food processing, were using slaves in their shops. The breadth of slavery's appeal among people in the crafts, merchants, and professionals possessed of taxable wealth underlines the muted, barely noticeable effect of early antislavery sentiment on the attitudes of Baltimoreans regarding the purchase and retention of African Americans before 1815.

Although there is no denying that manumission occurred more frequently in the city than in rural areas, a reading of the manumission documents suggests that reducing risks of slave flight and spurring higher production were far more important to most slaveholders than dissociation from an evil institution. Few Baltimore slaveholders recorded humanitarian impulses as a basis for their actions, and the conditional nature of most deeds belies giving any great weight to unstated motives of generosity or assuaging guilt. The popularity of self-purchase arrangements, of long-delayed grants of freedom conditional on faithful service, of freeing mothers but attempting to hold as yet unborn children in slavery, and the frequency with which manumitters serially freed slaves and purchased new ones, all suggest that we should understand manumission not primarily as an exit from slaveholding but rather as a reluctant, minimal shifting of strategies in employers' attempts to retain control of their labor supply. The fact that holders of larger numbers of slaves, those who could best afford to indulge themselves in manumission as a way of expressing humanitarian or republican beliefs, freed fewer slaves proportionally than small holders reinforces this understanding of the institution's purposes for masters.

Viewed in this light, African American attempts to escape from slavery, whether by flight or by the less risky strategy of negotiating manumission, played a more complex part in the fate of slavery in the city than the overused word "resistance" can capture. Although masters may have been driven to manumission bargains with slaves to counter flight or improve production, the creation through delayed manumission of the category of term slaves appears initially to have helped spread slavery to a wider domain in the city's workforce, by creating a form of coerced labor affordable to craftsmen and manufacturers of modest circumstances.

On the other hand, the resulting diffusion of slaves across a wide stratum of wealth holders brought about a change in the pattern of slaveholding: now, most Baltimore slaveholders owned only one to four slaves. For owners of a few slaves, seeking maximum gain from slaveholding by purchasing slaves for life, or by refusing to manumit slaves on any terms, or both, also maximized risks of slave flight and attendant loss of much if not all of their capital. Accordingly, such owners tended to follow a more cautious course, replicating the patterns of delayed manumission that had first become popular in the 1790s. The distribution of income-producing slaves to women also worked against amassing large slave holdings in the city, by creating another subclass of only modestly wealthy slave owners who found controlling adult male slaves especially difficult, because of their inability to dominate such chattels physically. As a result, women masters, an ever-growing subset of the city's slaveholding class, were even more likely to manumit male slaves or to fail to pursue runaways, thereby contributing indirectly to the dissolution of slavery in the city.

But these problems with using slave labor to accumulate and maintain wealth were neither unique to the urban setting nor so insurmountable as to constitute a full explanation of why slavery ultimately failed in Baltimore. Planters in Maryland as well as urban craftsmen had to be hard-driving to keep hold of freedom-seeking slaves and fortunate enough to avoid losses from illness or accident, if they were to build up a large and stable holding of slave wealth. Ironically, the decisions of those planters regarding slavery appear to have been at least as critical to the institution's survival in Baltimore as those of city slave owners.

Planters' needs to trim their slave workforces, flowing from the disruptions in the European tobacco market and the consequent shift away from tobacco after 1770, may have initially stimulated slavery in the city: slave workers as a result of those changes became generally available for purchase to substitute for European indentured servants and redemptioners who were no longer available because of the Revolutionary and Napoleonic wars. The attractiveness of such purchases to urban buyers can only have been increased to the extent that rural slaveholders were willing to sell slaves with craft skills. Planters seeking to diversify their activities had begun to train slave carpenters, tanners, shoemakers, and the like in increasing numbers in the last third of the eighteenth century, just as the movement of slaves to Baltimore began. But planters not only sold off slaves; they also engaged in selective manumission, as indicated by the data from rural counties. To be sure, rural planters, having larger holdings and facing perhaps less severe threats from slave flight, manumitted slaves far less often than urban slaveholders did; each county yielded only a small trickle of freed blacks relative to its slave population. From Baltimore's perspective, however, a series of trickles became a torrent of free and would-be free blacks flowing into the city from every county of the state, as evidenced by certificates of freedom and prison records indicating free black birthplaces.[7]

Although this flow of freed people may have been a safety valve for slavery in the countryside, it blew up the boiler of slave relations in the city. Controlling slaves became much more difficult because the rising numbers of urban free blacks facilitated flight to locations within the city, especially after 1810. More owners were thereby induced to entertain the gradual manumission strategy for managing slave workers, thus further destabilizing the master's long-term control. By 1820 the expansion of slavery had ceased, and much of the work formerly done by slaves was being performed by freed blacks.

The flexibility of master-slave relations, then, as embodied in complex bargains over sale and manumission, acted before 1810 to spread slavery within the city. That process helped to draw rural slaves to Baltimore, to the extent that they could influence their masters' plans for sales or hire. In any event, viewing the city and its surrounding counties as a market region, Baltimore's magnetic pull on rural slaves exemplified the portability of wealth held in slaves that has been characterized as one of the chief economic attributes of slavery.[8]

This market-driven accession of slaves to the city and the arrangements for self-hire, self-purchase, and the like made between city owners and African Americans did not fatally weaken slavery or provide enough free but propertyless black workers to replace slavery's role in the city's labor market. Slavery in Baltimore did not wither from internal failure; it was a casualty of the continued weakness of slavery in the Maryland countryside and of the continued flow of freed people arising therefrom.

The case study of the Maryland Chemical Works permits us to speculate on alternative developments in Baltimore's labor market that might have occurred, had slavery retained more strength rurally. The operators of the firm invested in significant numbers of slave workers, and despite some retrenchments, they continued to rely significantly on coerced labor in combination with mostly casual wage workers. This workforce produced chemicals and medicines in a highly capitalized business employing the most modern technologies of the day. After experimenting with slaves employed under a variety of terms, McKim chose to bank on slaves he owned and to extract as much labor as he could from them through wage incentives and, in the case of Scipio Freeman, the possible negotiation of an accelerated manumission by self-purchase. McKim appears to have initiated no manumissions; as a large slaveholder he effectively chose to self-insure against losses from flight rather than minimizing risk by promising freedom. Had demand for slave labor remained higher in Maryland's agricultural counties, with a consequently smaller flow of free blacks into the city and a lesser degree of threat to the retention of profitable slaves, the 1820s and 1830s might well have seen more Baltimore industries relying on a mix of slaves and free whites, as McKim's chemical works did.

The records of the chemical company thus sketch out ways in which industrial capitalists could quite advantageously combine wage labor and slave labor to attain their ends. They also testify, by their silence, to the feasibility of commingling free whites and enslaved blacks in the workplace without racial strife. Nor is this an isolated case; as the combined data on slaveholding, indentures, and apprenticeship in the crafts demonstrate, slaves worked with whites in most if not all of the trades before 1820. By comparison, the virtual exclusion of free blacks from craft apprenticeship suggests that white workers were far more troubled by working with or in the same trade as free blacks than with slaves.

Reflections on white attitudes toward free blacks, as delineated in the previous chapter, do little to dispel this speculation. Feared as a threat to a devoutly wished for social and political uniformity in the republic, suspected both of producing and consuming too little for the enhancement of the nation's political economy, free people of color could displace slave workers in Baltimore's economy precisely because they, like slaves, remained dependent on white employers. Such dependency may have arisen from debts acquired in purchasing freedom, or from the desire to buy out other family members, or as a consequence of race-based antagonisms that walled off some occupations and crowded free people of color into others. Whatever its origins, that dependency on the part of legally free persons fed resentment of free blacks. Slaves could safely be pitied, but propertyless free blacks could only be viewed as failures and hence burdens on society in the emerging categories of political economic thought.

As the record of the 1840s and the 1850s shows, free black workers themselves were replaced by European immigrants as the city's proletarian workers, a pattern that would be repeated in slave state cities in which free blacks, by whatever process, had replaced slave workers. In regions where slavery remained well entrenched in its rural strongholds, numbers of urban free blacks were smaller, urban slavery remained viable, and white immigrants were fewer.

These shifting patterns of labor usage suggest that the fate of slavery in nineteenth-century cities may not be fully explained either by its theoretical incompatibility with industrial capitalism or by the relative robustness of market demand for slaves in field labor. Baltimore's experience shows that slaves could be and were used quite profitably in enterprises with all the hallmarks of industrial capitalism. Likewise, the records of slave sales in the city indicate that although trade within Maryland was quite vigorous, prices responded imperfectly at best to interregional stimuli. Here, the ability of slaves to threaten flight if sold away from kin may have significantly influenced the behavior of some sellers.

What emerges from this study of early-nineteenth-century Baltimore and Maryland is the criticality of black efforts to obtain freedom; those efforts in combination with rural planters' decisions drove events in the city. Individual slaveholders in Baltimore could, and for a time did, transform the outlines of slavery without discarding it; indeed, their interactions with slaves seeking autonomy may have helped spread a transmuted form of slavery as a stage of life rather than as a lifelong institution. In this regard the struggles of Baltimore's masters to maintain control and African Americans' efforts to win autonomy may have been working toward a dynamic equilibrium in which a modified form of slavery would have thrived.

But Baltimore's masters could not cope with the consequences of their rural counterparts' similar strategies. While selective practices of manumission and sale stabilized slavery in all but Maryland's northern counties, the continued migration of large numbers of free people of color to Baltimore at once rendered slave labor less valuable and made its profitable exploitation more risky, given the aid offered by freed people to slaves.

Thus, masters' efforts to manipulate and control dependent black labor by retaining modified forms of slavery, applied consistently in both the city and the country, were partially frustrated, as black migration and mutual aid all but ended slavery in antebellum Baltimore. By winning through to freedom, Baltimore's blacks eliminated any likelihood of Baltimore's becoming a slave labor city, an outcome that white political economists might well have applauded. But in a final irony, the economic dependency of free black workers, in part a by-product of the process of self-purchased emancipation, formed grounds for the theoretical condemnation of free blacks, adding strength to racist sentiments that themselves may have fed on white resentment at Baltimore blacks' largely self-led liberation. Escaping slavery, however ambiguous the outcome, proved easier than shedding racism.

APPENDIX A

BALTIMORE SLAVEHOLDERS, 1790-1820: CRAFT AND TRADESPEOPLE, NUMBER OF SLAVEHOLDERS AND PROPORTION OF ALL PRACTITIONERS

| | Slaveholders | | | | | | | |
| Occupation | 1790 | | 1800 | | 1810 | | 1820 | |
	N	%	N	%	N	%	N	%
Baker	1	2	5	9	12	24*	5	8
Blacksmith	1	2	7	15	12	18*	8	7
Block maker	2	7	2	15	4	24	2	25*
Brass founder	0	0	2	67*	2	20	2	13
Bricklayer	2	50*	9	24	4	7	4	10
Brick maker	1	17	1	6	4	15	11	20*
Brush & comb maker	0	0	2	18*	2	18*	2	9
Butcher	0	0	2	8	5	17*	5	10
Cabinetmaker	1	3	6	19	8	21*	8	13
Carpenter	6	3	19	10	30	14*	45	11
Carver	0	0	0	0	1	17*	0	0
Chair maker	0	0	3	21	7	37*	4	21
Coach maker	0	0	0	0	0	0	1	4*
Coach trimmer	0	0	0	0	1	100*	0	0
Confectioner	0	0	0	0	1	8*	0	0
Cooper	3	8	6	12	12	16*	10	9
Coppersmith	1	17	3	75*	3	50	2	33
Cordwainer	6	6	15	10	18	11*	21	7
Currier	1	12	5	28	7	30*	6	22
Distiller	2	40*	3	25	3	23	4	17
Gunsmith	0	0	0	0	1	13*	0	0

Occupation	1790		1800		1810		1820	
	N	%	N	%	N	%	N	%
Hatter	2	9	6	19	6	14	8	23*
Jeweller	0	0	0	0	2	40*	1	14
Last maker	0	0	0	0	1	50*	0	0
Mattress maker	0	0	0	0	1	100*	0	0
Millwright	0	0	0	0	2	25*	3	20
Nail mfr.	1	25	0	0	4	67*	1	33
Painter	2	8	4	11*	4	10	6	7
Paperhanger	0	0	0	0	1	100*	1	33
Plane maker	0	0	0	0	1	33	1	50*
Plasterer	0	0	3	13*	2	8	3	10
Plumber	0	0	0	0	1	33*	1	14
Printer	0	0	2	18	5	38*	5	14
Rigger	1	5	6	21*	2	6	0	0
Rope maker	1	12	2	29*	2	12	3	11
Saddler	0	0	6	38*	7	35	3	11
Sail maker	2	12	4	24*	3	12	3	8
Ship carpenter	12	19	18	23	32	32*	34	30
Ship chandler	0	0	5	33	8	47*	4	44
Silk dyer	0	0	0	0	1	50*	0	0
Silversmith	0	0	2	18	6	35*	2	17
Soap & Candle maker	0	0	4	29	6	55*	3	30
Stonecutter	1	10	2	40*	4	24	5	28
Sugar refiner	0	0	1	50*	2	25	3	14
Tailor	7	8	10	9	20	24*	10	8
Tanner	1	11	5	50*	3	27	2	11
Tinplate worker	0	0	0	0	3	18*	2	13
Tobacco mfr.	1	9	4	21	6	23*	7	13
Trunk maker	0	0	0	0	1	20*	0	0
Turner	0	0	1	20	2	40*	0	0
Turpentine distiller	0	0	0	0	1	50*	0	0
Umbrella mfr.	0	0	0	0	2	25*	0	0

Occupation	1790		1800		1810		1820	
	N	%	N	%	N	%	N	%
Upholsterer	0	0	1	25*	2	17	2	18
Watchmaker	2	15	7	44*	3	23	4	27
Weaver	0	0	0	0	2	17*	0	0
Wheelwright	0	0	3	25*	1	8	1	4
Whip mfr.	0	0	0	0	1	25*	0	0
Other craft	0		25		28		43	
Total	60	11	211	14	315	19*	301	11

NOTE: *Denotes decade with highest slaveholding percentage.

This list includes different names for given occupations under single headings. Baker includes biscuit, cake, and loaf bread bakers. Block maker includes block and pump makers. Carpenter includes house carpenters and house joiners. Cooper includes oak and cedar coopers. Cordwainer includes boot maker, shoemaker, and ladies' shoemaker. Saddler includes harness makers. Ship carpenter includes boat builders, shipbuilders, ship joiners, and shipwrights. Soap and candle manufacturer includes chandler. Tinplate worker includes tin man, tinner, and tin manufacturer.

APPENDIX B

OCCUPATIONAL CATEGORIES:
CRAFT WORKERS AND OTHERS

The occupations marked with an asterisk were counted as artisans or manufacturers in analyses of who held slaves.

Accountant		Brass founder	*
Anchor mfr.	*	Bricklayer	*
Apothecary		Brick maker	*
Architect		Bridge builder	*
Assayer	*	Bridle maker	*
Auctioneer		Broker	
Baker	*	Brush maker	*
Bandbox maker	*	Butcher	*
Banker		Cabinetmaker	*
Barber	*	Cake baker	*
Billiard table keeper		Calico printer	*
Birdcage maker	*	Canvas mfr.	*
Blacking mfr.	*	Captain	
Blacksmith	*	Carpenter	*
Block & pump maker	*	Carpet mfr.	*
Boardinghouse keeper		Carpet weaver	*
Bookbinder	*	Carter	
Bookseller		Cartwright	*
Bookkeeper		Carver	*
Bootblack		Cashier	
Boot & shoe maker	*	Caulker	*
Botanist		Chair maker	*
Box maker	*	Chemical mfr.	*

170

Chocolate mfr.	*	Drum maker	*
Clergy		Dyer	*
Clerk		Ebonist	*
Clothier		Engineer	
Coach painter	*	Engraver	*
Coach maker	*	Fan maker	*
Coach trim mfr.	*	Farmer	
Cobbler	*	Farrier	*
Coffeehouse keeper		Fender mfr.	*
Collector	*	Fisherman	*
Comb maker	*	Founder	*
Confectioner	*	Gauger	*
Constable		Gentleman	
Conveyancer		Glass cutter	*
Cook		Glover	*
Cook shop keeper		Grocer	
Cooper, cedar	*	Gunpowder mfr.	*
Cooper	*	Gunsmith	*
Copperplate printer	*	Hack driver	
Coppersmith	*	Hairdresser	*
Cordwainer	*	Harness maker	*
Coroner	*	Hatter	*
Cotton mfr.	*	Hauler	
Cotton thread mfr.	*	Hotel keeper	
Crier		Huckster	
Currier	*	Importer	
Customs official		Innkeeper	
Dealer		Inspector	
Dentist		Instrument maker	*
Doctor		Insurer	
Dressmaker	*	Intelligence office	
Drover		Iron founder	*
Druggist		Ironmonger	

Japanner	*	Milliner	*
Jeweller	*	Millstone maker	*
Joiner	*	Millwright	*
Laborer		Miner	*
Last maker	*	Morocco dresser	*
Laundress		Musician	*
Lawyer		Nail mfr.	*
Leather mfr.	*	Nailer	*
Letter carrier		Naval officer	
Letter cutter	*	Notary public	
Letterer	*	Observatory keeper	
Limner	*	Officials	
Livery stable keeper		Ornamenter	*
Locksmith	*	Oyster house keeper	
Looking glass mfr.	*	Painters & glaziers	*
Lottery & exch. ofc.		Paperhanger	*
Machine maker	*	Paver	*
Magistrate		Pedlar	
Mahogany sawyer	*	Penitentiary keeper	
Maltster	*	Perfumer	*
Mantua maker	*	Pewterer	*
Marble cutter	*	Piano maker	*
Mariner		Pile driver	*
Marshal		Pilot	*
Mason	*	Plane maker	*
Mattress maker	*	Plasterer	*
Meal seller		Plater	*
Measurer		Plough maker	*
Merchant		Plumber	*
Merchant, dry goods		Porter	
Merchant, lumber		Porter bottler	*
Midwife	*	Potter	*
Miller	*	Printer	*

Prison guard		Stage owner	
Pump maker	*	Starch mfr.	*
Quarrier	*	Stationer	
Rectifyer		Stay maker	*
Reed maker	*	Stevedore	
Rigger	*	Stonecutter	*
Rope maker	*	Storekeeper	
Saddler	*	Sugar refiner	*
Saddletree maker	*	Surveyor	
Sail maker	*	Tailor	*
Salesman		Tanner	*
Sash maker	*	Tavern keeper	
Sawyer	*	Teacher	
Scourer	*	Tin man	*
Scow owner		Tin painter	*
Seamstress	*	Tinplate worker	*
Shingle dresser	*	Tobacco mfr.	*
Shipbuilder	*	Trunk maker	*
Ship carpenter	*	Turner	*
Shopkeeper		Turpentine distiller	*
Silk button mfr.	*	Type founder	*
Silk dyer	*	Umbrella mfr.	*
Silk maker	*	Veterinarian	
Silverplater	*	Victualler	
Silversmith	*	Waiter/servant	
Skinner	*	Warehouse keeper	
Slater	*	Watchman	
Soap & candle maker	*	Watch & clockmaker	*
Soldier		Wax worker	*
Spectacle maker	*	Weaver	*
Spinning wheel maker	*	Weigh master	*
Spinster		Well digger	*
Stage driver		Wharf builder	*

Wheelwright   *   Wire weaver   *

Whip & glue mfr.   *   Wood corder

Whitewasher   *   Woolen manufacturer   *

Widow

APPENDIX C

SALE PRICES OF TERM SLAVES
AND SLAVES FOR LIFE

These charts compare prices of slaves sold for a term of years with those sold for life, controlled by age, sex, and time period. The column on the right shows the difference expressed as a percentage.

1787-1809

Sales of Female Slaves

Age Group	Term Slaves No. Sold/Avg.Price	Slaves for Life No. Sold/Avg. Price	% Discount
0-4	0	0	—
5-9	2/ $80	4/$132	39
10-14	8/$107	9/$200	46
15-19	4/$190	14/$207	8
20-29	7/$122	10/$246	50
30+	2/$165	6/$262	37
Unknown	11/ $97	35/$141	31

Sales of Male Slaves

Age Group	Term Slaves No. Sold/Avg.Price	Slaves for Life No. Sold/Avg. Price	% Discount
0-4	1/ $40	1/$120	67
5-9	2/$155	4/$115	-35
10-14	6/$194	9/$203	5
15-19	6/$193	9/$302	36
20-29	5/$236	11/$293	19
30+	4/$208	7/$276	25
Unknown	17/$201	39/$235	17

1810-1818

Sales of Female Slaves

Age Group	Term Slaves No. Sold/Avg.Price	Slaves for Life No. Sold/Avg. Price	% Discount
0-4	1/$100	2/$125	20
5-9	3/ $90	6/$125	28
10-14	4/$188	12/$196	4
15-19	9/$153	18/$245	38
20-29	5/$143	17/$278	49
30+	4/$158	7/$208	24
Unknown	6/$122	15/$205	40

Sales of Male Slaves

Age Group	Term Slaves No. Sold/Avg.Price	Slaves for Life No. Sold/Avg. Price	% Discount
0-4	0	0	—
5-9	7/ $84	5/$106	21
10-14	12/$213	10/$194	−10
15-19	5/$230	14/$380	39
20-29	6/$290	15/$384	24
30+	4/$212	9/$321	34
Unknown	10/$245	14/$320	23

1819-1830
Sales of Female Slaves

Age Group	Term Slaves No. Sold/Avg.Price	Slaves for Life No. Sold/Avg. Price	% Discount
0-4	1/ $10	5/ $40	75
5-9	6/$122	10/ $98	-24
10-14	13/$102	16/$165	38
15-19	21/$122	43/$226	46
20-29	14/$112	20/$220	49
30+	6/ $72	17/$172	58
Unknown	23/$114	22/$190	40

Sales of Male Slaves

Age Group	Term Slaves No. Sold/Avg.Price	Slaves for Life No. Sold/Avg. Price	% Discount
0-4	4/ $40	8/ $61	34
5-9	5/$110	7/$125	12
10-14	14/$128	14/$215	40
15-19	17/$176	20/$264	33
20-29	30/$162	44/$342	53
30+	2/$225	12/$304	26
Unknown	21/$171	30/$282	39

NOTES

Abbreviations are listed at the beginning of the bibliography.

INTRODUCTION

1. See Greene, *Pursuits of Happiness,* esp. 190-93.
2. See Davis, *Problem of Slavery in the Age of Revolution,* and Davis, *Problem of Slavery in Western Culture.*
3. Eric Williams, *Capitalism and Slavery: The Caribbean,* (1944; reprint, London, 1964).
4. Haskell, "Capitalism and Humanitarian Sensibility."
5. Chaplin, "Slavery and the Principle of Humanity."
6. Frey, *Water from the Rock.*
7. For a good recent exposition of this view see Freehling, *The Road to Disunion.*
8. See K. Carroll, "Maryland Quakers and Slavery," and his "Religious Influences on the Manumission of Slaves."
9. See Nash and Soderlund, *Freedom by Degrees,* White, *Somewhat More Independent,* and Graham Hodges, *Slavery & Freedom in the Rural North: African Americans in Monmouth County, New Jersey, 1665-1865* (Madison, Wisc., 1996).

1. SLAVERY IN EARLY NATIONAL BALTIMORE AND RURAL MARYLAND

1. In Baltimore County outside the city, the number of slaves increased by 12 percent between 1790 and 1810, while city numbers more than tripled. Statewide over the same period the slave population increased 8 percent to approximately 111,000. See table 1.
2. See J. Wright, *Free Negro in Maryland,* 86-88 (tables).
3. Some 2,000 original bills of sale for the period 1785-1830 provide a sample of transactions. Official chattel records for Baltimore County between 1785 and 1850 survive only for 1813-14. These records include 126 slave bills of sale and 78 manumissions. By comparison, the original documents for this period describe 58 sales (46 percent of the transactions officially recorded) and 64 manumissions (82 percent of the official entries.) The original documents are representative of the larger official group by sex and age.
For the years 1790-1810, eighty bills of sale show a city dweller buying a slave from a resident out in the county; another 73 record a purchase from a master living outside the county. Only 16 sales of slaves from the city to elsewhere survive for the same time period. The 153 sales of slaves to city owners represent 27 per cent of all slave sales that identify buyer's and seller's place of residence. Compiled from Slave Bills of Sale, 1790-1810, Baltimore County Court, Maryland State Archives (hereafter MSA) and from Chattel Records, 1813-1814, Baltimore County Court.
4. See L.S. Walsh, "Rural African Americans," and Russo, "A Model Planter," for discussions of the reconfiguration of slave labor in late-eighteenth-century and early-nineteenth-century Maryland. Also see Paul Clemens, The Atlantic Economy

& Colonial Maryland's Eastern Shore: *From Tobacco to Grain,* Ithaca, NY, 1980 passim, for a comprehensive discussion of the agricultural restructuring of the late-eighteenth-century Eastern Shore. For the economic dislocations of the 1780s, see Maganzin, "Economic Depression in Maryland and Virginia."

5. See Declarations of Slaves, 1793-1800, Baltimore County Court.

6. See Laws of Maryland, 1792, chap. 56; 1797, chap. 75, MSA.

7. See Declarations of Slaves, 1793-1820, Baltimore County Court. One of Baltimore's largest slaveholders was Mme. Jean de Volunbrunn, a former resident of New York City whose departure with her slaves had provoked a riot there. See White, *Somewhat More Independent,* 144-45.

8. More than four hundred such private bills were legislated in the first half of the nineteenth century. In 1821 Baltimore's John Pendleton Kennedy sought a revision of the importation ban to regularize existing practice, prompted by the legislature's passage of seventeen private bills granting exemptions from the importation ban in 1820 and fourteen more the next year. See the *Baltimore Morning Chronicle* of Jan. 30, 1821, for Kennedy's remarks before the House of Delegates. For the bills, see Session Laws, 1800-1850, Laws of Maryland.

9. Names of all the slaveholders in the town or city of Baltimore for the first four federal censuses, as well as those on the city tax lists in 1804 and 1813, were matched against city directories to create occupational profiles. The directories used were Thompson and Walker's *Baltimore Town and Fell's Point Directory* of 1796, Warner and Hanna's *New Baltimore Directory and Annual Register* for 1800-1801, *Fry's Baltimore City Directory* for 1810, and *The Baltimore Directory,* compiled by Jackson and printed by Richard Matchett, for 1819-20. Occupational data for the 1790 census was augmented by searches of newspaper advertisements. For the 1813 tax records, I used the *Baltimore Directory and Register* of 1814, by Lakin, printed by J.C. O'Reilly, and for the 1804 tax list, *The Baltimore Directory for 1803,* by Stafford.

10. Of fifty-seven craft occupations appearing in city directories between 1790 and 1820, thirty-six (63 percent) showed the greatest concentration of slaveholders in 1810. Fifteen occupations (36 percent) had the highest proportion of slaveholding craftsmen in 1800, four (7 percent) in 1810, and only two (4 percent) in 1820. See appendix A for a chart of all the occupations.

11. Name matching with city directories identified about three-fifths (247 of 390) of slaveholders, who held about two-thirds of the slaves living in Baltimore town in 1790. Of those slaveholders, 60 worked in crafts or manufacturing and held 154 slaves. There were 188 other slaveholders with definable occupations, who owned 508 slaves. For 1800 645 of the 991 slaveholders were matched. Of these, 210 worked in crafts or manufacturing; they held 522 slaves. Other occupations together accounted for 435 slaveholders with 1,357 slaves. In all, just under two-thirds of the slaveholders, holding just over two-thirds of the slaves in the city, could be identified. In 1810 name matching defined 325 slaveholders (with 776 slaves) as in the crafts or manufacturing; 612 slaveholders, with 1,792 slaves, were in other identifiable occupations. Again, slaveholders with known occupations accounted for three-fifths of all slaveholders and slaves held. In 1820 name matches found 299 workers in crafts and 1,069 other slaveholders, holding 720 and 2,717 slaves, respectively. These made up three-fourths of slaveholders and nearly four-fifths of all slaves.

12. Between 1773 and 1800, 50 of 214 male runaways from masters in Anne Arundel and Prince George's Counties were advertised in the *Annapolis Maryland*

Gazette as possessing a craft skill, a proportion of 23 percent. From 1800 to 1815 only 8 of 102 (8 percent) were so advertised.

13. See Marks, "Skilled Blacks," 550.

14. A sample of 286 indentures from Talbot and Prince George's Counties between 1795 and 1830 showed that whereas 56 percent of all indentures registered before 1815 promised craft training, only 41 percent of those registered after 1815 did so. The annual volume of craft apprenticeships declined by roughly a third after 1815, from an average of twenty-four per year in the two counties combined, to an average of about sixteen. Data from Indentures, 1795-1828, Prince George's County Orphans' Court, MSA; Indentures, 1800-1830, Talbot County Orphans' Court, MSA.

15. See Temperley, "Capitalism, Slavery, and Ideology," esp. 96, for an idea of manumission as a device to attract free laborers. Temperley's frame of reference was the abolition of quasi-slavery among Scottish colliers in the late eighteenth century.

16. Account books that record slave hires and rentals include the Despeaux Account Book, MS. 294, Maryland Historical Society, Baltimore (hereafter MHS), for Joseph Despeaux, a shipbuilder in Baltimore ca. 1802-20, and the Allbright Account Book, MS. 12, MHS, for John Allbright, a brick maker, ca. 1790-1810. Also see Steffen, "Changes in the Organization of Artisan Production," 105-7. The Baltimore County Register of Wills (Petitions) and Guardian Accounts, both in the MSA, also contains references to the hiring of slaves to craftsmen.

17. See Hughes, "Slaves for Hire"; Starobin, *Industrial Slavery,* 128-37.

18. Of 1,078 slave sale or purchase advertisements, 178 (16.5 percent) indicated a desire to hire or hire out a slave. Advertisements tabulated from the *Maryland Journal and Baltimore Commercial Advertiser,* 1773-95; the *Federal Gazette,* 1796-1820, and the *Baltimore American and Commercial Daily Advertiser* (hereafter *American*), 1799-1820.

Of 492 runaway advertisements between 1790 and 1820 that identified the slave in any way other than appearance, 48 (9.7 percent) remarked on the slave's hired status.

19. See the *American* of Jan. 28 and Mar. 26, 1813. By 1821 the "General Intelligence Office" offered to find servants and replace them on request. See the Sept. 12, 1821, *American.*

20. See Laws of Maryland, 1817, chap. 104.

21. Data from Assessment Record, 1813, Baltimore City Commissioners of the Tax, MSA. Other similarly circumstanced women typically owned one to three slaves, but Rachel Nelson owned 9, Sarah Goldsmith 8, Isabella Hall 6, and Martha Coffield 5. Each of these women held over 70 percent of her wealth in slaves. Given their moderate means (all four were assessed at under six hundred dollars), their in-town residence, and the number of slaves each owned, it is hard to believe that they were not hiring out at least some of their chattels. Some widows may have been employing their slaves directly in the crafts in which their husbands had worked. Baltimore city directories virtually never listed women as craft practitioners; the lone exception, proving that such women existed, as might be expected, is Cornelius W. Stafford's *Baltimore Directory for 1803.*

22. See Sheller, "Artisans, Manufacturing, and the Rise of a Manufacturing Interest," 52-53, citing the Cox Account Book, MS. 262, MHS.

23. Winkle was one of thirteen inn, tavern, or boardinghouse keepers for whom slaves composed a majority of taxable wealth.

24. The pay book of the Maryland Chemical Works records payments to Madame DeLozier in 1828 and Simon Wilmer in 1830 for "the use of . . . hands." McKim had also bought slaves from innkeepers—James Renshaw and Enoch Churchman—in 1826 and 1827. See the Maryland Chemical Works Account Books, MS. 547, MHS.

25. The balance of this group came from the ranks of teachers, government officials, and gentlemen.

26. Hay's claim stressed the importance of the loss of Perry's hiring in her family's economy. She appears on the rolls of the Federal Direct Tax of 1798 as an owner of two taxable slaves and in the census of 1800 with four slaves. The city directory of 1800 lists her as a seamstress. See Miscellaneous Papers, 1798, Baltimore County Court.

27. There are no slaveholders named "Conner" or "Connor" who could have been sea captains in either the 1798 Federal Direct Tax List or the 1800 census.

28. The assessment of 1813 was part of a statewide revaluation of taxable property, causing the assessors to be unusually thorough in their listing of assets. See Laws of Maryland, 1812, chap. 191. City assessors recorded real property owned, as well as animals, furniture, silver, and the name, sex, age, and assessed value of any slaves held by taxpayers. See Assessment Record, 1813, Baltimore City, Commissioners of the Tax.

29. Although this represents an undercounting of slaves, the distribution of occupations among slaveholders, the sex and age distribution of slaves, and the average size of holdings are similar to those of the 1820 census. The assessors' lists are sufficiently complete and consistent to warrant their use as a survey of slave ownership in Baltimore in 1813.

According to law, most property was assessed at market value, but slaves were rated on fixed scales; a maximum valuation of $125 applied to men between the ages of fourteen and forty-five, with values ranging down to $20 for children and slaves over forty-five. Slave bills of sale and valuations for the decade 1810-19 suggest an average market value of more than $250 for an adult female slave and roughly $350 for an adult male slave. See Miscellaneous Court Papers, Baltimore County Court; Proceedings, Orphans' Court, Baltimore County Court. The statutory limits effectively granted tax relief for about two-thirds of the slaves' real market value, hardly surprising in a legislature dominated by slaveholding planters from southern Maryland's tobacco counties and the Eastern Shore.

30. Name matching with city directories identified occupations of 2,045 persons, just under 61 percent of the 3,367 wealth holders. See appendix B for a full listing of the occupations encountered and an explanation of craft/noncraft breakdowns in this and other tables.

31. Slaveholders in the lowest wealth quintile had less wealth than the $125 assessed value of an adult male slave and owned an adult female slave or a child.

32. For craftsmen, the decadal averages were 2.6 in 1790, 2.5 in 1800, and 2.4 in 1810 and 1820. For merchants and other nonartisanal or manufacturing slaveholders, the mean holding remained unchanged at 2.7 slaves for 1790, 1800, and 1810 and then dropped to 2.4 in 1820.

33. The number of slaveholders listed in the 1790 census was 390, of whom 113 appeared in the 1800 census. That census listed 991 Baltimore slaveholders, of whom 231 held slaves in the city in 1810. Of 1,360 slaveholders on the 1810 census rolls, 314 could be found in the 1820 census.

34. Michael B. Katz's study of Hamilton, Ontario, *The People of Hamilton, Canada West: Family and Class in a Mid-Nineteenth-Century City* (Cambridge, Mass., 1975), 122-31, found that no more than 35 percent of heads of household appeared in two city censuses ten years apart in the period 1851-61; thus, Baltimore's rates are not unusually low.

35. Persistence data do not include slaveholders who owned slaves in two successive censuses but who ceased to work in the crafts. Since far more slaveholders moved out of craft occupations into higher-status occupations of the day, such as "merchant" or "gentleman," than the reverse, the higher persistence rate of craft slaveholding before 1810 is even more remarkable.

36. Surviving bills of sale for the period 1785-1830 show only slightly more women (1,031) than men (953) being sold. See Slave Bills of Sale, Miscellaneous Papers, Baltimore County Court.

37. The ratios are based on 815 manumissions and 191 declarations of slaves. See Manumissions and Declarations of Slaves, Miscellaneous Court Papers, Baltimore County Court.

38. See Buckingham's *Journey through the Slave States,* passim. Also see Green, "Urban Industry, Black Resistance, and Racial Restriction," 314ff., for tables relating to the participation of male and female slaves in tobacco manufacture and other industries.

39. Thirteen of seventeen brick makers found in the 1813 tax list lived in ward 1 or ward 2, which then covered the southwest quarter of the city. Baltimore newspapers reported fires on an almost daily basis in the first two decades of the nineteenth century. As early as 1805, the city council passed fire prevention ordinances, and by 1826 it banned new construction in wood. See the Baltimore *American* of Apr. 17, 1805, and Ordinances of the Baltimore City Council, 1826, no. 57, Baltimore City Archives, MSA.

40. See Nelson, "Brickmaking in Baltimore."

41. Slaveholding shipbuilders included William Price, owner of twenty-five slaves, James Biays, who owned twenty-one slaves, and Joseph Despeaux, an emigrant from Saint Domingue who owned eleven slaves in 1813. In the 1800 census David Stoddert, builder of the U.S. frigate the *Constellation,* appeared as the owner of seventeen slaves.

42. Keith Aufhauser has pointed out that if technologies of work allow for its simplification into discrete, low-skilled activities, they contain nothing antithetical to efficient production with slave labor, unless the technology also reduces skill and strength requirements to the point where even cheaper forms of labor—such as women and children—can do the work. See Aufhauser, "Slavery and Technological Change." Shipyards of the early nineteenth century present an example supportive of these views.

43. Citywide, ten of twenty-nine wealth-holding blacksmiths owned slaves.

44. For Chenowith's advertisements, see the *American* of Jan. 1, 1814. See Jackson's *Baltimore Directory,* 1819, for Chenowith's new occupational title. The 1820 census shows him with two adult male slaves under forty-five and a boy under fourteen.

45. Adam Smith argued that bondmen were unproductive workers with no incentive but to "work as little and consume as much as possible." But in writing about the impact of divided labor on workers, Smith also worried about the dulling mental effect of segmented, repetitive work. The use of slaves by Baltimore concerns whose scale facilitated a division of labor suggests an alternative point of

view. Slaveholders may have regarded the use of slaves in mentally numbing jobs as an advantage, providing a better fit between those jobs and the supposed mental limitations of the black worker and allowing white craftsmen to be employed at more demanding jobs. See A. Smith, *Wealth of Nations,* 80, 363-67.

46. Seven nail makers appeared on the 1813 tax rolls, of whom three owned slaves, including Enoch Betts with slaves assessed at $825, 86 percent of his taxable wealth.

47. The data for coppersmiths and brass founders follow a similar pattern: four of five in the top two quintiles of wealth held slaves, but only one of six in the lower three groupings.

48. Three of five bakers in the fourth quintile of wealth held slaves; overall 54 percent (15 of 28) did so. Four of sixteen carpenters in the lowest wealth quintile held slaves, a rate virtually identical to the 26 percent (25 of 96) that prevailed for all carpenters. Only four of twenty-two painters held slaves, and three of them were in the lowest wealth quintile, as was the only slaveholding potter among four who appeared in the 1813 tax list. Four of six soap and candle manufacturers owned slaves—the two with the most and the two with the least wealth.

49. Of ninety-six carpenters with taxable wealth, twenty-five held slaves (26 percent). Bricklayers (24 percent) and painters (18 percent) were still farther below the 38 percent average of slaveholding among craftsmen and manufacturers.

50. In 1808 a writer to the Baltimore *American* noted that a leather-making entrepreneur "pays nothing for labor but what feeds and clothes his apprentices, slaves, horses, &c." See the *American,* Jan. 20, 1808.

51. Nine of fifteen tanners and curriers owned slaves, including ten adult men. By contrast, only sixteen of sixty-two boot makers, cordwainers, and glovers did so, a rate of 26 percent compared to the 60 percent of their leather suppliers. Charles Ridgely's Northampton Furnace, just north of the city, operated with a mixed slave-free workforce of considerable extent—he manumitted more than eighty slaves at his death in 1828. See Baltimore County Certificates of Freedom for 1828-31, MSA.

52. Over 80 percent of De Volunbrunn's assessed wealth lay in the ten men, nine women, and three children she owned.

53. Sampling one-fifth of Baltimore newspapers between 1790 and 1830 yielded 1,025 advertisements for the sale of slaves, exclusive of repetitions. Of these, 324 (32 percent) identified the slave to be sold as entitled to freedom in the future.

Over the same time period, 410 of 1,984 slave bills of sale (21 percent) registered with the Baltimore County Court involved a slave entitled to freedom. See Miscellaneous Papers, 1790-1830, Baltimore County Court.

54. James Winchell, a Baltimore baker, purchased Harry Gray in November 1811 for $250, Harry then having a fourteen-year term to serve. Eight months later, Winchell sold Harry to the bakers Lovell and Saltzer, for the same price. See Slave Bills of Sale, Miscellaneous Court Papers, 1811 and 1812, Baltimore County Court. David McKim of the Maryland Chemical Works owned James Jacobs, whose term had fifteen years to run at the time of purchase, for about fifteen months; he sold Jacobs in 1828 for the same $200 he had paid for him. See Maryland Chemical Works Account Books, MHS.

55. Price ranges for slaves are based on approximately 2,100 bills of sale recorded with the Baltimore County Court between 1790 and 1830. Sales involving

two or more slaves or sales that did not reflect market values were not considered. The latter category included sales among heirs of deceased slaveholders, sales between white parents and children, and conditional sales between borrowers and lenders as a form of collateral loan security. There remained nearly 900 sales of individual slaves, of which 312 were sales for a term of years.

Baltimore sales were grouped into three time periods: pre-1810, 1810-18, and 1819-30. In the first period slave prices rose slowly. In the next, slave prices rose again, but in the 1820s prices flattened or fell slightly.

Slaves were divided into seven age groupings: 0-4, 5-9, 10-14, 15-19, 20-29, 30 or older, and unspecified, and subdivided by sex for each age bracket. The resulting 42 pairs of cells exhibit a fairly uniform pattern of price differentials between slaves for life and for a term of years.

Purchase of a slave for an average term, ranging from five to twenty years depending on the slave's age, generally cost from 30 to 50 percent less than purchase of a comparably aged slave for life. Eighteen of the 42 paired cells showed price differentials in this range; 6 more revealed price reductions of more than 50 percent in favor of term slaves, and a further 6 showed savings in the 20 to 30 percent range. Five more cells showed savings of less than 20 percent; 5 showed no savings, and 2 cells had no sales for comparison.

Seventeen of the 20 sex and age pairs for female slaves showed term slaves to be more than 20 percent cheaper than slaves for life; for men this threshold was reached in only 13 of 20 cases. Given the relatively small numbers of cases in each cell (typically fewer than 40), these findings must be regarded as tentative indicators.

The matrix appears in appendix A.

56. Apprenticeship contracts stipulated the child's age, the maintenance, wages, education, and freedom dues he or she was to receive, and the craft to be taught. I examined each indenture recorded in thirteen sample years between 1800 and 1830: 1800, 1802, 1805, 1808, 1810, 1813, 1816, 1818, 1820, 1823, 1826, 1828, and 1830. During the sample years from 1800 to 1818, 2,432 boys were bound out, 304 per year, at a median age of fifteen; 1,571 (65 percent) were bound out between the ages of thirteen and seventeen. With an average term of service of six or seven years, about 1,800 to 2,000 boys were serving apprenticeships at any one time.

See Steffen's *The Mechanics of Baltimore,* 27-50, and Tina Sheller's "Artisans, Manufacturing, and the Rise of a Manufacturing Interest," 3-17, for discussions of apprenticeship in Baltimore.

57. The ensuing discussion relies on data from apprenticeships recorded in the eight sample years before 1820.

58. Occupational profiles for the extent of apprenticeship rely on the comparison of three indices. Estimates of the number of practitioners of each craft derive from counting city directory occupational entries. Tallies were also made of the number of masters binding apprentices by craft and, finally, of the total number of apprentices bound in those crafts.

By comparing the number of apprentices bound with the number of adult practitioners, we can gain a sense of the importance of apprentice labor in each trade. The ratio of apprentices bound to the number of binding masters generates a crude index of scale of operation, with a high ratio suggesting that the trade was being carried on in large shops, and vice versa. Finally, by comparing the propensity of masters to bind apprentices to their propensity to hold slaves by craft, we can speculate whether slave labor and apprentice labor competed with or complemented each other.

59. Across all crafts, the number of binding masters in a decade averages just over four-fifths of the number of craft participants (84 percent). The number of apprentices bound slightly exceeds the number of craft participants, in a ratio of 123:100. The ratio of apprentices to binding masters, across all the crafts, is just under three to two, at 148:100. Departing from this general pattern, it appears that ship carpenters and joiners rarely resorted to apprentice labor: in the 1810-19 decade, only 7 percent of them bound an apprentice, and the apprentice-to-practitioner ratio was a microscopic 10:100. Sail makers, on the other hand, were more likely than the average to use apprentices, with an apprentice-to-practitioner ratio of 160:100.

60. For brick makers, the apprentice-to-practitioner ratio was about half the average, at 56:100, as was the ratio of binding masters to practitioners, at 45:100. Bakers, though less well off than brick makers in general, were equally uncommon users of apprentice workers, with an apprentice-to-practitioner ratio of 63:100 and a master-to-practitioner ratio of 46:100. Only three boys were bound out as soap and candle makers in all the sample years between 1800 and 1820, for an apprentice-to-practitioner ratio of 12:100.

61. Camp bound seventeen boys in an eight-year sample of indentures with the Baltimore County Orphans' Court. With an average indenture length of six years, this works out to twelve or thirteen apprentices serving him at any one time. Camp was assessed in 1813 at $1,856, making him the second wealthiest cabinetmaker in Baltimore. For Camp's purchase of Ashberry, see Miscellaneous Papers, 1815, Baltimore County Court.

62. Examples include Joseph Cox, a hatter, who bound twelve apprentices before 1820 and owned two adult male slaves in 1813; he purchased a twenty-one-year-old man, Charles Wilson, in 1817. Cox participated in the Census of Manufactures of 1820 and at that time employed eight men, three women, and twelve boys. Cox also owned women slaves who may, too, have been making hats. William Branson, hatter, bound five apprentices before 1820 and owned two adult male slaves in 1813. John Oldham, chair maker, bound five apprentices and owned three slaves. Peter Hoffman, Jr., bound five apprentices as paper makers and owned six slaves, including three adult men, in 1813. Robert Quail, a cooper, had seven white boys and men of ages ten to twenty-five in his household in 1810, plus two slaves. James Sloan, cordwainer and merchant, owned five adult male slaves in 1813 and had seven apprentice-age boys in his household in 1810. Richard K. Heath, tanner, bound seven apprentices out before 1820 and also purchased two male slaves, Prince and Ignatius, for $500 in 1813.

63. See indentures of Joseph Wood to Joseph Cox, hatter, in 1816; Charles Ruckel to Richard K. Heath, in 1813; and James Maydwell to James Sloan, in 1813. For examples of apprentices promised training in only part of the cordwaining or hatting trades, see indentures of Frisby Robbins, 1816, or Charles Bowers, 1813. These all are found in Baltimore County Indentures, MSA.

64. See the indenture of Negro Juliet, Baltimore County Indentures, 1805.

65. See Indenture of Charles Brown, Baltimore County Indentures, 1810.

66. See Indenture of Jacques Zacharie, Baltimore County Indentures, 1805.

67. See Indenture of Negro Joseph, 1811, and Indenture of Negro Ann, Baltimore County Indentures, 1809.

68. See Indenture of John Richardson, Baltimore County Indentures, 1805.

69. Edwards manumitted all her slaves prospectively on June 30, 1812; the bindings of George, Morris, and John occurred on the same day. The boys' freedom dates were set to coincide with their twenty-first birthdays. See Miscellaneous Court Papers, 1812, Baltimore County Court, and Indentures of Negro George, Negro John, and Negro Morris, 1812, Baltimore County Indentures.

70. Certificates of Freedom recorded in Baltimore between 1805 and 1830 identify about one-fifth of the bearers as having been born outside Baltimore County. Certificates from Dorchester and Prince George's Counties show virtually no inmigration of free blacks. Deeds of manumission and slave bills of sale that note the slaveholder's residence often indicate that a slave's point of origin was outside Baltimore.

71. For Talbot County, sampling all indentures registered at five-year intervals from 1800 to 1830, 38 of 147 indentures, or 26 percent, involved free black children. This roughly matched free blacks' 28 percent share of the free population of the county in 1830. In Prince George's County, following the same method, free blacks accounted for 27 of 141 indentures, or 19 percent, despite representing less than 14 percent of the free population in 1830. For another Eastern Shore county, see Daniels, "Alternative Workers in a Slave Economy."

72. Between 1800 and 1830 the free black population of Baltimore City more than quintupled. By comparison, free black populations increased only 30 to 50 percent during those years in Dorchester, Kent, and Talbot Counties, with white numbers in these counties declining or showing nominal growth at most. Eight Maryland counties, including Calvert, Caroline, Charles, Harford, Kent, Queen Anne's, St. Mary's, and Talbot, had lower white populations in 1830 than in 1790 or 1800.

73. The apprenticeship law was modified in 1808 to empower the orphans' court to bind out the children of "lazy, indolent, and worthless free negroes"; it was changed again in 1818, to permit the binding of any free black child "not at service or learning a trade." See Laws of Maryland, 1808, chap. 54, and 1818, chap. 189.

74. See Laws of Maryland, 1796, chap. 67, for the bar on free black franchise. Maryland established a nearly universal white male suffrage in 1802.

75. Ibid., 1801, chap. 109.

76. Ibid., 1818, chap. 197, and 1825, chap. 93. The 1818 law allowed courts to order corporal punishment or banishment for free blacks convicted of a wide variety of felonies for which whites would be sent to the penitentiary. The 1825 law went further and allowed re-enslavement as a punishment, but it was repealed in 1826. The corporal punishment law remained in effect throughout the antebellum period.

77. Between 1798 and 1830 some 480 masters bound two or more boys, the maximum number seventeen by William Camp, cabinetmaker. Four percent of all craft bindings in this sample were of free blacks. Given that masters who bound more than one apprentice averaged about four bindings, one would expect to find about 84 percent of the multiple groupings to be all white (.96 x .96 x .96 x .96 = .8435). In fact, 468 of the 480 cases, or 97.5 percent, involved only white boys, an underrepresentation of free blacks statistically significant at the .02 level.

Even masters who employed very large numbers of apprentices, and who appear to have used slave labor as well, had no free black apprentices. The cabinetmaker William Camp, the sail maker Benjamin Buck, hatters Jacob Rogers and Joseph Cox, and the chair maker Jacob Daley each bound ten or more apprentices in the indenture years sampled, and all owned slaves; none of them bound any free black apprentices.

78. In Talbot and Prince George's Counties, free blacks were bound in numbers matching or exceeding their population share. But of those thirty-two masters who had bound two or more boys, only one apprenticed both whites and blacks. A random distribution of black and white apprentices in these counties would have yielded eleven masters who apprenticed both black and white boys; the shortfall shows a significant correlation between disinclination to bind blacks and the presence of white apprentices.

79. See Laws of Maryland, 1818, chap. 189. See Berlin, *Slaves without Masters,* 226-27, and Fields, *Slavery and Freedom on the Middle Ground,* 35, for arguments that apprenticeship laws were used to control the labor of free black children against their parents' will.

80. In the years sampled, 57 percent of 3,148 bindings of white boys and 50 percent of 208 bindings of black boys were voluntary. Although the white rate is higher, the degree of significance fails to meet even the weakly correlated .10 level on a chi-square test. For girls the voluntary binding rate over the same period was 40 percent for whites in 538 cases and 34 percent for blacks in 98 cases, again a distinction without statistical significance.

For a discussion of the attitudes of free blacks toward apprenticeship, see Matthews, "Race, Sex, and the Dimensions of Liberty," 284-86.

81. In 1810 388 indentures of apprentice boys were recorded by the Baltimore courts, a rate of 9 per 1,000 of the city's population. At that time apprentices may have equaled about 10 percent of the city's male population of approximately 24,000.

In 1830 the 215 bindings entered represent an indenture rate of 2.7 per 1,000 and a total apprentice population equal to about 3 percent of the city's roughly 41,000 male residents.

82. The Union Manufacturing Company got under way in 1810 and bound more than 60 boys before 1815 to learn "cotton manufacturing, including carding, spinning, and weaving, or any of those trades." See the indenture of David Stinchcomb to the Union Manufacturing Company, Baltimore County Court Indentures, 1810. Other cloth makers also engaged apprentices: the Baltimore Manufacturing Company's agent Nathan Levering indentured 41 boys, Edward Gray and Company 19, and the Washington Cotton Manufacturing Company 13. All of these indentures occurred between 1808 and 1817 and are recorded in the Baltimore County Indenture records.

83. The Union Manufacturing Company had 104 girls tending its bobbins but only 16 boys and 10 men; the Baltimore Steam Works engaged 50 girls and no boys at all. Edward Gray's Patapsco Cotton Factory employed boys and girls in equal numbers, 35 of each, but had not indentured any children in the previous four years. Likewise, Nathan Levering, then acting as proprietor of both the Powhatan Cotton Mills and the Washington Cotton Factory, was no longer indenturing new apprentices; he had a large proportion of girls in his mills. These data are drawn from the 1820 Census of Manufactures for Baltimore City and Baltimore County; U.S. Census Office. Fourth Census, 1820, Records of the 1820 Census of Manufactures, Schedules for Maryland (Washington, D.C., 1821.).

84. Prior to 1820 an average of 53 girls were indentured per year. Over nine-tenths of them were to be taught housekeeping, with or without specific instruction in sewing or needlework. See Baltimore County Indentures.

2. INDUSTRIAL SLAVERY IN BALTIMORE

1. Starobin, *Industrial Slavery,* 115.

2. Wade, *Slavery in the Cities,* chaps. 4, 6. Wade did not assume that industrial slavery was by definition urban, but the conditions that, in his view, fatally eroded the master's control of the urban slave—especially slave hiring—applied to industrial slavery whether urban or rural.

3. Ibid., 230.

4. Goldin, *Urban Slavery in the South,* 51-75, 123-26.

5. Fred Bateman and Thomas Weiss, *A Deplorable Scarcity: The Failure of Industrialization in the Slave Economy* (Chapel Hill, N.C., 1981), 157-63. See also their article, coauthored with Foust, "Participation of Planters in Manufacturing."

6. See Dew, "Slavery and Technology," 107-26 (quotation on 113).

7. The Baltimore County Land Records, book 178, folios 392 and 393, Nov. 23, 1825, record Sims's assignment of his interest in the factory buildings and leased land to John McKim, Jr., to secure a forty-thousand-dollar loan. The McKim sons formed McKim, Sims, and Company with Howard Sims after the loan came due. The McKims assumed majority ownership and direction of the company; Sims was to control production, while the McKims managed procurement, sales, and accounting. See the Articles of Agreement of McKim, Sims, and Co., McKim Collection, MS. 547, MHS.

8. McKim, Sims, and Company incorporated by an act of the legislature in 1827. See Laws of Maryland, 1826, chap. 195. The McKims squeezed Howard Sims out of the partnership within two years. By early 1828 Sims had ceased to be a partner and had become a salaried plant manager; by late 1828 he was gone altogether. The Baltimore *American* of Jan. 3, 1828, reported that the Maryland Chemical Works had won a silver medal for high-quality alum and an honorable mention for its magnesium sulfate (Epsom salts), in a competition sponsored by the Franklin Institute. For early chemical production in America, see Haynes, *American Chemical Industry,* vol. 1, *Background and Beginnings,* 179, 184; also see *Niles' Weekly Register* of Jan. 6, 1816, 9:329-30, and Griffith, *Annals of Baltimore,* 228. For a general account of early manufacturing in Maryland, see Griffin's "Industrial Revolution in Maryland." For a contemporary description of the uses of alum, see Muspratt, *Chemistry,* 1:149-76, article on alum.

9. The Maryland Chemical Works (MCW) journal, or general ledger, itemized slave expenses for the year 1828 and recorded the price of each slave bought by the firm. The pay book denotes days worked, absences, overtime worked, earnings, and tasks undertaken for both slave and free workers from 1827 to 1832. The MCS journal and pay book are in the Maryland Chemical Works Account Books collection, MS. 547.2, MHS.

10. See the MCW journal for January 1828.

11. A ground plan of the MCW shows forty structures, including furnaces, mills, drying rooms, and production rooms for alum, Epsom salts, Prussian blue, calomel, and other chemicals, as well as a dwelling for the plant manager, the Negro house, a stable, an office, and a variety of packing and storing rooms. A contract of June 26, 1827, engaged Watchman and Bratt to "put up a first rate low pressure Steam Engine of twenty-four horse power on the Bolton and Watt principle," at a cost of six thousand dollars. McKim Collection, MHS. Edward Stewart was paid $250 and $227 for time and materials on the Negro House. MCW journal, February and May, 1828.

12. *American,* Dec. 20, 1827. McKim's reference to a year-long contract signaled his desire to obtain slave workers. Free workers, white or black, had no promise of employment beyond week-to-week.

13. The MCW pay book for January 1828 shows seventy employees "at work on the Merchandise," comprising forty-two free workers and twenty-eight slaves.

14. Medicines produced included calomel, tartar emetic, and Epsom salts. Pigments included Prussian blue, chrome yellow and green, and copperas. In addition to alum, the firm manufactured producer goods such as bleaching powder, muriatic acid, and sulfuric acid. See "Maryland Chemical Works Prices Current," undated, McKim Collection.

15. The MCW journal lists agents in Boston, Providence, New York, Philadelphia, Richmond, Norfolk, Charleston, Savannah, New Orleans, and Pittsburgh. Local customers of the firm included chair makers, paperhangers, morocco leather dressers, bookbinders, paint manufacturers, cordwainers, white lead manufacturers, glass makers, and distillers, as well as retail merchants. Local business was also transacted through a company store near the wharves of the Basin (today's Inner Harbor). See the MCW journal for January of each year, 1828-33.

16. The chemical works remained tightly linked to J.K. McKim and Sons, which monopolized procurement and long-distance sales of the firm. Most of the book value of the Maryland Chemical Works continued to be capital advanced by, and drawing interest for, the firm of J.K. McKim and Sons, secured by mortgages held by John K. McKim, Jr. Baltimore County Land Records, book 189, folio 205, Nov. 15, 1827, MSA.

17. Muspratt's *Chemistry* was used to enlarge upon and clarify the marginalia in the MCW pay book referring to production methods.

18. Alum generated the greatest sales for the company. See the MCW journal for 1828, pp. 11-80, and the annual summary for 1828 appearing in January 1829, p. 81.

19. Muspratt, *Chemistry,* 149-76, vol. 1, notes that lixiviation may be speeded by heat; the MCW plant diagram shows a long room labeled "furnaces" situated next to a room for "cylinders." It is likely that waste heat from the furnaces was employed to keep warm the cylinders or steeping cisterns for alum. The MCW pay book indicates that slaves were paid "extras" for night work in alum production. The process resembled the churning of butter; an illustration in Muspratt shows a covered steeping cistern with a large hole in the center of the cover. A worker stands on the cover and is plunging or stirring a long rod through the hole into the cistern.

20. The works diagram identifies the single largest room in the plant as the "alum room." Muspratt emphasizes the large amounts of space needed to allow alum to dry in long, shallow beds; the plant's alum room was in all likelihood a covered drying shed. See Muspratt, *Chemistry,* 160, 163, vol. 1.

21. The MCW journal lists soap and candle makers as suppliers to the firm. See account summaries for January of 1829, 1830, and 1831.

22. Residual mother liquor was reused in intermediate steps of alum making, or in the manufacture of Epsom salts if the silica of the clay had contained magnesium. See Muspratt, *Chemistry,* 169-71, vol. 1.

23. Many antebellum industrial concerns operated intermittently. Factories relying on water power shut down when streams froze and water wheels iced up. Difficulties in transporting or stockpiling raw materials in winter also hampered

year-round operations; iron production in particular was constrained by seasonal limitations on making and storing charcoal. But the Maryland Chemical Works' steam engine and wood fires were not affected by the seasons, and many raw materials were obtained locally from Baltimore butchers, tanners, and soap makers. The costs of factory construction, some of which could be attributed to facilitating a year-round production environment, exceeded fifty thousand dollars; the value of raw material inventories at the plant ranged from five thousand to eight thousand dollars. See the MCW journal, January entries for 1828 and 1829.

24. See Starobin, *Industrial Slavery,* 28-29, 293-95.

25. MCW pay book, January and February of 1828.

26. Slaves figured prominently in late-eighteenth- and early-nineteenth-century production of iron, another capital-intensive, heat-powered industry. See Lewis, *Coal, Iron, and Slaves,* chap. 1.

27. Matchett's city directories for Baltimore in the 1820s and the U.S. Census of Manufactures for 1820 for the city and county of Baltimore list manufacturers in these lines. See also Griffith's *Annals of Baltimore* and Varle's *Baltimore.*

28. The MCW pay book lists 299 persons earning wages, many of whom worked two, three, or four separate stints at the plant. In all, 363 hiring actions occurred in order to keep an average of thirty-eight positions filled, an average of eighty-three employees per year for thirty-eight jobs, and a turnover rate of 118 percent per year.

29. The slave pay records also accounted for a few free black workers, mainly carpenters or coopers. MCW pay book, 1827-32.

30. Marginalia separate from the employee's hours and wage rate entry denote payments for specified additional tasks. Maintenance of two sets of incentive pay records suggest that two different measures of employee effort, time worked and items produced, were in use. A further point in favor of regarding the "extra" as a unit of time is that much labor, especially in the nearly interminable alum-making process, had no easily measurable product and could be compensated only by payments geared to time worked. See the MCW pay book, 1827-32.

31. Table 5 shows high turnover for free workers; table 6 shows that this turnover took place in a free workforce of relatively stable size. Taken together, these facts support the view that turnover represented voluntary resignations and not firing of casual labor. A week-by-week review of free-worker records further substantiates this point. The chemical works did have a real and persistent free-worker turnover from 1827 onward. It seems reasonable to posit that this problem had also existed in 1825 and 1826 and played a part in McKim's decision to obtain slave labor.

32. This preference for owned slaves was atypical. See, for example, Starobin, *Industrial Slavery,* 28-37, and Lewis, *Coal, Iron, and Slaves,* 82-103.

33. The MCW journal lists fifteen slaves purchased for the firm in 1826 or 1827. Baltimore County manumission deeds show that David McKim freed two slaves who were not among the original fifteen, at dates subsequent to his sale of the plant. My assumption is that these seventeen slaves are all the firm ever owned. Pay book margin notes identify some other slaves on board in 1828-30 as hires. After 1830 all of the slaves at the plant were owned by David McKim. Sales and manumissions for slaves in Baltimore County are found among Miscellaneous Papers, 1785-1847, Baltimore County Court.

34. McKim paid a total $2,950 for ten slaves for life in 1826 and 1827. He obtained the other five slaves for less because they were slaves for a stipulated

term of years pending manumission. Average prices for male slaves for life between ages eighteen and thirty-five were $347 in 1828, $295 in 1829, $310 in 1830, and $317 in 1831; they averaged $320 for the four-year period. Prices for female and juvenile male slaves exhibit the same flatness for these years. Data drawn from Miscellaneous Papers, 1828-31, Baltimore County Court.

35. Although this point may seem entirely unremarkable, it is worth stating that McKim focused his attention not only on slave prices and total slave production but on individual slave productivity as well.

36. McKim may not have been surprised by the absenteeism of the wage workers if they displayed the typical "pre-industrial" disdain for regularity. See Herbert G. Gutman, *Work, Culture, and Society in Industrializing America: Essays in American Working-Class and Social History* (New York, 1976), 15-32; Alan Dawley and Paul Faler, "Working-Class Culture and Politics in the Industrial Revolution: Sources of Loyalism and Rebellion," *JSH* 9 (June 1976): 466-68; Bruce Laurie, *Artisans into Workers: Labor in Nineteenth-Century America* (New York, 1989), 37-46. For study showing that significant cultural transformation was not necessarily required to generate reliable factory hands, see Sisson, "From Farm to Factory."

37. Slaves were scheduled to work a total of 20,604 days; days worked totaled 18,671; absences equaled 1,933, 9.4 percent. Free workers were slated for 51,198 days of work, and had 4,893 absences, or 9.6 percent of their scheduled work days. MCW pay book, 1827-32.

38. Three slaves employed by the plant hired their own time. The pay book noted a weekly salary for these men, as for free workers, but it listed them in the slaves' column. MCW pay book, 1828-32.

39. Ibid., 1827-32.

40. The pay book notes one-time payments to slaveholders "for the use of their hands," suggesting that McKim was paying by the day for short-term replacements for slaves. See MCW pay book, 1827-31.

41. A slave's median weekly likelihood of being absent one or more days was 19 percent. Eleven of fourteen slaves who stayed at the firm more than eighteen months had absentee rates lower than the median; nineteen of thirty slaves who worked less than eighteen months had above-median rates. MCW pay book, 1827-32.

42. William Adams missed more than eight months of work consecutively in 1831 because of sickness; Perry Tilghman missed thirteen weeks in 1830 because of a scalded leg. Neither Adams nor Tilghman tended to have frequent one- or two-day absences. MCW pay book, 1830-31.

43. The lead linings of the cisterns and evaporating pans needed constant repair; William Adams's skill as a lead caster no doubt counted for a great deal in McKim's decision to retain him. See Muspratt, *Chemistry,* 1:159-62, for discussions of replacing lead linings in maintaining equipment.

44. Thomas Hawthorn, who worked more than four years in the Epsom salts room, rose from the standard $4.50 a week in 1827 to $8.00 by 1831. Perhaps Hawthorn assumed status as "first hand" or "foreman" of the Epsom salts room. John McCoy, who worked more than three years at the plant in the evaporating chamber of the alum room, earned $6.00 a week by 1831. MCW pay book, 1827-31.

45. John Sewell had made chrome yellow, then worked in the alum room, then burned magnesium, and in 1831 was calcining alum. Scipio Freeman had moved from the Epsom salts room to the alum furnace and had then been assigned

to burn alum clay; he also earned extra pay by digging clay. Nelson Farewell made blue vitriol, evaporated alum, and burned magnesium, holding each of these jobs at two different intervals in his four-and-one-half years at the plant. See the MCW pay book for Sept. 15, 22, Dec. 8, 1827; July 18, 1829; May 8, June 5, Aug. 7, 1830; Jan. 1, 1831; see also marginal notes throughout the 1827-32 run of the pay book.

46. Dew's examination of the Buffalo Iron Forge found that daily iron production quotas remained at the same level over a forty-year period. He attributed this phenomenon to successful slave resistance to demands for greater production. Dew, "Slavery and Technology," 121.

47. McKim purchased Jacobs for two hundred dollars on March 22, 1827, from Caleb Dougherty, for a term of fifteen years, Jacobs then being twenty-five years old. Jacobs's bill of sale stipulated his manumission at the age of forty, in 1842. See the MCW journal, loose documents.

48. On November 21, 1828, David McKim sold James Jacobs to John Caton for two hundred dollars. Miscellaneous Papers, Nov. 21, 1828, Baltimore County Court.

49. The pay book does not indicate what James Jacobs did between March and November of 1828. David McKim may have hired him out on a short-term basis.

50. Winder's age is described in his bill of sale to David McKim of Jan. 9, 1827, found as a loose paper in the MCW journal.

51. The MCW pay book contains the entry "Run" to explain Winder's day-and-a-half absence in the week of February 7, 1829.

52. Austin Woolfolk, a slave dealer, sold a man named James Winder, age about twenty-five, in August of 1830 to a Kentucky buyer. See Miscellaneous Papers, 1830, Baltimore County Court. See Calderhead, "Professional Slave Trader," for more on Woolfolk. Also see Bancroft, *Slave-Trading in the Old South,* 37-44; and Dillon, *Benjamin Lundy,* 118-20.

53. David McKim sold at least three other slaves besides James Winder. All but Winder were sold to Baltimoreans, including the other recaptured runaway, Allen Henson. Slave bills of sale from David T. McKim to John Caton, 1828, and David T. McKim to Edward Spedden, 1829, Miscellaneous Papers, Baltimore County Court.

54. Henson ran off in August 1828, was caught within a week, and earned extras for months thereafter, before he too was sold off by McKim in July 1829. MCW pay book for August 1828 to July 1829.

55. George Boardly and Scipio Freeman, for example, earned extras in forty-nine weeks of 1829. MCW pay book, 1829.

56. McKim employed four plant managers in five years, beginning with Howard Sims. The second and third managers lasted less than a year altogether. The fourth manager confessed to "pilfering more than $250.00 of goods by his own account" in 1832. Given this experience, McKim was probably not eager to search for another supervisor to watch over the nighttime activities of the slaves. See the MCW pay book, 1827-1832. See Starobin, *Industrial Slavery,* 105-9 and 169-73, for slaves as supervisors or managers.

57. The plant diagram identifies a dwelling other than the Negro House, which may have housed the manager, and the pay book shows occasional purchases of food for him. See the MCW pay book, Mar. 15, 1828, or Nov. 26, 1831. The "At What Employed" lists give no hint that the plant retained a nighttime

supervisor. Given the frequency and volume of slave extras, it is most likely that the slaves worked their extra time without white supervision.

58. See Starobin, *Industrial Slavery,* 100-103; Lewis, *Coal, Iron, and Slaves,* 118-27; and Dew, "Disciplining Slave Ironworkers," esp. 406-9.

59. Extras were calculated in wholes, halves, and quarters. Free workers earned pay for whole, half, and quarter days worked; extras most likely represented the same units of time.

60. See Lewis, *Coal, Iron, and Slaves,* 117-26; Dew, "Sam Williams, Forgeman."

61. McKim expended about fifty to fifty-five cents per day for each day of slave labor performed. Extras brought him more labor at a much lower incremental cost.

62. Among slaves, the median propensity to work one or more extras in a week was 66 percent. Ten of fourteen (71 percent) of slaves who worked more than eighteen months exceeded this level; only twelve of thirty (40 percent) who stayed less than eighteen months did so. Six slaves bought by David McKim in 1826 and 1827 worked for the full fifty-six months recorded in the pay book; all six missed work less often and worked more extras than most other slaves. See MCW pay book, 1827-32.

63. Lewis, in *Coal, Iron, and Slaves,* 82-103, cites numerous examples of such strategies.

64. See Dew, "Slavery and Technology," 118-21.

65. See MCW pay book of 1828 for records on Stephen Dorsey; MCW pay book of 1828-29 for records on Fender and Murphy.

66. The MCW pay book for July 18, 1829, shows seven slaves getting seventy-five cents for two extras "at Tub in Alum Room" and later documents the higher rate for work at the magnesium furnace and for casting lead. See MCW pay book, 1829.

67. Extra pay rates and comments are all from the MCW pay book, 1829-32. The daily labor rate for white workers remained at seventy-five cents a day from 1827 through 1832.

68. One may wonder why McKim clung to a policy of cheap or underpaid extras. First, he may have felt uncomfortable paying full white wage rates to slaves in the absence of a visible output measure to assure him of their hard work. His willingness to pay slaves by the task for digging alum clay and casting lead indicates that he had may have preferred output-oriented compensation, when feasible. Second, McKim did get some positive responses to his cheap extras; many slaves worked extras almost every week and did not fall sick or run away.

69. No year-long hires were made after January 1830. See MCW pay book, 1831-32.

70. MCW pay book, Jan. 21 to Apr. 28, 1832.

71. Slaves receiving the fifty-cents-per-week "wage" also earned pay for extras in 90 percent of the pay book entries made on or after Jan. 21, 1832.

72. At twenty-five cents per extra, the average cash income of a slave at the Maryland Chemical Works was $.52 per week in 1831. Taking into account extras paid at $.375 each, the actual average pay for extras was about $.55. MCW pay book, 1831-32.

73. See the MCW journal, loose papers.

74. Freeman earned three or more extras 84 out of 235 weeks on the pay books, or 36 percent of the time. MCW pay book, 1827-32.

75. Freeman began earning extra money digging or hauling clay in late 1829. By early 1831 he was hauling $1.50 worth of clay per week, over and above his other labor. From January 8, 1831, onward Freeman received a base payment of $3.00 a week, $1.50 for the clay and $1.50 for boarding himself. MCW pay book, September 1829 to April, 1832.

76. *Matchett's Baltimore City Directory* for 1833. Maryland law treated manumission as a deed of gift rather than as a contract and thus did not insist on any statement of the terms thereof other than the date on which freedom was conferred.

77. MCW pay book, 1830-32. On September 4, 1830, the firm began paying Philip Payne boarding money "for his wife to board servants." Freeman started to get his $1.50 a week on September 11.

78. Prices for slaves for a term of years ranged between those of slaves for life and the annual hire price for slaves of similar sex, age, and condition. Freeman, twenty-nine years old in 1833, would have commanded perhaps $60 a year as a hire. With two years to serve in 1833, Freeman's price would in all likelihood be just under his hire price of $120 for those two years. Price data derived from Miscellaneous Papers, 1785-1835, Baltimore County Court.

79. Self-purchasing slaves sometimes paid as much as 50 to 100 percent more than normal prices for slaves of their age and sex. Miscellaneous Papers, 1785-1830, Baltimore County Court.

80. Freeman earned $118.75 for extras from 1827 to 1832 and $128.44 for digging clay. He boarded himself for eighty-five weeks, receiving $127.50. Altogether, he obtained $374.69; a purchase price of $100 is 27 percent of that amount, and $120 is 32 percent. Earnings figures from the MCW pay book, 1827-32.

81. At $4.50 per week, a white laborer working fifty weeks a year would have cost McKim $1,350 for six years. McKim would have expended another $468 for the two extras per week, or $1,818 for all work time over six years. When the $120 Freeman earned for clay digging is added in, McKim's total expenditure to buy Freeman's labor on the market would have been $1,938. For Freeman, McKim spent $374.69 in actual payments for extras, self-boarding, and clay digging, plus $588.72 for six years of direct maintenance costs at $98.12 a year. Add a further $200 for Freeman's purchase price, plus capital opportunity costs of $12 (6 percent) a year, totaling $83 over six years, compounded. Subtract the $100 realized by selling Freeman's remaining time, and McKim's net cost for Freeman's labor was $1,146, a savings of 40 percent, or nearly $800, compared to the cost of free labor. Cost figures drawn from the MCW journal's slave expense accounts for 1828, and earnings from the pay book, 1827-32.

82. The worth of slave labor is calculated on the assumption that a slave for life would actually work forty-seven weeks a year—the average annual absentee rate for slaves at the works being five weeks—at a value of 4.50 per week, for a total of $1,269. Direct costs for maintaining a slave for six years would have been about $588. Had Freeman been a slave for life, McKim would have expended perhaps $320 to obtain him, with opportunity costs over six years of $133, for a total cost of $1,041. A slave for life could have been sold for perhaps $200, in which case the cost of six years of labor by a slave for life would be $841, 66 percent of $1,269, and about $400 less than the cost of free white labor.

83. He spent $136.75 for shoes and $289.45 for two sets of drawers, shirts, and stockings per man. MCW journal, slave expense account, January and February, 1828.

84. All cost data in this discussion are drawn either from the MCW journal for 1828, slave expense account, or from the 1828 MCW pay book entries.

85. By the 1820s and 1830s, owners commonly and successfully insisted that hirers of slaves provide medical care. See Starobin, *Industrial Slavery,* 62-70, and Lewis, *Coal, Iron, and Slaves,* 154-55. Also see Savitt, "Slave Life Insurance."

86. Average costs of $200 for slaves for a term of years, $350 for a slave for life, and $55 for a slave hired for one year were derived from the firm's experience, as was the 6 percent interest rate, used in the journal for all interest calculations, whether for interest-bearing stock, notes held by creditors, accounts receivable, or unpaid obligations.

87. For term slaves I assumed an average term of eight years; for slaves for life an average working span of twenty-five years. The former is based on Baltimore County deeds of manumission and bills of sale. The latter assumes that slaves could not be expected to be fully productive after the age of forty-five. Maryland's manumission laws forbade the manumission of slaves over this age, on the assumption that such freedmen would be unable to work and maintain themselves (see Laws of Maryland, 1796, chap. 67). Depreciation is assumed to occur in equal decrements. An argument could be made for using a depreciation-by-age curve with little or no year-by-year loss of value for adult slaves in their twenties and a gradually steepening dropoff in value thereafter; for the illustrative purposes of these tables, a straight line depreciation is sufficiently accurate.

88. For contemporary estimates of the cost of slave labor, see the Baltimore *Genius of Universal Emancipation,* Sept. 15, 29, Oct. 6, Nov. 24, 1827. These issues discuss tax rates and assume, as does table 8, that the hirer of a slave paid the taxes thereon.

89. Wage laborers were paid only for days actually worked; their absences had no impact on labor costs.

90. These figures apply only to adults. McKim did hire boys, who commonly earned $1.50 a week. MCW pay book, 1827-32. McKim never employed any slave boys, implying that the cost advantage for slaves disappeared when comparing purchase and maintenance costs with a $1.50 a week free labor cost.

91. Henson was sold along with Edward Norris in 1829 for $200, $125 less than their combined purchase prices in 1827. See David T. McKim to Edward Spedden, July 1829, Miscellaneous Papers, Baltimore County Court. Both men were slaves for a term of years, but the shortening of their terms by two years each would not normally account for a 40 percent drop in value. It is plausible that Henson lost value disproportionately if the purchaser knew of his escape attempt.

92. See Hungerford, *Baltimore and Ohio Railroad,* 26, vol. 1. For the value of J.K. McKim's estate, see Baltimore County Wills, folio 487, book 18, and see his inventory in Baltimore County Inventories, folios 51, 60, 482, book 52.

93. The MCW pay book provides at least one example of McKim's cost consciousness. After boarding the sick William Adams in the city infirmary for nine weeks (cost $27.86) McKim arranged to have Adams sent to the Eastern Shore, where he could be boarded for $1.00 a week. Adams remained there for a further seven weeks and then came back to Baltimore (passage $1.50) to resume work. McKim may have believed that Adams would recover faster away from the heat and contagion of the city and its infirmary; the pay book notes only the $11.00 McKim saved by shipping the sick man back and forth across the Chesapeake Bay to cheaper lodgings.

94. Henson ran the week of August 23, during which he had worked four

and a quarter days and earned one extra. Rea received a reward of $2.625 in early September. The pay book records expenses for locks and fetters in September and October. MCW pay book, Aug. 23, Sept. 13, 20, Oct. 4, 1828.

95. Hall Brittain had been hired to the plant for all of 1828 and rehired in 1829. Nicolas Ford had come to the plant in the second week of February and had been there five weeks when he ran. The pay book for the week of March 21 lists Brittain's name just above Ford's; given the pattern of pay book entries, they probably worked at the same task. Brittain was "discharged" the same week Ford ran off, a usage that connotes a dismissal for unsatisfactory behavior. MCW pay book, 1828-29.

96. Smith was purchased for $275 from James Renshaw on November 14, 1826, as recorded in a loose bill of sale in the MCW journal.

97. No record indicates whether McKim reimbursed Ford's owner. Only if McKim could demonstrate that he had taken reasonable care to prevent Ford from running off and had made prompt and reasonable efforts to recover Ford would he avoid having to reimburse Ford's owner for the loss of the slave. See judgment of the court in *Hay v. Conner,* Miscellaneous Papers, 1798, Baltimore County Court, for a discussion of this subject.

98. Winkelman earned fees of $10.00 and $10.50 for two visits to the Negro House in July of 1829. The final entry in the pay book regarding Sewell records $7.50 spent for his "coffin, grave, bearers, and Minister." The other slaves at the plant received a half holiday to attend Sewell's funeral. MCW pay book, July and August 1829.

99. MCW pay book, 1829-30. The number of slaves at work never rose above fourteen for more than a week or two at a time after Sewell's death.

100. A doubling of slave prices would have doubled capital opportunity and depreciation costs but would have left maintenance costs untouched. Under those conditions, slave labor in 1828 would still have been about 20 percent, or a dollar a week cheaper, than free labor.

3. THE BLACK DRIVE FOR AUTONOMY AND MASTERS' RESPONSES

1. See the *Maryland Journal and Baltimore Commercial Advertiser,* July 24, 1794.

2. See Jones, *Born a Child of Freedom, yet a Slave,* 37-64. Jones concludes that "the threat of sale was the most effective long-term mechanism of control" (p. 63).

3. Carville Earle has argued that the slowness of the shift from slavery to free labor in Chesapeake areas switching from tobacco to wheat culture can be attributed to fairly close marginal costs of maintaining slaves year round as opposed to hiring free labor for seasonal work. Planters might have avoided complete dissociation from slavery lest unforeseen rises in free labor costs make slavery once again the cheapest system. See Earle, *Geographical Inquiry,* 226-57.

4. See the October 4, 1796, advertisement of Solomon Etting in the *Federal Gazette,* concerning the runaway Darkey.

5. Between 1777 and 1783, Maryland newspapers carried twenty-seven runaway advertisements that declared a slave had fled "to the British" or "to the Army." The earliest ads appeared in conjunction with the passage of a British fleet up the Chesapeake in 1777 in preparation for a march on Philadelphia; thereafter

there were repeated British raids throughout the region. Compiled from Windley, *Runaway Slaves.*

6. Rochambeau's troops marched north along Maryland's Western Shore in the summer and fall of 1782. During this period eight runaway ads speculated that a slave had fled "to the French." Compiled from Windley, *Runaway Slaves.*

7. See Hoffman, "The 'Disaffected' in the Revolutionary South," for a discussion of Maryland's Eastern Shore during the Revolution.

8. See Laws of Maryland, 1663, chap. 30.

9. Ibid., 1681, chap.4.

10. See *Butler v. Boarman,* September 1770, Harris and McHenry, *Maryland Reports.*

11. Butler lived in Saint Mary's County, where a courthouse fire had destroyed all records from the relevant period.

12. See Harris and McHenry, *Maryland Reports,* 1787, 2:214.

13. See Harris and McHenry, *Maryland Reports,* 4:295. For a recent and thorough examination of this case, see Papenfuse, "From Recompense to Revolution." Papenfuse contends that reactions to the Saint Domingue revolt keyed a reaction against freedom petitions that worked against the Mahoneys.

14. This practice was struck down by the U.S. Supreme Court in 1813. See Helen Caterall, *Judicial Cases concerning Slavery,* 4:45.

15. See the *Annapolis Maryland Gazette* of Jan. 19, 1792, advertisement of G.R. Brown for the runaway Jemima. Nine runaway advertisers of the 1790s noted that an escapee would try to pass for free "as a Butler." Compiled from Baltimore newspapers and the *Annapolis Maryland Gazette.*

16. The society was founded in 1789. See Berlin, *Slaves without Masters,* 28, for an occupational breakdown of the society's original members. See Finnie, "Anti-Slavery Movement in the Upper South," 322-25, for a discussion of the society.

17. See "Report of a meeting of the Maryland Society for Promoting the Abolition of Slavery."

18. See Laws of Maryland, 1796, chap. 67, secs. 21-27. The law also restricted petition filings to county courts, likely to provide a cheaper and friendlier venue for slaveholders than the appellate courts.

19. See Caterall, *Judicial Cases concerning Slavery,* vol. 4, passim.

20. The *Maryland Gazette* carried ads for eighteen runaways in conjunction with a pending or unsuccessful freedom petition, between 1791 and 1800. Rawlings's ads appeared in issues of July 1797 and October 1800, respectively.

21. See Manumissions, Anne Arundel County, MSA. Carroll's manumission of five Mahoney brothers and two other slaves occurred in 1808, that of John Joice in 1802. Ashton manumitted Daniel Mahoney in 1806. See also Papenfuse, "From Recompense to Revolution," 53-54, for Carroll's interest in the Ashton-Mahoney case.

22. See Manumission of James Chaplain to Negro Job, Dorchester County Land Records, 1823, MSA.

23. The society appears to have ceased operations by 1798. See Guy, "Maryland Abolition Society."

24. For the ban on manumission by will see Laws of Maryland, 1752, chap. 1; for the repeal statute passed in 1790, chap. 9. For Pennsylvania's *post-nati* law, see Nash and Soderlund, *Freedom by Degrees,* 74-99.

25. Speech of William Pinkney in the Maryland House of Delegates, of Nov. 1, 1789, in the Anti-Slavery Collection, Enoch Pratt Free Library, Baltimore.

26. By 1820 Pinkney, then a U.S. senator, favored Missouri's entrance as a slave state, endorsing the "diffusion" argument as his state's best hope for drawing down its numbers of slaves and free blacks.

27. The legislature never made the ban permanent. For renewals, see Laws of Maryland, 1755, chap. 12, 1758, chap. 9, 1766, chap. 1, 1786, chap. 35, and 1789, chap. 61. For the repeal statute, see 1790, chap. 9.

28. See *Negro Peter and Others v. John Elliott's Executors,* Harris and McHenry, *Maryland Reports,* 1793, vol. 2.

29. See Laws of Maryland, 1796, chap. 67.

30. Ibid., sec. 13.

31. See *Burrough's Administrator v. Negro Anna,* in *Cases in the Court of Appeals of Maryland,* June 1817, MSA. Burroughs had left his slave woman Anna "her liberty . . . , a young bay mare, . . . four barrels of Indian corn, and three hundred weight of pork." The appeals court ruled her still a slave.

32. See Harris and Johnson, *Maryland Reports,* 1820, 5:59. In this case a Mr. Goslee freed his slaves at specified ages and identified certain of them to serve his widow during their remaining years of servitude. The widow claimed her thirds and revoked this bequest.

33. See "Opinion of Francis Scott Key on the Manumission Deed of George Calvert," June 24, 1825, Scharf Papers, MSA.

34. The principal sources are newspaper advertisements from 1773 to 1830, as they relate both to the purchase, sale, hiring, and flight of slaves and to apprentices, indentured servants from Europe, sailors, and convicts. Additional material has been drawn from runaway dockets, court cases, and occasional newspaper articles. Runaway ads have been mined heavily to establish runaway typologies (a young adult male who runs away alone, for example), and as "witnesses in spite of themselves" about the lives of slaves (references to physical and psychological scars have been catalogued and analyzed). Historians of the slave family have noted that runaways frequently sought to reunite with kinfolk. Recently, cultural historians have focused on runaways' clothes, hair, speech, and mannerisms in order to understand contemporary cultural attitudes of and toward African Americans. For a comprehensive discussion see G. Mullin, *Flight and Rebellion.* Regional studies touching on runaways include Nash, *Forging Freedom,* 136-54; White, *Somewhat More Independent,* 114-49; Wood, "Female Resistance to Chattel Slavery." Fields, *Slavery and Freedom on the Middle Ground,* principally deals with the demise of slavery in Maryland post-1850, but see chap. 1, esp. 16-17. Prude, "To Look upon the 'Lower Sort,'" focuses on perceptions of runaways revealed through physical descriptions. Collections of runaway ads include Smith and Wojtowica's *Blacks Who Stole Themselves* and Windley, *Runaway Slaves.*

35. Ebbing runaway rates from Baltimore during 1800-1810 coincided with declining growth in the free black population of Philadelphia, as depicted by Nash in *Forging Freedom,* 137, table 4. The correlation between fewer Maryland runaways being reported headed for Philadelphia and lower free black growth rates in Philadelphia lends support to the hypothesis of Baltimore slaveholders that more runaways were hiding out in Baltimore and its environs.

36. Between 1791 and 1820, 237 of 525 male runaways (45 percent) were identified by advertisers as possessing a skill. Most numerous were brick makers (25), sailors (24), forge and furnace hands (22), and shoemakers (11). Others included bakers (8), blacksmiths (8), ship carpenters (7), rope makers (5), carpenters (5), cigar makers (5), nailers (5), barbers (4), tailors (4), caulkers (4), and watermen (4).

37. See the Baltimore *American* of June 27, 1811.

38. Ibid., Feb. 9, 1818.

39. Total black population in Baltimore in 1810 was 10,591 and in 1820, 14,615. Cited from U.S. Census Office, Third Census, 1810, Population Schedules of the Third Census of the U.S., 1810, Maryland (Washington, D.C. 1810), and Fourth Census, 1820, Population Schedulees of the Fourth Census of the U.S., 1820, Maryland, (Washington, D.C. 1820).

40. See the *American,* July 12, 1817, ad for Mary Brown.

41. See Nash and Soderlund, *Freedom by Degrees,* esp. chaps. 1, 2.

42. See advertisement of William Norris, Jr., in the *American* of June 24, 1818. For jailed runaways, see the Baltimore City Gaol, Runaway Docket, 1831, MSA. The docket lists more than 150 Negroes jailed as suspected runaways; slightly less than half were released to local owners.

43. The rural runaways were taken from a sample of 615 advertisements in the *Annapolis Maryland Gazette* from 1773 to 1815. The Baltimore sample of 721 advertisements was drawn from 1773 to 1820, from the *Maryland Journal and Baltimore Commercial Advertiser* (1773-95), the *Federal Gazette* (1796-99 and 1801-4), and the *American* (1799-1801 and 1804-20).

44. The maximum sliding-scale reward offered for male runaways from Baltimore between 1811 and 1820 averaged $73, based on a sample of 241 advertisements in the *American.* This maximum figure would typically be paid for a slave recaptured more than fifty miles from Baltimore, or "out of the state of Maryland."

45. See advertisement of Anthony Mann for the recovery of John Davis, in the *American* of July 16, 1808.

46. See advertisement of Christopher Hughes in the May 4, 1798, edition of the Baltimore *Federal Gazette.*

47. See Petition of James Hughes, Petitions, 1791, Baltimore County Orphans' Court, MSA.

48. For examples, see the Petition of Helen Burk (October 1797), of Elizabeth Hayes (November 1807), or of John Gorham (November 1816), Petitions, Baltimore County Orphans' Court.

49. See Petition of Negroes Basil and Philip, Pardon Papers, 1794, Maryland Governor and Council, MSA.

50. See the advertisement of Alexander Lawson of Jan. 29, 1796, in the *Federal Gazette* and that of Joseph Biays of Mar. 23, 1792, in the *Maryland Journal and Baltimore Commercial Advertiser.*

51. See the *American* of Feb. 11, 1820.

52. See Bancroft, *Slave Trading in the Old South,* 28-42. Most of Bancroft's evidence came from the 1830s and later.

53. Other interpretations of what advertisers meant by a desire to avoid "trouble" are unconvincing. Because slaves were generally sold for cash, ascertaining creditworthiness would not normally be at issue. Nor did Maryland law impose special fees or documentary requirements on out-of-state sales of slaves.

54. Woolfolk and Anderson advertised in Baltimore newspapers during the period 1816-18. See the *American* of Mar. 7 or Oct. 12, 1818.

55. Slave population declined 7 percent in Baltimore from 1810 to 1820; the flat numbers of sale ads do indicate an unchanging overall frequency of slave sale.

56. Of 523 male runaways advertised between 1791 and 1820, 259 (49 percent) were said to be between the ages of fifteen and twenty-four. In the years 1816-18 that proportion increased to 52 of 90 (58 percent).

57. See Laws of Maryland, 1817, chap. 112.

58. Records checked include those of the Baltimore city and county courts for 1818-30 and the Prisoner Records of the Maryland Penitentiary. Seven persons served time for the offense of kidnapping, that is, the attempt to transport a term slave. See Prisoner Records, 1811-30, Maryland Penitentiary, MSA. Pardon petitions reveal six cases in which a convicted kidnapper avoided imprisonment through the governor's intervention but no cases indicative of any prosecution of the original seller of a term slave. See Pardon Papers, 1818-30, Governor and Council.

59. Report of the Grand Jury of Baltimore County, July term, 1816, printed in the *Federal Gazette* of Oct. 29, 1816.

60. See Laws of Maryland, 1817, chap. 112, and 1818, chap. 208.

61. The Woolfolks sold slaves to Georgia and Louisiana from 1816 to 1830. David Anderson, of Tennessee, traded in slaves well into the 1820s. In an 1822 runaway advertisement he sought to recover eight bondmen who had escaped from the Baltimore City Jail. See the *American* of Sept. 5 and Sept. 20, 1822.

62. See Laws of Maryland, 1817, chap. 112, sec. 6. For the debate, see the *Federal Gazette* of Sept. 13, 1810.

63. See the *American,* Nov. 30, 1816.

64. Ibid.

65. See the *American,* July 18, 1818.

66. Kidnapping flared up again in the 1820s, leading to an unsuccessful proposal to allow slaves and free blacks to testify against whites in kidnapping cases. See the *American* of Aug. 9, 1822. Also see "A Further Supplement to the Act entitled, an Act Relating to Servants and Slaves," pamphlet 2708, MHS.

67. Of the 197 advertisements for runaway women, only 19 (10 percent) indicate that a fugitive took children with her.

68. The 1813 tax rolls listed 825 slave children under the age of fourteen and 962 women over that age. See Baltimore City, Commissioners of the Tax, Assessment Record, 1813, MSA. The 1820 census reported 1,552 slave women age fourteen and older and 1,562 slave children below that age. That census showed 859 slave women (55 percent) living in households with a total of 989 slave children under fourteen and 693 slave women (45 percent) in households with no children under fourteen. The census data show 573 of 1,552 slave children (37 percent) living in households with no black woman. Compiled from the Baltimore city census, Fourth Census of the United States, 1820.

69. See the *American,* Sept. 26, 1809; Dec. 12, 1812; Oct. 3, 24, 1806; *Federal Gazette,* June 17, 1796; *American,* Nov. 29, 1816.

70. See ad of F.B. Brunelot in the *American,* Oct. 15, 1814.

71. See the *American,* Jan. 3, 1818, ad to sell a hostler.

72. See the case of *Ridout, Jubarre, et al., vs. Richard Caton, Robert Oliver, John Oliver, the Cape Sable Co., et al.,* in Maryland Chancery Papers, case 17898-9015, MSA. The first quotation is from a letter of Apr. 24, 1816, from Thomas H. Dorsey to Gerrard Troost. The second quotation is from a deposition of Margaret Troost, of Apr. 9, 1817.

73. See the complaint of Job Garretson in *Garretson v. Hollis,* Maryland Chancery Papers, case 17898-2064, filed Jan. 3, 1802.

74. See the *American,* Jan. 7, 1810, concerning an eighteen-year-old wagoner; May 23, 1809, concerning a twenty-one-year-old Negro man with nine years to serve; and July 31, 1811, concerning a Negro woman skilled in gardening.

75. See the *American,* Sept. 8, 1818, an advertisement regarding a woman, a cook, and a man who was a driver, on board the *Two Brothers.*

76. See the *American,* Jan. 10, 1812, advertisement of Thomas Shaw and John Murray, executors of William Weatherly's estate.

77. See the *Federal Gazette* of Dec. 29, 1797.

78. See Duvall's notice of Pitt in the *American,* June 20, 1817.

79. See *Maryland Journal and Baltimore Commercial Advertiser,* September 1785, for Gough's advertisement to recover "Will," a blacksmith.

80. Ibid., May 3, 1791. The median reward offered in 158 runaway advertisements from the 1790s was twenty dollars. Gough promised Will Bates's captor twice as much as all but one other reward offered in the decade.

81. See the Laws of Maryland, 1804, chap. 90, and 1833, chap. 224.

82. See W. Green, *Life of William Green.*

83. I have found no successful freedom petitions that turned on a master's failure to manumit a term slave on schedule. See Caterall, *Judicial Cases concerning Slavery,* 4:49-71, for Maryland cases involving freedom petitions.

84. See *Gibson Readle v. Ninian Willett,* Maryland Chancery Papers, Feb. 21, 1810. Also see *Hood v. Weems,* Maryland Chancery Papers, 1816. Hester Hood alleged that she had sold her slave Harry to John C. Weems in 1807 on condition that he free Harry in three years. In 1816 Harry was still not free, and Hood contended that Weems was planning to sell Harry out of the state.

85. Keith Hopkins sees gradual self-purchase as a form of insurance against the death of a slave. See *Conquerors and Slaves,* 127-29. The logic fits well for small slaveholders in the upper South.

86. See the *American,* Mar. 9, 1815, ad of Joseph Hart, offering a one-hundred-dollar reward for the capture of Moses Lemmon.

87. See Lewis, "The Darkest Abode of Man;" Lewis, "Slave Families at an Early Chesapeake Ironworks." Also see Dew, "David Ross and the Oxford Iron Works," and Dew, "Disciplining Slave Ironworkers," for examples in Virginia and Maryland.

88. See the *American* of Dec. 4, 1813.

89. I have found no cases in the court reports for Maryland in which a slaveholder recovered damages from an unauthorized employer of a slave.

90. Self-hiring did entail risks, especially the threat of kidnapping. The Protection Society of Baltimore, formed in 1816, noted that kidnappers preyed on slaves as well as on free blacks, particularly by luring them to secluded locales with offers of work chopping wood, mowing, or picking fruit. See the *American* of Sept. 26, 1816.

91. The 1790 census data for Baltimore town show .6 percent of 1,255 slaves living in all-black households; for 1800 the proportion is 1.7 percent of 2,843 slaves, for 1810 1.3 percent of 4,657 slaves, and for 1820 5.5 percent of 4,289 slaves.

92. See Laws of Maryland, 1796, chap. 67. This law lowered the upper age limit on emancipations from fifty to forty-five.

93. See Laws of Maryland, 1796, chap. 68, sec. 17, and 1817, chap. 112.

94. The twenty cases derive from a review of 2,331 wills filed with the Baltimore County Court between 1790 and 1825. Of these, 597 specifically disposed of slave property.

95. See the will of John Battee, registered in 1800, in Baltimore County Wills, 1797-1802, p. 259, MSA.

96. See Frederick Douglass, *The Life and Times of Frederick Douglass* (1892; reprint, New York, 1967), 99.

97. See *Niles' Weekly Register,* Dec. 2, 1815, 9:231.

98. See Petition of Negro Rachel, Petitions, 1820, Baltimore County Orphans' Court.

99. See the *American,* Sept. 12, 1818, ad of Joshua Barney.

100. Ibid., Apr. 14, 1819.

4. MANUMISSION AND THE TRANSFORMATION OF SLAVERY

1. The literature on manumission in the ancient world and in Latin America is voluminous. For Roman society, see W.D. Phillips, *Slavery from Roman Times,* 25-39, and Bradley, *Slaves and Masters in the Roman Empire,* 81-112. Garlan discusses manumission in Attic Greece in *Slavery and Ancient Greece,* 73-84. For an urban setting in Latin America, see Karasch, *Slave Life in Rio de Janeiro,* esp. 335-68. Descriptions relating to other parts of Latin America include Klein, *Slavery in the Americas,* 62-65, 196-200; Scott, *Slave Emancipation in Cuba,* passim, esp. 149-57; Bowser, *The African Slave in Colonial Peru,* 273-301; Schwartz, *Sugar Plantations in Brazilian Society,* 439-65; Sharp, *Slavery on the Spanish Frontier,* 127-47. Cooper, *Plantation Slavery on the East Coast of Africa,* 243-68, discusses manumission in nineteenth-century Zanzibar. For a theoretical treatment, see Patterson, *Slavery and Social Death,* 209-39.

2. Berlin, in *Slaves without Masters,* 30, argues that "equalitarian ideals motivated most manumitters in the years following the Revolution," whereas nineteenth-century emancipators were "motivated more by cold utility than by libertarian ideals" (p. 150). See pp. 15-50, 138-160. Robert Fogel and Stanley Engerman, in "Philanthropy at Bargain Basement Prices," 377-401, focus on northern gradual emancipation laws and conclude that freeing slaves at age twenty-six or older provided full compensation to slaveholders for the loss of ownership of the slave's labor power. Matison notes this distinction in motivation ("Manumission by will was an act of charity; manumission by deed often meant self-purchase.") in "Manumission by Purchase," 164.

For manumission in New York and Philadelphia, see White, *Somewhat More Independent,* esp. chaps. 1 and 2; Nash and Soderlund, *Freedom by Degrees,* esp. chaps. 2 and 4. K. Carroll states in "Religious Influences on the Manumission of Slaves" that in Eastern Shore Maryland, manumission "received its start and gained its main strength from religion." He discusses Quakers, Methodists, and Nicholites, whose sects had opposed perpetual slavery.

3. Frank Tannenbaum, *Slave and Citizen: The Negro in the Americas* (New York, 1946). See pages 50-71 for his discussion of manumission.

4. The 14,800 free blacks residing in Baltimore in 1830 far exceeded the roughly 3,000 manumissions by deed and will registered for the city *and* county, during the years 1789-1830.

Place-of-birth data on certificates of freedom suggest that fewer than one Baltimore free black in ten had been born and raised in the city itself. See the Register of Certificates, Clerk of Baltimore County, 1806-1816, microfilmed under the title "Negroes Manumitted and Born Free, 1806-1864," Baltimore City Archives. This list of certificates of freedom identifies place of birth for 195 people. Of these, 176 were raised outside Baltimore County; only 19 persons are listed as having been raised in Baltimore City.

5. Residents of Baltimore city manumitted 1,080 slaves by will and deed over the first three decades of the nineteenth century, an annual average of 36, or a rate of 9 per 1,000 per year. For Prince George's County, all recorded manumissions equaled 543, or 18 per year, a rate of less than 2 per 1,000 over the years 1800-1830. Dorchester County's 1,186 manumissions, or 39 per year, begin to approach the city's level, at 7 per 1,000. The Maryland State Colonization Society noted 2,342 manumissions throughout the state in the decade 1831-41, a statewide rate of 2 slaves per 1,000 per year. See the *Maryland Colonization Journal,* June 1841, p. 11, MHS.

6. See Zilversmit's *The First Emancipation.* Also see Berlin, *Slaves without Masters,* 15-50, for a discussion of the First Emancipation in both northern and southern states. See pp. 137-38 for subsequent southern efforts to restrict emancipation.

7. Of 9,606 manumissions by deed recorded in eight Maryland counties between 1770 and 1830, 4,835 (50.3 percent) freed female slaves and 4,771 (49.7 percent) liberated males. Those who found that outside the United States about two-thirds of manumittees were women include Brana-Shute, "Approaching Freedom"; Karasch, *Slave Life in Rio de Janeiro,* 336; L.L. Johnson, "Manumission in Colonial Buenos Aires," 262; Handler, *The Unappropriated People;* Cox, *The Free Coloreds in the Slave Societies of St. Kitts and Grenada;* Klein, *African Slavery in Latin America and the Caribbean.* Klein claims that "all recent studies" support the two-thirds ratio (p. 227). Also see Ingersoll, "Free Blacks in a Slave Society," and Kotlikoff and Rupert, "The Manumission of Slaves in New Orleans."

8. Many studies of manumission in Latin America and the Caribbean have found that people of mixed race were more likely to become free than darker-skinned slaves. According to Stephen Small, this pattern is also to be found in North America but has been overlooked by earlier investigators. He cites manumission records from Georgia and planter records from Virginia as support. See his "Racial Group Boundaries and Identities."

9. About 29 percent of 1,044 free people of color and term slaves sentenced to the state penitentiary before 1830 were categorized by their keepers as mulatto or yellow, and 24 percent of 83 slaves for life were so described, showing a difference not statistically significant. There is no guarantee that these populations were representative samples of their larger groups, of course, but the hypothesis that lighter skin color worked in favor of one's gaining freedom is certainly not supported by these data, as compiled from Prisoner Records, 1811-30, Maryland Penitentiary.

10. Of 7,549 manumissions by deed in seven rural counties, 2,744 (36 percent) took effect immediately and 4,805 (64 percent) required a term of servitude pending emancipation.

11. From 1800 to 1814, 442 of 844 Baltimore manumissions by deed (52 percent) were immediate. From 1815 to 1830, 768 of 1,195 Baltimore manumissions (67 percent) were immediate.

12. Overall, about 7 percent of manumitters noted reasons of conscience in deeds granting freedom (694 of 9,606). With the exception of eighteenth-century Talbot County, where about 40 percent of manumitters evinced such reasons (357 of 891), no more than 10 to 15 percent of any county's manumitters expressed opposition to slavery while liberating slaves.

13. The firm of Warner and Hanna printed one-page manumission forms as early as 1789. By the early 1800s, a majority of original manumissions were filed on forms.

14. See American Methodist Episcopal church class membership lists for Baltimore City Station, and East Baltimore (Fell's Point) for the years 1799-1825. For the Friends' Society (Quakers), see the records of the Baltimore Yearly Meeting. Both are in the microfilm collections, MSA. The manumission lists are from those deeds found in the Miscellaneous Papers, Baltimore County Court, for the years 1785-1830. Of over 2,000 manumission deeds, only 156 manumissions could positively be attributed to a Quaker or a Methodist.

15. See Baltimore Yearly Meeting for Sufferings, Minutes on Negroes and Slaves, and the Slave Trade, Etc., microfilm reel 1401, MSA, pp. 360-75.

16. For changes in the Methodist discipline on slavery, see Daniel Hitt and Thomas Ware, eds., *Minutes of the Methodist Conference Annually Held in America from 1773 to 1813, Inclusive* (New York, 1813). See also Mathews, *Slavery and Methodism.*

17. Summarized from the Journal of the Baltimore Annual Conference, Methodist Episcopal Church, vols. 1 and 2, 1817 and 1844, dealing with the period 1800-1833. For bringing slaves forward to "have their time judged," see Baltimore Circuit of the Methodist Episcopal Church, Quarterly Conference Minutes, for the period 1799-1816. Both items are at the United Methodist Historical Society, Lovely Lane Museum, Baltimore.

18. Name matching between church membership records and Baltimore slaveholders in the second and third censuses revealed 44 of 990 slaveholders in 1800 to be Methodists (4.4 percent) and 59 of 1,362 in 1810 (4.3 percent). In 1820 there were 145 Methodists out of 1,777 slaveholders in the city (8.2 percent). Considering the emphasis of the Methodist discipline on recording manumissions, it is not likely that surviving records significantly underrepresent Methodist action.

19. This number derives from name matching of congregation members listed in the City Station and East Baltimore class lists to manumitters in Baltimore county. Matching efforts revealed 108 sales and 104 purchases of slaves by Methodists over the same time span, suggesting that compliance with nonslaveholding rules was imperfect.

20. The first president of the Baltimore and Ohio Railroad, Philip Evans Thomas, and its first chief construction engineer, Caspar Wever, were both Quakers, who barred the use of slave labor in constructing the road. See Hungerford, *Baltimore and Ohio Railroad.* The Ellicott brothers operated forges, foundries, mills, and naileries; they neither owned nor hired slaves in Maryland.

21. See Manumission of Denwood Jones to Negro Kit, Dorchester County Land Records, 1821.

22. See Laws of Maryland, 1832, chap. 296. The willingness to "grandfather" the right of those buying liberty in installments to remain suggests that gradual self-purchase was widespread.

23. Matison, in "Manumission by Purchase," noted that only Delaware, Tennessee, and Louisiana characterized self-purchase as a contract between master and slave.

24. Slaves over the age of forty-five could not be freed, and any slave manumitted had to be "capable by labour . . . to procure sufficient food and raiment." See Laws of Maryland, 1796, chap. 67, sec. 29.

25. Miscellaneous Papers, 1820, Baltimore County Court.

26. Ibid., 1817.

27. Ibid., 1819.

28. Manumission of Robert Tilley to Negro William Carroll, Chattel Records, 1802, Prince George's County, MSA.

29. Manumission of Michael Lucas to Thomas Perry, Land Records, 1801, Dorchester County.

30. See Manumission of Edward Griffith to Sundry Negroes, Land Records, 1823, Dorchester County.

31. Manumission of Edward Wrotten to Negro David, Land Records, 1800, Dorchester County.

32. Manumission of Richard Mackall to Sundry Negroes, Miscellaneous Papers, 1808, Baltimore County Court. See also manumissions by Mackall to James Byas (1809) and Bigs Butler (1809) and of Isaac (1811) for shortening of terms.

33. Manumission of Edward Griffith to Sundry Negroes, Land Records, 1824, Dorchester County, manumission of James Chaplain to Negro Job, Laud Records, Dorchester County, 1823.

34. Of 429 female and 370 male slaves manumitted immediately by deed in Baltimore city and County between 1789 and 1830, for whom an age was specified, 225 women (52 percent) were thirty or older, as were 234 men (63 percent). The modal age of forty defined 36 women and 33 men.

35. See Laws of Maryland, 1817, chap. 112.

36. See the supplement to the Baltimore Yearly Meeting Records, Baltimore Yearly Meeting for Sufferings, Minutes on Negroes and Slaves, 1816, microfilm reel 1401, MSA.

37. The Act concerning Negroes of 1715 decreed that children born of white mothers and black fathers be bound to service until the age of thirty-one. It was in effect until 1796.

38. See Miscellaneous Papers, 1804, Baltimore County Court. Turnbull set terms of service as long as forty-two years.

39. See Manumission of Charles Goldsborough to Negro Benjamin Jackson, Land Records, 1822, Dorchester County. Goldsborough also sold at least two other elderly female slaves to their kin, although neither of these transactions were formally linked to manumissions of the purchasers.

40. See Manumission by Henry Darden, William Vanderford, and Henry Downes of Negro Benjamin, Land Records, 1811, Queen Anne's County, MSA.

41. See Laws of Maryland, 1796, chap.67. Regarding reregistration or tardy registration of manumissions, see Manumission by Elizabeth Hutchings of Sundry Negroes, Land Records, 1807, Queen Anne's County, for a typical example. At least one hundred of the manumissions in the eight counties surveyed in this work represented "perfections" of previous deeds that were defective because they had been registered too late or not at all.

42. See Manumission by William Browne of Negro Phill, Land Records, 1800, Queen Anne's County.

43. See Manumission by Joseph Blackiston of Negro John, Land Records, 1805, Kent County, MSA. Also see manumissions by Thomas Granger of Sundry Negroes, 1785 and 1790, and of Milcah, 1814, Land Records, Kent County.

44. See Douglass, *Life and Times,* 95-97, regarding division and redivision of slaves. The Baltimore County Orphans' Court Proceedings bulge with slave valuations filed by court-appointed appraisers as a prelude to the sale of slaves to divide an estate. See Proceedings, Baltimore County Orphans Court. This discussion relies on a study of these records from 1790 to 1830.

45. Guardian Accounts filed with the Baltimore County Orphans' Court

between 1800 and 1825 yielded 130 notations of annual hire rates for slaves. The median value was $60, the mean value $59. Hire rates of as much as $240 per year were obtained for a few slave blacksmiths and shipwrights. See Guardian Accounts, 1800-25, Baltimore County Register of Wills.

46. See Mortgages, 1800-30, Miscellaneous Papers, Baltimore County Court. In a sample of one hundred mortgages, interest of 6 percent was charged more than 90 percent of the time.

47. For income-generating slaves, also see William Gwynn's guardianship of Bridget Tull, from 1807 through 1812; Zachary Miles for the grandchildren of William Preston, between 1800 and 1811, Edward Pannell for heirs of John Pannell, from 1801 to 1810, Benjamin Ricaud for Mary Ann Hyatt from 1806 to 1815, and John Wooden for the heirs of Joseph Bowen, from 1808 to 1822, in Guardian Accounts, 1800-22, Baltimore County Orphans' Court.

48. See Baltimore County Wills, 1797-1802, p. 552. Also see Guardian Accounts, 1803-09, Baltimore County Orphans' Court, for the value of DeRochebrune's slaves and their earnings as hirees.

49. For Hewitt, see Baltimore County Wills, 1802-5, p. 356. Hopkinson's account is in Guardian Accounts, 1812, Baltimore County Orphans' Court.

50. See Baltimore County Wills, 1802-5, p. 99. For Piper as a Methodist, see class lists of Baltimore City Station, Methodist Episcopal Church, 1799 and 1800, microfilm rolls M408-11.

51. Wills filed in Baltimore between 1791 and 1820 record 189 promises of manumission, of which 29 (15 percent) granted freedom at the testator's death. Of 821 deeds of manumission granted between 1790 and 1830, 486 (59 percent) granted freedom immediately. See Baltimore County Wills, 1791-1820, and Miscellaneous Papers, 1790-1830, Baltimore County Court.

52. Residents of Baltimore city granted 23 percent of their manumissions by will, compared to 29 percent in Dorchester County, 38 percent in Prince George's County, and 44 percent in outlying Baltimore County, during the period 1790-1830. See Baltimore County, Dorchester County, Prince George's County Wills, MSA. Chi-square tests reveal the lower ratio of manumissions by will in Baltimore city to be significant at the .01 level.

53. Other indicators of concern about slave flight include injunctions against selling slaves out of Maryland and allowing favored slaves to choose a master from among several heirs.

54. The 1790, 1800, 1810, and 1820 censuses list a total of 4,844 heads of household in which a slave resided in Baltimore. This figure does not eliminate duplicate listings of the same slaveholding person in successive censuses. Nor can it include those who held slaves for a few years but were never recorded in a decennial census. The 277 households with 7 or more slaves represent 5.7 percent of all slaveholding households. In calculating manumission rates, I presumed that each census listing indicated holding each slave for ten years, as an average. Altogether, large holders owned 2,504 slaves, for whom 85 recorded manumissions survive, over the entire time span 1790-1830, a rate of 3.4 manumissions per 1,000 slaves per year.

I constructed a sample of 170 small slaveholders, defined as those owning three or fewer slaves, stratified across the first four censuses but selected randomly from within each census roll.

The small slaveholders displayed a manumission rate of 8.6 per 1,000 slaves per year.

55. In 1790 27 of 390 slaveholders listed for Baltimore town (6.9 percent) were women; they owned 6.8 percent of the city's slaves. For 1800, women were 10.5 percent of the slaveholders and owned 10.3 percent of the slaves; for 1810 they made up 11.7 percent of the slaveholders and owned 10.9 percent of the slaves. By 1820, women were 13.2 percent of all slaveholders (234 of 1,777) and owned 13 percent of the slaves (556 of 4,289). Data compiled from microfilm copies of the first through fourth censuses of the United States for Baltimore City. U.S. Bureau of the Census, Heads of Families at the First Census of the U.S. Taken in the Year 1790: Maryland (Baltimore, 1965; originally published Washington, D.C., 1907). For information on third and fourth U.S. censuses, see note 39 above.

Regarding manumissions, women freed 247 of 1,080 slaves between 1790 and 1830, comprising both deeds and wills in which the manumitter could positively be identified as living in Baltimore city. Data derived from Miscellaneous Papers, Baltimore County Court, and Baltimore County Wills, 1790-1830.

56. The percentages quoted represent the proportion of taxable wealth in slaves held by the median woman or man on lists of taxables rank-ordered by the percentage of wealth so held. The 1813 tax list identifies 123 women and 974 men who resided in Baltimore city and who were assessed taxes on slaves. Data compiled from the Assessment Records, 1813, Baltimore City Commissioners of the Tax.

57. The male average was $1,429 and the female average, $654.

58. The first four censuses for Baltimore list 62 white female heads of household owning five or more slaves. These women collectively constitute 11.7 percent of the 533 women listed in the first four censuses for Baltimore. The 496 slaves they held make up 31 percent of the 1,481 slaves residing in households headed by white women.

59. Slaves were assumed to have been held an average of ten years by a woman who lived throughout the period 1790-1830 and who appeared once on the census list. Women whose death dates were known and who disposed of slaves in their wills were assumed to have held slaves for the period between their first appearance in the census and their death, plus a period of five years before their first appearance.

The sample of women owning three or fewer slaves was drawn at random from each of the first four censuses, after stratifying the number to be taken from each roll with a view to obtaining a 20 percent sample of all "smallholding" female masters.

60. See Miscellaneous Papers, 1811, Baltimore County Court, regarding the sale of the slave Jerry by Stephen Hill, for an example. Phrases like "whom I formerly purchased from Jacob Myers" or "who was raised by William Price" occur in perhaps a third of the Baltimore County bills of sale.

61. See Douglass, *Life and Times,* 78.

62. See Proceedings, Jan. 1, 1827, Baltimore County Orphans' Court. Court-appointed estate appraisers reported, "We have appraised them two ways, for a term of years and for life." Here are their figures: For life: Elisha, 32, $300; Joshua, 30, $300; Catherine, 5, $100. For a term of years: Elisha, 32, to serve 5 years, $150; Joshua, 30, to serve 5 years, $150; Catherine, 5, to serve 25 years, $75.

63. See the MCW journal.

64. See the *Federal Gazette* of Jan. 7, 1802; the woman was advertised as "about 30, with seven years to serve." The second ad appeared in the Baltimore *American* of Sept. 8, 1818, and was placed by the captain of the schooner *The*

Two Brothers. Advertisements to sell slaves placed by Baltimore masters frequently mentioned a desire to find a local buyer, in order to accommodate the slave's wish to stay in the city.

65. Total black population in Baltimore in 1810 was 10,591; for 1820 it was 14,615. Cited from the third and fourth federal censuses.

66. An analysis of runaway skills also suggests that gradual manumission or self-purchase did not fully forestall slave flight. Slaves in the crafts had greater opportunities to earn cash and buy themselves than most, but although no more than 37 percent of the slave population were ever owned by persons in the crafts, craft workers made up 45 percent of runaways with a specified skill.

67. Letter of Judge Nicholas Brice, dated Dec. 11, 1827, and reprinted in *Genius of Universal Emancipation,* Baltimore, Mar. 1, 1828.

68. Ibid.

69. See Laws of Maryland, 1833, chap. 224, secs. 1, 4, 6. After 1817, when the ban on was first imposed, concern was expressed repeatedly that the freedom of term slaves sold out of state was inadequately protected. For a comprehensive argument on the matter, see the *Genius of Universal Emancipation,* ed. Benjamin Lundy, of Jan. 20, 1827, and Feb. 10, 1827.

70. See Laws of Maryland, 1833, chap. 224, sec. 2. The records of the Baltimore County Orphans' Court for the 1830s and 1840s contain many cases in which estate administrators or guardians petitioned the court to extend terms or sell term slaves out of state; in these cases the court called in outside witnesses to speak concerning either the slave's behavior or the slaveholders' claims to have notified slaves of their possible sale out of state, or both matters.

71. This account follows that of Klein in *Slavery in the Americas,* 196-200. For *coartación* in New Orleans, see Ingersoll, "Free Blacks in a Slave Society."

72. See Bradley, *Slaves and Masters in the Roman Empire,* 81-112, esp. 108-10 on the *peculium.*

73. See Scott, *Slave Emancipation in Cuba,* 74-77, on age restrictions for *coartados* and Bradley, *Slavery and Society at Rome,* 154-65, on restrictions on the number and proportion of a master's slaves who could be freed by will in imperial Rome.

74. See Bradley, *Slavery and Society at Rome,* 156-57.

75. In Baltimore County, 1789-1830, 410 of 1,984 surviving sales records were for a term of years. In Dorchester County 74 of 1,515 sales and in Prince George's County 22 of 1,004 sales were for a term of years.

76. See Miscellaneous Papers, Baltimore County Court. Manumissions filed from 1789 to 1825 and bills of sale filed from 1789 to 1830 were examined to provide at least a five-year period of search for later purchases after each manumission.

77. Deeds of manumission identify 46 grantors as free people of color, virtually all of whom were manumitting spouses or children. About one-quarter of all manumitters were women, of whom only 4 percent reacquired slaves; very few of them practiced a traditionally male craft; employment of bound labor in the crafts was a male preserve.

78. Imagine a universe of 200 manumitters and 200 purchases of slaves, which includes 20 manumissions followed by repurchases, a 10 percent repurchase rate. If 100 records of each set become lost, a search of surviving records would find, on average, 10 of the 20 manumissions that could be paired with repurchases. Since half the bills of sale would also be missing, only 5 of 10 possible

pairs would be found, on average. The researcher working with these smaller data sets could conclude that only 5 percent—5 of 100—of manumitters repurchased.

Significant proportions of Baltimore's slave records have failed to survive. Most official court copies of slave sales and manumissions were destroyed many years ago; what survives are random original records preserved as miscellaneous court papers. Comparison of these originals with a rare surviving volume of chattel records for 1813-14 revealed that only 55 percent of the bills of sale recorded in the chattel records and about 80 percent of the manumissions could be found in extant miscellaneous original papers.

79. In Dorchester county, where large proportions of manumissions were inspired by religious principles, the reacquisition rate of 12 percent for white males nonetheless matches that found in Baltimore, even without excluding Quaker manumissions. In Prince George's County, a rural tobacco county where masters' labor needs varied less than those of urban employers, 16 percent, or one in six men, bought more slaves after a grant of freedom, again a higher rate than in Baltimore. If rates in these counties exceed those for Baltimore, it seems quite likely that the Baltimore rates may be artificially low because of lost or unrecorded transactions.

80. For the law, see Laws of Maryland, 1817, chap. 112. In 1817 51 bills of sale were recorded with the Baltimore County Court; in 1818, 77. The number of gradual manumissions recorded in 1818 also jumped from 27 to 43 in 1818.

81. Cook's manumission and all three bills of sale are in the Miscellaneous Papers, Baltimore County Court, in their respective years.

82. John Kelso appears as a class member on the City Station member lists of Baltimore's Methodist church for the years 1810, 1813, and 1820.

83. The Woodard and Hill sales of Jerry are in the Miscellaneous Papers for the Baltimore County Court, for 1807 and 1811. If Jerry was in fact over fifty by 1811, as the Woodard sale of 1807 suggests, then Hill lied to evade the law banning manumissions of slaves over forty-five. Such cases may not have been uncommon: in addition to hundreds of manumissions that did not state the slave's age, an average of one or two a year in Baltimore followed Hill's formula of simply asserting that the slave was "under 45" or "about 45." Baltimore editor Hezekiah Niles claimed that many "overage" slaves were manumitted. See *Niles' Weekly Register,* Jan. 16, 1825, vol. 27.

84. See William Haslett's manumission and sale of James. The buyer, James Pannell of Baltimore City, paid $275 for the right to command James for a term of twelve years. Miscellaneous Papers, 1814, Baltimore County Court.

85. The Baltimore Conference kept its rules against selling slaves for life at least as late as 1820. See Armstrong, *History of the Old Baltimore Conference,* 199.

86. Soper bought Margaret in 1813 from John Pool. Pool commuted Margaret's servitude from life to six years as part of the transaction and received $180 from Soper. See Miscellaneous Papers, 1813, Baltimore County Court.

5. FREE BLACK FAMILY STRATEGIES FOR GAINING FREEDOM

1. Daniel Vickers, *Farmers and Fishermen,* (Chapel Hill, N.C., 1994), provides a first-rate overview of family-based economic activity in seventeenth- and eighteenth-century New England, as well as a good review of the extensive literature on this subject.

2. See Manumission by Robert Goldsborough of Negro Chloe, Land Records, 1806, Queen Anne's County. The accounting of Sam Stewart's payments for Chloe's freedom are recorded on the back of the manumission deed.

3. See Manumission by George Gilbert of Sundry Negroes, Land Records, 1801, Queen Anne's County. Also see Manumission by Free Negro Isaac Bellows of Negro Lydia, Manumissions, 1793, Anne Arundel County.

4. See Manumission by Jesse Higgins of Jane Gibbs et al., Land Records, 1799, Kent County. See Manumission by Phill Howard of Mary and Mary Ann Howard, Manumissions, 1817, Ann Arundel County, and Manumission by Phill Howard of George and Rachel Howard, Manumissions, 1818, Ann Arundel County.

5. See Manumission by Free Negro Peter Porter to Harry, Land Records, 1797, Talbot County, MSA.

6. Affidavits regarding Negro Jane, Miscellaneous Papers, 1815, Baltimore County Court.

7. See Laws of Maryland, 1809, chap. 171.

8. Of 641 prospective manumissions of women that determined the condition of unborn children, only 60 (9 percent) freed such children at birth. The median term length for unborn children was 25-29 years for males and 20-24 years for females. Seventy-four manumitters (11 percent) stated that the terms applied to children would also apply to grandchildren. Data drawn from eight Maryland counties over the period 1770-1830 (Anne Arundel, Baltimore, Dorchester, Harford, Kent, Prince George's, Queen Anne's, and Talbot). For an example, see Jurningham Drury, Manumission of Negro Sarah, Manumissions, 1820, Anne Arundel County.

9. See Manumission of John Jones to Negro Dafney, Land Records, 1824, Dorchester County. For a similar transaction, see the assignment by Joseph Bowzer of his children to Letitia Pierce, in which Bowzer acknowledges that Pierce or her heirs could claim his children without "any charge for keeping the children." The assignment, dated 1831, is in the Gorsuch Family Papers, MHS.

10. See Harris and Johnson, *Maryland Reports,* 1823, *Hamilton v. Cragg,* for a challenge to a manumission of minor children as violating the self-maintenance requirements for freed persons.

11. These data derive from manumissions of 2,598 male and 2,663 female slaves whose age was specified in a deed filed between 1770 and 1830. For men, 1,237 (48 percent) were over thirty, and 1,872 (72 percent) were over twenty-five. For women, 1,042 (39 percent) were over thirty, and 1,608 (60 percent) were over twenty-five. Data from the eight Maryland counties cited in note 8 above.

12. J.E.K Walker, in *Free Frank,* 38-42, describes how Frank spent over $14,000 to purchase freedom for himself, his wife, and his descendants to the *fourth* generation.

13. See U.S. House, *Annals of Congress,* 20th Cong., 2d sess., Jan. 7, 1829, 182-83.

14. See Manumission of Fielder Dorsett to Negro Jones, Chattel Records, 1803, Prince George's County, MSA.

15. See Manumissions, 1802, Anne Arundel County.

16. See Manumission by Isaac Hackett of Negro Delia, Manumissions, 1793, Kent County, and Manumission by Thomas Sluby of Negro Delia, Manumissions, 1795, Kent County, MSA.

17. See Manumission by James Carey of Negro Moses, Miscellaneous Pa-

pers, 1789, Baltimore County Court. See Manumission by Morgan Brown to Negro William Berry, Manumissions, 1783, Kent County.

18. Philip Fiddeman registered manumissions in the Queen Anne's County Land Records in 1790, 1796, 1799, 1801, 1803, 1808, 1809, 1811, 1813, 1814, and 1816.

19. Thomas's statement appears in Petition for Pardon of Free Negro Henry Toomey, Pardon Papers, Governor and Council of Maryland, box 17, folder 2.

20. See Manumission by Thomas Burgess of Sundry Negroes, Land Records, 1808, Queen Anne's County, and Mortgage by George Garnet to Joseph Blake and Richard Rochester, 1810, Land Records, 1810, Queen Anne's County.

21. Petition of John Dubernat, February 1819, Petitions to the Judges, Baltimore County Orphans' Court.

22. Data for the next three tables were drawn from Baltimore manumission records and these rural counties: Anne Arundel, Dorchester, Harford, Kent, Prince George's, Queen Anne's, and Talbot. They represent manumissions surviving in these counties' land or manumission records from 1770 to 1820. All cases are included in which a child's sex was specified, as well as his or her age at the time the deed was recorded.

23. An examination of bills of sale for slaves in Baltimore County between 1787 and 1830 reveals 23 cases in which children under five years of age were sold for a discrete price (as opposed to group sales with their mother and siblings). Boys were more likely than girls thus to be purchased, by a margin of 14 to 9, and sold for about 50 percent more, that is, an average price of $61 compared to $40 for girls. Data from Bills of Sale, Miscellaneous Papers, Baltimore County Court.

24. See the last will and testament of Thomas Pitt, Baltimore County Wills, 1819.

25. See the will of Don Carlos Hall, 1823; of Frank Armstrong, 1816; and of Amy Scoggins, 1820, all in Baltimore County Wills.

26. Grantors of 384 manumissions by deed were positively identified as free people of color. Of these manumissions, 83 (22 percent) postponed freedom until after completion of a term of servitude.

27. See Manumission by David Polk of Negroes David and Benjamin, Miscellaneous Papers, 1816, Baltimore County Court.

28. There were 54 cases in which free black men manumitted males identified as age nineteen or under at the time of the recording of the deed. Of these, 27 (50 percent) became term slaves before obtaining free status.

29. The data are: Baltimore, 7 of 68 black manumissions of children delayed; other Maryland counties, 73 of 316; Kent County, 31 of 99. Regarding the proportion of African Americans indentured by the courts, Baltimore blacks never composed as much as 10 percent of those bound out before 1830, as discussed in chapter 1. In Dorchester and Prince George's Counties, by contrast, over one-quarter of all indentures were of black children. For Kent County, see Daniels, "Alternative Workers in a Slave Economy," passim.

30. See Petition of Thomas Winston, Petitions, 1846, Baltimore County Orphans' Court.

31. See M. Johnson and Roark, "Strategies of Survival."

32. Of 1,581 bills of sale for slaves in Baltimore County between 1790 and 1830, only 32 involved identifiable free people of color as purchasers; of these, 26 specified a familial relationship with the slave being bought. See Miscellaneous Papers, Baltimore County Court.

6. POLITICAL-ECONOMIC THOUGHT AND FREE BLACKS

1. For a sample of southern attitudes toward free black labor after the Civil War, see Roark, *Masters without Slaves,* esp. 111-56. For Cuba, see Scott, *Slave Emancipation in Cuba.* For a good overview of the literature, also see Scott, "Exploring the Meaning of Freedom."

2. Free day laborers earned $4.50 for a six-day week. Self-purchase for $350, a midrange price for a healthy adult male slave, would require a laborer to save fifteen to twenty-one months' full-time earnings. In 1813 the median wealth of Baltimore's taxable households was $342. Price data derived from slave bills of sale and manumissions in Miscellaneous Papers, 1790-1830, Baltimore County Court. Tax data from Assessment Record, 1813, Baltimore City Commissioners of the Tax.

3. See Raymond, *Elements of Political Economy,* 2:415. Raymond was born and educated in Connecticut and moved to Baltimore around 1814. His opposition to the unrestricted admission of Missouri appeared in a pamphlet entitled *The Missouri Question.* Also see Paul Conkin, *Prophets of Prosperity,* 77-111. The second quote is from Hezekiah Niles, *Niles' Weekly Register,* May 22, 1819.

4. See *Annapolis Maryland Gazette,* Nov. 12, 1790. Bettye Gardner has tentatively identified "A Freeman" as Ezekiel Cooper, a Methodist preacher. See her "The Free Blacks of Baltimore," Ph.D. diss., George Washington University, 1973.

5. See *Annapolis Maryland Gazette* of Nov. 26, 1790.

6. Ibid., Dec. 2, 16, 1790.

7. Ibid., Jan. 13, 20, 1791.

8. See *American Museum,* May 10, 23, 1788, 414-17 and 509-12. "Othello" signed himself as being "of Baltimore."

9. See Drew McCoy, *The Elusive Republic: Political Economy in Jeffersonian America* (Williamsburg, 1980), esp. 13-47.

10. The 1790 census listed 8,043 free blacks in the entire state of Maryland, 7 percent of the black population of the state.

11. See Laws of Maryland, 1801, chap. 109; 1805, chap. 66, 80; 1808, chap. 81.

12. See Laws of Maryland, 1806, chap. 56; for tumultuous meetings and the gun ban, see Laws of Maryland, 1806, chap. 81.

13. See Pardon Papers, 1782-1829, Governor and Council of Maryland. The foregoing comments are based on an examination of 1,371 petitions for pardon, including 1,151 for whites, 156 for slaves, and 64 for free persons of color.

14. Gary Nash's examination of free blacks in Philadelphia notes that falling real wages after the year 1800 may have contributed to similar negative perceptions there of free blacks. See his *Forging Freedom,* 144-45.

15. See Harper, "Letter from General Harper," 8-9.

16. *Niles' Weekly Register,* May 22, 1819.

17. For Raymond's comments on the respective roles of production and consumption, see *Elements of Political Economy,* 2:108-57.

18. See *Niles' Weekly Register,* May 15, 1819, 16:193.

19. For the outline of his demographic argument, see Raymond, *The Missouri Question,* 8-20. Earlier antislavery writers had also compared northern growth to southern stagnation. See Dillon, *Slavery Attacked,* 120-22.

20. See Raymond, *Missouri Question,* 26-29.

21. See Learned, "A View," 7-8, 13-18.

22. Ibid., 24-25.

23. See Harper, "Letter from General Harper."

24. Ibid., 6-7. Harper had in his youth endorsed more optimistic sentiments. In an address made in his native South Carolina in 1788, Harper stated, "Can we imagine one being more superior to another than a Franklin a Witherspoon, or a Jefferson, to a negro just landed from the Coast of Africa? Yet these creatures are of the same species; they came into the world in all respects alike, except in the colour of their skin, and the difference between them, great as it appears, arises wholly from education." Cited from "A discourse on Learning," Mar. 15, 1788, Ms. Caroline T. Fisher Collection of Robert Goodloe Harper Papers, Special Collections 2360, MSA.

25. Harper, "Letter from General Harper," 8-9.

26. Ibid., 9-11.

27. Ibid., 8, 13-14.

28. Ibid., 25.

29. See Fredrickson, *The Black Image in the White Mind,* 3-22, and Finnie, "Anti-Slavery Movement in the Upper South," 324, for more extensive discussions of colonization.

30. See "Emancipation of the Blacks," in *Niles' Weekly Register,* Aug. 1, 1818, 14:382.

31. See Harper, "Letter from General Harper," 7.

32. "Mitigation of Slavery" appeared in eight parts in *Niles' Weekly Register,* between May and August of 1819. See *Niles' Weekly Register,* vol. 16. Niles, born in 1777, had been raised as a Quaker in Wilmington, Delaware. He edited a Federalist-sponsored newspaper in Baltimore, *Baltimore Evening Post,* from 1806 to 1811, leaving it to found the *Weekly Register,* a nationally circulated newspaper that he edited until his death in 1839. In politics Niles moved from Federalism to support for National Republican and Whig measures, especially the development of home markets and domestic manufacturing. See Stone, *Hezekiah Niles as an Economist.* Niles was a moderate antislaveryite whose strongest attacks were launched against the slave trade. See the *Weekly Register* of 1817-18, 12:287, 323; 13:80, 332, 377; 14:280; and 15:267-68, 384, for examples.

33. See *Niles' Weekly Register,* June 26 and May 15, 1819.

34. Ibid., May 15, 1819 and May 22, 1819.

35. Ibid., Mar. 30, 1822, Mar. 11, 1826. See also *African Repository,* July 1826, 2:152-54. During the first twenty years of its existence, 1,130 of the 2,270 incarcerations (49.8 percent) in the Maryland Penitentiary involved prisoners identified as black, mulatto, or "yellow." Data compiled from Prisoner Records, 1811-1830, Maryland Penitentiary.

36. See Laws of Maryland, 1818, chap. 197. For the debate, see the *American,* Feb. 1, 1819, and the *Annapolis Maryland Republican,* Jan. 9, 1819.

37. See Raymond, *Elements of Political Economy,* esp. 406, vol. 2.

38. Ibid., 413-18, vol. 2.

39. See *Niles's Weekly Register,* May 22, 1819.

40. Niles claimed that removal of twelve thousand slave girls per year from the southern states would "eliminate" the slave population over time, or so reduce black numbers as to eliminate fears of insurrection. See the *Weekly Register* of July 17, 1819, for Niles's statistical analysis, predicated on the dubious assumption that each slave woman bore an average of ten surviving children.

41. See *Niles' Weekly Register,* May 8, 1819, 16:13, Aug. 14, 1819, 16:401,

and July 17, 1819. For a discussion of early-nineteenth-century views of the impact of climate and environment on skin color, see Stanton, *The Leopard's Spots,* esp. 3-23.

42. See *Niles' Weekly Register,* Aug. 14, 1819.

43. For an exposition of early-nineteenth-century attitudes toward women as inculcators of republican virtues, see Linda K. Kerber's *Women of the Republic: Intellect and Ideology in Revolutionary America* (Chapel Hill, 1980), esp. 283-87.

44. Raymond, *Elements of Political Economy,* 2:413-21. These views were not simply a mask for race prejudice; Raymond also opposed lotteries, because instant wealth "demoralized" winners. Raymond's visceral distaste for rapid change slanted his analysis of manumission: over four-fifths of manumissions recorded in Baltimore city and county wills between 1790 and 1825 required a term of service before granting freedom, as did a majority of manumissions by deed.

45. Kennedy spoke on a bill designed to compel slaves manumitted by will in the future to leave the state. Kennedy successfully opposed banishment, urging voluntary colonization as a more humane alternative. See the Baltimore *American* of Jan. 23 and 30, 1821.

46. See the Baltimore *Genius of Universal Emancipation,* Jan. 12, 1828. The author was probably William Watkins, then an emerging leader of the free black community in Baltimore.

47. E. Tyson, "Farewell Address to the Free People of Color," 8-9. Also see J.S. Tyson, *Life of Elisha Tyson,* and Graham, *Baltimore,* 35-92.

48. See the Baltimore *Genius of Universal Emancipation,* Sept. 12, 1825.

49. Ibid., Aug. 12, 1826.

50. Ibid., July 7, 1827.

51. See Laws of Maryland, 1833, chap. 224, which modified the law of 1817, chap. 112. The new law allowed courts to consider owners' petitions to sell ungovernable or absconding term slaves.

52. For the petition and its defeat, see *Genius of Universal Emancipation,* Jan. 12, Apr. 26, 1828.

CONCLUSIONS

1. See *Niles' Weekly Register* of July 12, 1828, 34:316-25, for a description of the parade and groundbreaking ceremonies for the railroad.

2. Carroll's father had been one of the founders of the Baltimore Iron Company. See K. Johnson, "Genesis of the Baltimore Iron Company."

3. Carroll was part owner of the Cape Sable Company, an alum manufacturing concern. He supplied the company with slaves as his contribution to the company's working capital. See Maryland Chancery Papers, Cape Sable Co., case 17,898-9015.

4. See *Niles' Weekly Register,* vol. 40, July 16, 1831.

5. See Steffen, *The Mechanics of Baltimore;* Laurie, *Artisans into Workers;* or Sean Wilentz, *Chants Democratic: New York City and the Rise of the Working Class, 1788-1850* (New York, 1984), for treatments of workers that give passing attention at best to African Americans.

6. Berlin's *Slaves without Masters* devotes one of eleven chapters to emancipation; Fields's *Slavery and Freedom on the Middle Ground* deals with the eman-

cipation struggle in Maryland during the Civil War as a central theme, but her chapter on Baltimore is largely a justification of ignoring early emancipation there, in order to focus on events of the 1850s and 1860s.

7. Certificates of freedom show that over 60 percent of Baltimore registrants had been raised elsewhere. Prisoner records of the Maryland Penitentiary for 1811-30 show that just under two-thirds of free black felons resident in Baltimore City when convicted had been born elsewhere. See Certificates of Freedom, 1805-1832, Baltimore County Court, and Prisoner Records, 1811-40, Maryland State Penitentiary.

8. See G. Wright, *Political Economy of the Cotton South,* esp. 128-57.

BIBLIOGRAPHY

ABBREVIATIONS

AgH	Agricultural History
AHR	American Historical Review
BHR	Business History Review
CWH	Civil War History
EEH	Explorations in Economic History
EPFL	Enoch Pratt Free Library, Baltimore, Md.
JAH	Journal of American History
JEH	Journal of Economic History
JER	Journal of the Early Republic
JNH	Journal of Negro History
JSH	Journal of Social History
JSouH	Journal of Southern History
LH	Labor History
MHM	Maryland Historical Magazine
MHS	Maryland Historical Society, Baltimore, Md.
MSA	Maryland State Archives, Annapolis, Md.
MVHR	Mississippi Valley Historical Review
PMHB	Pennsylvania Magazine of History and Biography
S&A	Slavery and Abolition
WMQ	William and Mary Quarterly

PRIMARY SOURCES

Newspapers

Annapolis Maryland Gazette, 1773-1830
Annapolis Maryland Republican, 1817-24
Baltimore American and Commercial Daily Advertiser, 1799-1830
Baltimore American Farmer, 1819-42
Baltimore Evening Post, 1805-11
Baltimore Federal Republican, 1808-13
(Baltimore) *Genius of Universal Emancipation,* 1824-30
Baltimore Maryland Censor, 1818-19
Baltimore Morning Chronicle, 1819-21, 1822-24
Baltimore Telegram, 1814-16
Baltimore Telegraphe, 1797-1806
Baltimore Whig, 1807-14
Federal Gazette and Baltimore Daily Advertiser, 1796-1825
Maryland Journal and Baltimore Commercial Advertiser, 1773-95
Niles' Weekly Register, 1811-39
(Washington, D.C.) *African Repository,* 1825-30

Baltimore City Directories

Baltimore Directory and Register for 1814-15, James Lakin
The Baltimore Directory, corrected up to June, 1819, Samuel Jackson
The Baltimore Directory for 1803, Cornelius W. Stafford
Baltimore Town and Fell's Point Directory for 1796, Thompson and Walker
Fry's Baltimore Directory for 1810, John Fry
Matchett's Baltimore Directory, 1827, 1829, 1833
The New Baltimore Directory, and Annual Register for 1800 and 1801, Warner and Hanna

Contemporary Books and Articles

The American Museum. Philadelphia, 1788-89.
Asbury, Francis. *The Journal and Letters.* 3 vols. New York, 1821; reprint, Nashville, 1958.
Bacon, Leonard. "Slavery in Maryland." In *Slavery Discussed in Occasional Essays from 1833 to 1836.* New York, 1846, EPFL.
Baltimore Weekly Magazine. Baltimore, 1800-1801.
Buckingham, James Silk. *Journey through the Slave States.* London, 1842.
Carey, John L. "Slavery in Baltimore Briefly Considered." Baltimore, 1845, EPFL.
Carey, Matthew. *Essays on Political Economy.* New York, 1822; reprint, New York, 1966.
———. "Reflections on the Causes That Led to the Formation of the Colonization Society: With a View of Its Probable Results." Philadelphia, 1832, MHS.
Green, William. *Narrative of the Events in the Life of William Green (Formerly a Slave).* Springfield, Mass., 1853.
Griffith, Thomas Waters. *Annals of Baltimore.* Baltimore, 1834, MHS.
Harper, Robert Goodloe. "A Letter from General Harper, of Maryland, to Elias B. Caldwell, Esquire, Secretary of the American Society for Colonizing the Free People of Colour, in the United States with Their Own Consent." Baltimore, 1818, MHS.
Learned, Joseph D. "A View of the Policy of Permitting Slaves in the States West of the Mississippi, Being a Letter to a Member of Congress." Baltimore, 1820, MHS.
Pennington, William C. "The Fugitive Blacksmith." London, 1849; reprinted in *Five Slave Narratives: a compendium.* Arno Press, N.Y., 1968.
Pinkney, William. Summary of remarks on manumission by will, delivered to the Maryland House of Delegates December 11, 1789. Baltimore, 1789, EPFL.
"Proceedings of a Meeting of the Friends of African Colonization Held in the City of Baltimore." Baltimore, 1827, MHS.
Raymond, Daniel. *The Missouri Question.* Baltimore, 1819, MHS.
———. *Elements of Political Economy.* 2d ed. 2 vols. Baltimore, 1823, MHS.
"Report of a Meeting of the Maryland Society for Promoting the Abolition of Slavery and the Relief of Free Negroes, and Others, Unlawfully Held in Bondage." Joseph Townsend, secretary. Baltimore, 1792, EPFL.
Smith, Adam. *An Inquiry into the Nature and Causes of the Wealth of Nations.* London, 1776; reprint, New York, 1937.
Steuart, R.S. "A Letter on Slavery." Baltimore, 1845, EPFL.

Tyson, Elisha. "Farewell Address to the Free People of Color of Baltimore." Baltimore, 1824, MHS.
Tyson, John. *Life of Elisha Tyson, the Philanthropist.* Baltimore, 1825, EPFL.
Varle, Charles. *A Complete View of Baltimore.* Baltimore, 1833.
Walsh, Robert, Jr. *An Appeal from the Judgments of Great Britain Respecting the United States of America.* Philadelphia, 1819, MHS.
Weld, Isaac. *Travels through the States of America and the Provinces of Upper and Lower Canada, 1795-1797.* London, 1806.

Unpublished Documents

Maryland Historical Society, Baltimore, Md.
   Allbright Account Book
   Baker Account Books
   Baltimore Assessment Record Book
   Baltimore Cash Book
   Bond Accounts
   Bond Family Papers
   Briggs-Stabler Papers
   Cox Account Book
   Deer Creek Iron Company Accounts
   Despeaux Account Book
   Despeaux, Joseph, Papers
   Elk Forge Account Book
   Hanson Family Papers
   Harper Letters
   Hollyday Papers
   Industrial Notes
   Kauffman Daybooks
   Kelso and Ferguson Account Book
   Krebs Account Book
   Long Family Collection
   Marine, Matthew, Account Books
   Maryland Chemical Works Account Books
   Maryland State Colonization Society Papers
   Maryland Tax Lists (Federal Direct Tax of 1798)
   McKim Collection
   McKim Papers
   Meredith Papers
   Phoenix Shot Tower Company Account Book
   Principio Company Papers
   Pringle, Mark, Letterbook
   Ridgely Account Books
   Ridgely Papers
   Scharf Papers
   Shriver Collection
   Williams, George, Business Papers
   Williamson Papers
Baltimore City Archives, Baltimore, Md.
   Ordinances of the Baltimore City Council (1797-1830)

Maryland State Archives, Annapolis, Md.
  Methodist Church Records
    Baltimore City Station
      Class Records (1799-1830)
      Trials and Judgments (1816-22)
    East Baltimore Station
    Church Register (1800-1830)
  Quaker Records
      Supplement to Baltimore Yearly Meeting Records Reports, Meeting
      for Sufferings, Miscellaneous Papers (1681-1812)
  Scharf Papers
  State of Maryland
    Chancery Papers (1783-1835)
    General Assembly, Law Record (1715-1830)
    Governor and Council
      Pardon Papers (1782-1830)
      Pardon Records (1782-1820)
    Laws of Maryland (1634-1860)
    Law Reports
      Maryland Reports, *1658-1799. 4 vols. Harris and McHenry*
      Maryland Reports, *1800-1826. 7 vols. Harris and Johnson*
      Maryland Reports, *1827-29. 2 vols. Harris and Gill*
    Penitentiary, Prisoner Records (1811-40)
  Anne Arundel County
    Manumissions (1784-1822)
  Baltimore County
    Baltimore City Commissioners of the Tax
      Assessed Persons List (1804, 1813)
      Assessment Record (1813)
    County Commissioners of the Tax
      Transfer Book (1814-27)
    County Court
      Certificates of Freedom (1805-30)
      Chattel Records (1763-73, 1813-14)
      Land Records (1790-1830)
      Miscellaneous Papers (1785-1830)
        Bills of Sale (Slaves)
        Declarations of Slaves
        Deeds of Gift
        Manumissions
        Mortgages
        Releases from Mortgages
      Naturalization Docket (1796-1835)
      Petition Docket (1812)
    County Jail
      City Criminal Docket (1827-32)
      Runaway Docket (1831-32)
    Orphans' Court
      Petitions (1781-1852)
      Proceedings (1794-1830)

Register of Wills
  Accounts of Sale (1785-1809)
  Guardian Accounts (1801-30)
  Indentures (1794-1830)
  Inventories (1790-1830)
  Wills (1790-1825)
Dorchester County
  Chattel Records
    Bills of Sale (Slaves) (1799-1830)
    Manumissions (1828-30)
  Land Records
    Manumissions (1799-1827)
  Harford County
    Manumissions (1775-91)
  Kent County
    Land Records
      Manumissions (1774-1819)
  Prince George's County
    Chattel Records
      Bills of Sale (Slaves) (1801-30)
      Manumissions (1801-30)
    Indentures (1795-1828)
  Queen Anne's County
    Land Records
      Manumissions (1777-1820)
  Talbot County
    Indentures (1800-30)
    Land Records
      Manumissions (1769-1820)
United Methodist Historical Society, Baltimore, Md.
  Journal of the Baltimore Annual Conference, Methodist Episcopal Church,
    (1800-1844)
  Quarterly Conference Minutes (1800-1844)

SECONDARY SOURCES

Abbott, Collamer. "Isaac Tyson, Jr., Pioneer Mining Engineer and Metallurgist."
    MHM 60 (1965): 15-23.
Adams, Alice D. *The Neglected Period of Anti-Slavery in America, 1808-1831.*
    Boston, 1908.
Adams, Donald. "Prices and Wages in Maryland, 1750-1850," *JEH* 46 (1986):
    623-44.
Anderson, Perry. *Passages from Antiquity to Feudalism.* London, 1974.
Anderson, Ralph V., and Robert Gallman. "Slaves as Fixed Capital: Slave Labor
    and Southern Economic Development." *JAH* 64 (1977): 24-46.
Andrews, Doris E. "Popular Religion and the Revolution in the Middle Atlantic
    Ports: The Rise of the Methodists, 1770-1800." Ph.D. diss., Univ. of Pennsyl-
    vania, 1986.

Armstrong, James. *History of the Old Baltimore Conference, 1773-1857*. Baltimore, 1907.

Aufhauser, Keith. "Slavery and Technological Change." *JEH* 34 (1974): 36-50.

Bagnall, W. *Textile Industries of the United States, 1639-1810*. Cambridge, Mass., 1893.

Bancroft, Frederic. *Slave Trading in the Old South*. New York, 1931.

Bateman, Fred, James Foust, and Thomas Weiss. "Large Scale Manufacturing in the South and West, 1850-1860." *BHR* 45 (1971): 1-17.

———. "The Participation of Planters in Manufacturing in the Antebellum South." *AgH* 47, no. 2 (1974): 277-97.

———. "Profitability in Southern Manufacturing: Estimates for 1860." *EEH* 12, (1975): 211-31.

Berlin, Ira. *Slaves without Masters: The Free Negro in the Antebellum South*. New York, 1974.

Berlin, Ira, and Herbert Gutman. "Natives and Immigrants, Free Men and Slaves: Urban Workingmen in the Antebellum American South." *AHR* 87 (1982): 1175-200.

Berlin, Ira, and Ronald Hoffman, eds. *Slavery and Freedom in the Age of the American Revolution*. Charlottesville, Va., 1983.

Bernard, Richard. "A Portrait of Baltimore in 1800: Economic and Occupational Patterns in an Early American City." *MHM* 69 (1974): 341-60.

Bibbins, Ruthella "The City of Baltimore, 1797-1850: The Era of the Clipper, the Turnpike, Mill, and Railroad: An Epoch of Commerce and Culture." In Baltimore: *Its History and Its People,* edited by Clayton Hall. Vol. 1. New York, 1912.

Bilhartz, Terry. *Urban Religion and the Second Great Awakening: Church and Society in Early National Baltimore*. Rutherford, N.J., 1986.

Bining, Arthur C. "Iron Plantations of Early Pennsylvania." *PMHB* 57 (1933): 117-37.

———. *Pennsylvania Iron Manufactures in the Eighteenth Century*. Harrisburg, Pa., 1938.

Bishop, J.L. *A History of American Manufactures from 1608 to 1860*. 3 vols. Philadelphia, 1868.

Blandi, Joseph. *Maryland Business Corporations, 1783-1852*. Baltimore, 1934.

Boles, John B. *The Great Revival, 1787-1805: The Origins of the Southern Evangelical Mind*. Lexington, Ky, 1972.

———. "Tension in a Slave Society: The Trial of the Reverend Jacob Gruber." *Southern Studies* 18 (1979): 179-97.

Bowser, Frederick. *The African Slave in Colonial Peru, 1524-1650*. Palo Alto, Calif. 1979.

Brackett, Jeffrey. *The Negro in Maryland*. Baltimore, 1889.

Bradford, S. Sydney. "The Negro Ironworker in Antebellum Virginia." *JSouH* 25, (1959): 194-206.

Bradley, Keith, R. *Slavery and Society at Rome*. Cambridge, U.K., 1994.

———. *Slaves and Masters in the Roman Empire: A Study in Social Control*. New York, 1987.

Brana-Shute, Rosemary. "Approaching Freedom: The Manumission of Slaves in Suriname, 1760-1828." *S&A* 10 (1990): 41-63.

Bridner, Elwood L., Jr. "The Fugitive Slaves of Maryland." *MHM* 66 (1971): 34-50.

Brooks, Lester Smith. "Sentinels of Federalism: Rhetoric and Ideology of the Federalist Party in Maryland, 1800-1815." Ph.D. diss., Univ. of Michigan, 1986.

Brown, George T. *The Gas Light Company of Baltimore.* Baltimore, 1936.

Browne, Gary L. *Baltimore in the Nation, 1789-1861.* Chapel Hill, N.C., 1980.

———. "Federalism in Baltimore." *MHM* 83 (1988): 50-57.

———. "The Panic of 1819 in Baltimore." In *Law, Society, and Politics in Early Maryland,* edited by Aubrey Land, Lois G. Carr, and Edward Papenfuse. Baltimore, 1976.

Bruce, Kathleen. *Virginia Iron Manufactures in the Slave Era.* New York, 1931.

Calderhead, William. "How Extensive Was the Border State Slave Trade: A New Look." In *Slave Trade and Migration,* edited by Paul Finkelman, 42-55. New York, 1989.

———. "The Role of the Professional Slave Trader in a Slave Economy: Austin Woolfolk, a Case Study." *CWH* 23 (1977): 195-211.

Campbell, Penelope. *Maryland in Africa: The Maryland State Colonization Society, 1831-1857.* Urbana, Ill., 1971.

Cappon, Lester. "The Trend of the Southern Iron Industry under the Plantation System." *Journal of Economic and Business History* 2, no. 1 (1930), 3-37.

Carroll, Douglas, and Blanche Coll. "The Baltimore Almshouse: An Early History." *MHM* 71 (1966): 135-52.

Carroll, Kenneth. "An Eighteenth Century Episcopalian Attack on Quaker and Methodist Manumission of Slaves." *MHM* 80 (1985): 139-50.

———. "Maryland Quakers and Slavery." *Quaker History* 72 (1983): 27-42.

———. "Religious Influences on the Manumission of Slaves in Caroline, Dorchester, and Talbot Counties." *MHM* 61 (1966): 176-97.

Cassell, Frank. "Slaves of the Chesapeake Bay Area and the War of 1812." *JNH* 57 (1972): 144-55.

Caterall, Helen. *Judicial Cases concerning American Slavery and the Negro.* 5 vols. Washington, D.C., 1936.

A Century of Population Growth, 1790-1900. Washington, D.C., 1909; reprint, Baltimore, 1967.

Chaplin, Joyce E. "Slavery and the Principle of Humanity: A Modern Idea in the Early Lower South." *JSH* 24 (1991): 299-315.

Clark, Victor. *History of Manufactures in the United States.* 3 vols. New York, 1929.

Collins, Herbert. "The Southern Industrial Gospel before 1860." *JSouH* 12 (1946): 386-402.

Conkin, Paul. *Prophets of Prosperity: America's First Political Economists.* Bloomington, Ind., 1980.

Conrad, Alfred H., and John R. Meyer. "The Economics of Slavery in the Antebellum South." *Journal of Political Economy* 66 (1958): 95-130.

Cooper, Frederick. *Plantation Slavery on the East Coast of Africa.* New Haven, Conn., 1977.

Cox, Edward L. *The Free Coloreds in the Slave Societies of St. Kitts and Grenada, 1763-1833.* Knoxville, Tenn., 1984.

Crapster, Basil. "Hampton Furnace in Colonial Frederick County." *MHM* 80 (1985): 1-8.

Crowl, Philip. *Maryland during and after the Revolution, a Political and Economic Study.* Baltimore, 1943.

Curry, Leonard. *The Free Black in Urban America, 1800-1850: The Shadow of the Dream.* Chicago, 1981.

———. "Urbanization and Urbanism in the Old South: A Comparative View." *JSouH* 40 (1974): 43-60.

Daniels, Christine M. "Alternative Workers in a Slave Economy: Kent County, Maryland, 1675-1810." Ph.D. diss., Johns Hopkins Univ., 1990.

Davidson, Philip G. "Industrialism in the Ante-Bellum South." *South Atlantic Quarterly* 27 (1928): 405-25.

Davis, David Brion. *The Problem of Slavery in the Age of Revolution, 1770-1823.* Ithaca, N.Y., 1975.

———. *The Problem of Slavery in Western Culture.* Ithaca, N.Y., 1966.

———. "Reflections on Abolitionism and Ideological Hegemony." *AHR* 92 (1987): 797-812.

———. *Slavery and Human Progress.* New York, 1984.

Della, M. Ray, Jr. "The Problems of Negro Labor in the 1850s." *MHM* 66 (1971): 14-32.

Demaree, L. Steven. "Maryland during the First Party System: A Roll Call Analysis of the House of Delegates, 1789-1824." Ph.D. diss., Univ. of Missouri, Columbia, 1984.

Dew, Charles B. "Black Ironworkers and the Slave Insurrection Panic of 1856." *JSouH* 41 (1975): 321-38.

———. "David Ross and the Oxford Iron Works." *WMQ* 31 (1974): 189-224.

———. "Disciplining Slave Ironworkers in the Antebellum South." *AHR* 79 (1974): 393-418.

———. *Ironmaker to the Confederacy.* New Haven, Conn., 1966.

———. "Sam Williams, Forgeman: The Life of an Industrial Slave in the Old South." In *Region, Race, and Reconstruction,* edited by J. Morgan Kousser and James McPherson, 199-239. New York, 1982.

———. "Slavery and Technology in the Antebellum Southern Iron Industry: The Case of buffalo forge," 107-26." In *Science and Medicine in the Old South,* edited by Ronald L. Numbers and Todd L. Savitt. Baton Rouge, 1989.

Deyle, Stephen. "The Irony of Liberty: Origins of the Domestic Slave Trade." *JER* 12 (1992): 37-62.

Dillon, Merton L. *Benjamin Lundy and the Struggle for Negro Freedom.* Urbana, Ill., 1966.

———. *Slavery Attacked: Southern Slaves and Their Allies, 1619-1865.* Baton Rouge, 1990.

Dockes, Pierre. *Medieval Slavery and Liberation.* Chicago, 1982.

Dorfman, Joseph. *The Economic Mind in American Civilization, 1606-1865.* 2 vols. New York, 1946.

Dowd, Mary Jane. "The State in the Maryland Economy, 1776-1807." *MHM* 57 (1962): 90-132, 229-58.

Dumond, Dwight. *Anti-Slavery: The Crusade for Freedom in America.* Ann Arbor, Mich., 1961.

Earle, Carville. *Geographical Inquiry and American Historical Problems.* Stanford, Calif., 1992.

———. "A Staple Interpretation of Slavery and Free Labor." *Geographical Review* 68 (1978): 51-65.

Earle, Carville, and Ronald Hoffman. "Staple Crops and Urban Development in the Eighteenth Century South." *Perspectives in American History* 10 (1976), 7-78.

———. "The Urban South: The First Two Centuries." In *The City in Southern*

History: The Growth of Urbanism in the South, edited by Blaine Brownell and David R. Goldfield. Port Washington, N.Y., 1977, 47-83.

Eaton, Clement. "Slave Hiring in the Upper South: A Step toward Freedom." *MVHR* 46 (1960): 663-78.

Engerman, Stanley L. "The Effects of Slavery upon the Southern Economy." *EEH* 4, no. 2 (1967): 73-97.

———. "A Reconsideration of Southern Economic Growth, 1770-1860." *AgH* 49, no. 2 (1975): 343-80.

Engerman, Stanley L., and David Eltis. "Economic Aspects of the Abolition Debate." In *Anti-Slavery, Religion, and Reform,* edited by Christine Bolt and Seymour Drescher. London, 1980, 272-93.

Essig, James D. *The Bonds of Wickedness: American Evangelicals against Slavery, 1770-1808.* Philadelphia, 1982.

Evans, Robert C. "The Economics of American Negro Slavery." In *Aspects of Labor Economics.* Princeton, N.J., 1962, 156-89.

Faust, Drew G. "'Trying to Do a Man's Business': Slavery, Violence and Gender in the American Civil War." *Gender and History* 4 (1992): 197-214.

Fields, Barbara Jeanne. *Slavery and Freedom on the Middle Ground: Maryland during the Nineteenth Century.* New Haven, Conn., 1985.

Finkelman, Paul. "Slaves as Fellow Servants: Ideology, Law, and Industrialization." *American Journal of Legal History* 31 (1987): 269-305.

Finley, Moses I. *Ancient Slavery and Modern Ideology.* New York, 1980.

Finnie, Gordon E. "The Antislavery Movement in the Upper South before 1840." *JSouH* 35 (1969): 319-42.

Fleisig, Haywood. "Slavery, the Supply of Agricultural Labor and the Industrialization of the South." *JEH* 36 (1976): 572-97.

Fogel Robert W. *Without Consent or Contract.* New York, 1989.

Fogel Robert W., and Stanley L. Engerman. "Philanthropy at Bargain Basement Prices: Notes on the Economics of Gradual Emancipation," *JEH,* 1974, VOL. 34, 377-401.

———. *The Reinterpretation of American Economic History.* New York, 1971.

———. *Time on the Cross: The Economics of American Negro Slavery.* Boston, 1974.

Foner, Eric. "Abolitionism and the Labor Movement in Antebellum America." In *Anti-Slavery, Religion, and Reform,* edited by Christine Bolt and Seymour Drescher. London, 1980, 254-71.

Foster, Gaines. "Guilt over Slavery: A Historiographical Analysis." *JSouH* 56 (1990): 665-94.

Foust, James D., and Dale E. Swan. "Productivity and Profitability of Antebellum Slave Labor: A Micro-Approach." *AgH* 44 (1970): 39-61.

Fox-Genovese, Elizabeth, and Eugene D. Genovese. *Fruits of Merchant Capital.* New York, 1983.

Fredrickson, George M. *The Black Image in the White Mind: The Debate on Afro-American Character and Destiny, 1817-1914.* New York, 1971.

Freehling, William W. *The Road to Disunion: Secessionists at Bay, 1776-1854.* New York, 1990.

Freudenberger Herman, and Jonathan Pritchett. "The Domestic United States Slave Trade: New Evidence." *Journal of Interdisciplinary History* 21 (1991): 447-77.

Frey, Sylvia. *Water from the Rock: Black Resistance to Slavery in the Revolutionary Age.* Princeton, N.J., 1991.

Galenson, David. *White Servitude in Colonial America.* Cambridge, U.K., 1981.

Gallman, Robert. "Slavery and Southern Economic Growth." *Southern Economic Journal* 45 (1979): 1007-22.

Gardner, William, and Edward Cooke. *Chemical Synonyms and Trade Names.* 6th ed. London, 1968.

Garitee, Jerome. *The Republic's Private Navy: Privateering Business as Practiced by Baltimore during the War of 1812.* Middletown, Conn. 1977.

Garlan, Yvon. *Slavery and Ancient Greece.* Ithaca, N.Y., 1984.

Genovese, Eugene D. *The Political Economy of Slavery.* New York, 1965.

——. Roll, Jordan, *Roll: The World the Slaves Made.* New York, 1974.

——. *The World the Slaveholders Made.* New York, 1969.

Gilbert, Arlan K. "Gunpowder Production in Post-Revolutionary Maryland." *MHM* 52 (1957): 187-201.

Gilchrist, David T., ed. *The Growth of the Seaport Cities, 1790-1825.* Charlottesville, VA., 1966.

Gilje, Paul. "'Le Menu Peuple' in America: Identifying the Mob in the Baltimore Riots of 1812." *MHM* 81 (1986): 50-66.

Glickstein, Jonathan. "Concepts of Free Labor in Antebellum America." Ph.D. diss., Yale Univ., 1989.

——. "Poverty Is Not Slavery: American Abolitionists and the Competitive Labor Market." In *Anti-Slavery Reconsidered: New Perspectives on the Abolitionists,* edited by Lewis Perry and Michael Fellman, 195-219. Baton Rouge, 1979.

Goldenberg, Joseph. *Shipbuilding in Colonial America.* Charlottesville, VA., 1976.

Goldfarb, Stephen. "Laws Governing the Incorporation of Manufacturing Companies Passed by Southern State Legislatures before the Civil War." *Southern Studies* 24 (1985): 407-16.

Goldin, Claudia Dale. *Urban Slavery in the American South, 1820-1860.* Chicago, 1976.

Goodrich, Carter, ed. *Government Promotion of American Canals and Railroads, 1800-1890.* New York, 1960.

Graham, Leroy. *Baltimore: The Nineteenth Century Black Capital.* Washington, D.C., 1982.

——. "Manumitted Free Blacks in Baltimore, 1806-1816." *Maryland Magazine of Genealogy* 5 (1982): 9-22.

Green, George D. *Finance and Economic Development in the Old South.* Palo Alto, Calif., 1972.

Green, Rodney Dale. "Black Tobacco Factory Workers and Social Conflict in Antebellum Richmond: Were Slavery and Urban Industry Really Compatible?" *S&A* 5 (1984): 183-203.

——. "Quantitative Sources for Studying Urban Industrial Slavery in the Antebellum US South." *Immigrants and Minorities* 5 (1986): 305-15.

——. "Urban Industry, Black Resistance, and Racial Restriction in the Antebellum South: A General Model and a Case Study in Urban Virginia." Ph.D. diss., American Univ., 1980.

Greenberg, Dolores. "Energy, Power, and Perception of Social Change in the Early Nineteenth Century." *AHR* 95 (1990): 693-714.

Greene, Jack P. *Pursuits of Happiness: The Social Development of Early Modern British Colonies and the Formation of American Culture.* Chapel Hill, N.C., 1988.

Gregg, William. "Practical Results of Southern Manufactures." *DeBow's Review* 18 (1855): 777-91.

Griffin, Richard W. "An Origin of the Industrial Revolution in Maryland: The Textile Industry, 1789-1826." *MHM* 61 (1966): 24-36.

———. "Sidelights: The Columbia Manufacturing Company and the Textile Industry of the District of Columbia, 1808-1816." *MHM* 48 (1953): 259-67.

Guy, Anita Aidt. "The Maryland Abolition Society and the Promotion of the Ideals of the New Nation." *MHM* 84 (1989): 342-49.

Hall, Robert L. "Slave Resistance in Baltimore City and County, 1747-1790." *MHM* 84 (1989): 305-18.

Handler, Jerome. *The Unappropriated People: Freedmen in the Slave Society of Barbados.* Baltimore, 1974.

Haskell, Thomas L. "Capitalism and the Origins of the Humanitarian Sensibility." *AHR* 90 (1985): 339-61, 547-66.

Haynes, Williams. *The American Chemical Industry: A History.* 6 vols. New York, 1954.

Haywood, C. Robert. "Economic Sanctions: Use of the Threat of Manufacturing by the Southern Colonies." *JSouH* 25 (1959): 207-19.

Helper, Hinton R. *The Impending Crisis of the South.* New York, 1857.

Hoffman, Ronald. "The 'Disaffected' in the Revolutionary South." In The American *Revolution: Explorations in the History of American Radicalism,* edited by Alfred F. Young, 273-316. Dekalb, Ill., 1976.

Hollander, J.H. *The Financial History of Baltimore.* Baltimore, 1899.

Hopkins, Keith. *Conquerors and Slaves: Sociological Studies in Roman History.* Cambridge, U.K., 1978.

Hughes, Sarah. "Slaves for Hire: The Allocation of Black Labor in Elizabeth City County, Virginia, 1782 to 1810." *WMQ* 35 (1978): 260-86.

Hungerford, Edward. *The Story of the Baltimore and Ohio Railroad, 1827-1927.* 2 vols. New York, 1928.

Ingersoll, Thomas N. "Free Blacks in a Slave Society: New Orleans, 1718-1812." *WMQ* 48 (1991): 173-200.

James, Alfred R. "Sidelights on the Founding of the Baltimore and Ohio Railroad." *MHM* 48 (1953): 267-81.

Jernegan, Marcus. "Slavery and the Beginnings of Industrialism in the American Colonies." *AHR* 25 (1920): 220-40.

Johnson, Keach. "The Genesis of the Baltimore Iron Works." *JSouH* 19 (1953): 157-79.

Johnson, Lyman L. "Manumission in Colonial Buenos Aires, 1776- 1810." *Hispanic American Historical Review* 59 (1979): 258-79.

Johnson, Michael, and James Roark. "Strategies of Survival: Free Negro Families and the Problem of Slavery." In *In Joy and in Sorrow: Women, Family, and Marriage in the Victorian South,* edited by Carol Bleser, 88-102. New York, 1991.

Jones, Norrece T. *Born a Child of Freedom yet a Slave: Mechanisms of Control and Strategies of Resistance in Antebellum South Carolina.* Hanover, N.H., 1990.

Jordan, Winthrop D. *White over Black: American Attitudes toward the Negro, 1550-1812.* Williamsburg, Va., 1968.

Karasch, Mary. *Slave Life in Rio de Janeiro, 1808-1850*. Princeton, N.J., 1987.

Kaufman, Allen. *Capitalism, Slavery, and Republican Values: Antebellum Political Economists, 1819-1848*. Austin, 1982.

Kerber, Linda K. *Federalists in Dissent: Imagery and Ideology in Jeffersonian America*. Ithaca, N.Y., 1970.

Klein, Herbert S. *African Slavery in Latin America and the Caribbean*. New York, 1986.

———. *Slavery in the Americas: A Comparative Study of Virginia and Cuba*. Chicago, 1967.

Klugh, Henry F. *Statistics: The Essentials for Research*. Hillsdale, N.J., 1986.

Kotlikoff, Laurence J., and Anton J. Rupert. "The Manumission of Slaves in New Orleans, 1827-1846." *Southern Studies* (Summer 1980): 172-81.

Kuhlmann, Charles B. *The Development of the Flourmilling Industry in the United States*. Boston, 1929.

Kulikoff, Allan. *Tobacco and Slaves: The Development of Southern Cultures in the Chesapeake, 1680-1800*. Williamsburg, VA., 1986.

Land, Aubrey. "Economic Behavior in a Planting Society." *JSouH* 33 (1967): 469-85.

———. "Genesis of a Colonial Fortune: Daniel Dulany." *WMQ* 7 (1950): 255-69.

Lander, Ernest M., Jr. "Ante-Bellum Milling in South Carolina." *South Carolina History and Genealogy Magazine* 52 (1951): 125-32.

———. "The Iron Industry in Ante-Bellum South Carolina." *JSouH* 20 (1954): 337-55.

———. "Slave Labor in South Carolina Cotton Mills." *JNH* 38 (1953): 160-73.

Lebsock, Suzanne. *The Free Women of Petersburg: Status and Culture in a Southern Town, 1784-1860*. New York, 1984.

Lewis, Ronald L. *Coal, Iron, and Slaves: Industrial Slavery in Maryland and Virginia, 1715-1865*. Westport, Conn., 1979.

———. "The Darkest Abode of Man: Black Miners in the First Southern Coal Field, 1780-1865." *VMHB* 87 (1979): 190-202.

———. "Slave Families at an Early Chesapeake Ironworks." *VMHB* 86 (1978): 169-79.

———. "The Use and Extent of Slave Labor in the Virginia Iron Industry." *West Virginia History* 38 (1977): 141-56.

Lewis, Ronald L., and John Newton, eds. *The Other Slaves: Manufacturers, Artisans, and Craftsmen*. Boston, 1978.

Linden, Fabian. "Repercussions of Manufacturing in the Ante-Bellum South." *North Carolina Historical Review* 17 (1940): 313-31.

Lindstrom, Diane. *Economic Development in the Philadelphia Region, 1810-1850*. New York, 1978.

Litwack, Leon. *North of Slavery*. New York, 1967.

Lovejoy, Paul. *Transformations in Slavery: A History of Slavery in Africa*. Cambridge, U.K., 1983.

Loveland, Anne C. *Southern Evangelicals and the Social Order, 1800-1860*. Baton Rouge, 1980.

Luraghi, Raymond. "The Civil War and the Modernization of American Society: Social Structure and Industrial Revolution in the Old South before and during the War." *CWH* 18 (1972): 230-50.

MacLeod, Duncan J. "From Gradualism to Immediatism: Another Look." *S&A* 3 (1982): 140-52.

———. *Slavery, Race, and the American Revolution*. Cambridge, U.K., 1974.

Maganzin, Louis. "Economic Depression in Maryland and Virginia, 1783-1787." Ph.D. diss., Georgetown Univ., 1967.

Mancini, Matthew. "Political Economy and Cultural Theory in Tocqueville's Abolitionism." *S&A* 4 (1983): 151-69.

Marks, Bayly Ellen. "Clifton Factory, 1810-1860: An Experiment in Rural Industrialization." *MHM* 80 (1985): 48-65.

———. "Skilled Blacks in Antebellum St. Mary's County, Maryland." *JSouH* 53 (1987): 537-64.

Martin, Thomas. "Neglected Aspects of the Economic Thought and Method of Condy Raguet." *History of Political Economy* 19 (1987): 401-13.

Mathews, Donald G. *Slavery and Methodism: A Chapter in American Morality, 1780-1845*. Princeton, N.J. 1965.

Matison, Sumner Eliot. "Manumission by Purchase." *JNH* 33 (1948): 146-67.

Matlack, L.C. *The Antislavery Struggle and Triumph in the Methodist Episcopal Church*. New York, 1881; reprint, N.Y. 1969).

Matthews, Jean. "Race, Sex, and the Dimensions of Liberty in Ante-bellum America." *JER* 6 (1986): 275-91.

McClatchy, Ricky. "The Demise of the Antislavery Movement among Baptists in America, 1783-1830." Ph.D. diss., Southwest Baptist Theological Seminary, 1990.

McClelland, Peter D., and Richard J. Zeckhauser. *Demographic Dimensions of the New Republic: American Interregional Migration, Vital Statistics, and Manumissions, 1800-1860*. Cambridge, U.K., 1982.

McKenzie, Edna C. "Self Hire among Slaves, 1820-1860: Institutional Variation or Aberration?" Ph.D. diss., Univ. of Pittsburgh, 1973.

McManus, Edgar J. *Black Bondage in the North*. Syracuse, N.Y., 1973.

Mendels, Franklin. "Proto-industrialization, the First Phase of the Industrialization Process." *JEH* 32 (1972): 241-61.

Miller, Randall M. "The Fabric of Control: Slavery in Antebellum Southern Textile Mills." *BHR* 55 (1981): 471-90.

Mitchell, Broaddus. "The Growth of Manufactures in the Old South." *Annals of the American Academy of Political Science*, no. 153 (1933): 21-29.

———. *The Rise of Cotton Mills in the South*. Baltimore, 1921.

———. *William Gregg: Factory Master of the Old South*. Chapel Hill, N.C., 1928).

Morris, Richard. "Labor Controls in Maryland in the Nineteenth Century." *JSouH* 14 (1948): 385-400.

———. "The Measure of Bondage in the Slave States." *MVHR* 41 (1954): 219-40.

Morris Thomas D. "'Society Is Not Marked by Punctuality in the Payment of Debts': The Chattel Mortgages of Slaves." In *Ambivalent Legacy: A Legal History of the South*, edited by David J. Bodenhamer and James W. Ely, Jr., 147-70. Jackson, Miss., 1984.

Mullin, Gerald W. *Flight and Rebellion: Slave Resistance in Eighteenth-Century Virginia*. New York, 1972.

Mullin, Michael. "Women and the Comparative Study of American Negro Slavery." *S&A* 6 (1985): 25-40.

Muspratt, Sheridan. *Chemistry, Theoretical, Practical, and Analytical, As Applied and Relating to the Arts and Manufactures*. 2 vols. Glasgow, U.K., 1860.

Nash, Gary B. *Forging Freedom: The Formation of Philadelphia's Free Black Community, 1720-1840*. Cambridge, Mass., 1988.

Nash, Gary B., and Jean R. Soderlund. *Freedom by Degrees: Emancipation in Pennsylvania and Its Aftermath*. New York, 1991.

Nelson, Lee H. "Brickmaking in Baltimore, 1798." *Journal of the Society of Architectural Historians* 18 (1959): 33-34.

North, Douglass C. *Economic Growth of the United States, 1790-1860*. Englewood Cliffs, N.J., 1961.

Oakes, James. *The Ruling Race: A History of American Slaveholders*. New York, 1983.

——. *Slavery and Freedom: An Interpretation of the Old South*. New York, 1990.

Olson, Sherry. *Baltimore, the Building of an American City*, Baltimore, 1980.

Pancake, John S. "Baltimore and the Embargo, 1807-1809." *MHM* 47 (1952): 173-85.

Papenfuse, Eric R. "From Recompense to Revolution: Mahoney v. Ashton and the Transformation of Maryland Culture." *S&A* 15 (1994): 39-63.

Parish, Peter. "The Edges of Slavery in the Old South: Or, Do Exceptions Prove Rules?" *S&A* 4 (1983): 106-25.

Parker, William N. "Slavery and Economic Development: An Hypothesis and Some Evidence." *AgH* 44 (1970): 115-25.

Paskoff, Paul. *Industrial Evolution*. Baltimore, 1976.

Patterson, Orlando. *Slavery and Social Death: A Comparative Study*. Cambridge, Mass., 1982.

Pearse, John. *A Concise History of the Iron Manufacture of the American Colonies up to the Revolution and in Pennsylvania until the Present Time*. Philadelphia, 1876.

Peterson, Arthur G. "Flour and Grist Milling in Virginia: A Brief History." *VMHB* 43 (1935): 97-108.

Phillips, Ulrich B. *American Negro Slavery*. New York, 1918.

Phillips, William D., Jr. *Slavery from Roman Times to the Early Transatlantic Trade*. Minneapolis, 1980.

Porter, Glenn, and Harold C. Livesay. *Merchants and Manufacturers*. Baltimore, 1971.

Preyer, Norris W. "The Historian, the Slave, and the Ante-Bellum Textile Industry." *JNH* 46 (1961): 67-84.

Provine, Dorothy. "The Economic Position of the Free Blacks in the District of Columbia, 1800-1860." *JNH* 45 (1960): 61-71.

Prude, Jonathan. "To Look upon the 'Lower Sort': Runaway Ads and the Appearance of Unfree Laborers in America, 1750-1800." *JAH* 78 (1991): 124-59.

Quarles, Benjamin. "The Colonial Militia and Negro Manpower." *MVHR* 46 (1959): 643-52.

Ramsdell, Charles W. "The Natural Limits of Slavery Expansion." *MVHR* 16 (1929): 151-71.

Ransom, Roger, and Richard Sutch. "Capitalists without Capital: The Burden of Slavery and the Impact of Emancipation." *AgH* 62 (1988): 133-60.

Rice, Otis K. "Coal Mining in the Kanawha Valley to 1861: A View of Industrialization in the Old South." *JSouH* 31 (1965): 393-415.

Roark James L. *Masters without Slaves: Southern Planters in the Civil War and Reconstruction*. New York, 1977.

Robert, Joseph C. *The Tobacco Kingdom*. Gloucester, Mass., 1938.

Robinson, Donald L. *Slavery in the Structure of American Politics, 1765-1820.* New York, 1971.

Rothbard, Murray N. *The Panic of 1819: Reactions and Policies.* New York, 1962.

Russel, Robert R. "The General Effects of Slavery upon Economic Progress." *JSouH* 4 (1938): 34-54.

Russo, Jean B. "A Model Planter: Edward Lloyd IV of Maryland, 1770-1796." *WMQ* 49 (1992): 62-88.

Saunders, A.C. DeC. M. *A Social History of Black Slaves and Freedmen in Portugal, 1441-1555.* Cambridge, U.K., 1982.

Saunders, Robert. "Modernization and the Free Peoples of Richmond: The 1780s and the 1850s." *Southern Studies* 24 (1985): 237-72.

———. "Modernization and the Political Process: Governmental Principles and Practices in Richmond, Virginia, from the Revolution to the Civil War." *Southern Studies* 24 (1985): 117-42.

Savitt, Todd L. "Slave Life Insurance in Virginia and North Carolina." *JSouH* 43 (1977): 583-600.

Sayre, Robert. "The Evolution of Early American Abolitionism: The American Convention for Promoting the Abolition of Slavery and Improving the Condition of the African Race, 1794-1837." Ph.D. diss., Ohio State Univ., 1987.

Schwartz, Stuart B. *Sugar Plantations in the Formation of Brazilian Society: Bahia, 1550-1835.* Cambridge, U.K., 1985.

Schwarz, Philip J. "Emancipators, Protectors, and Anomalies: Free Black Slaveowners in Virginia." *VMHB* 95 (1987): 317-38.

Schweikart, Larry. "Southern Banks and Economic Growth in the Antebellum Period: A Reassessment." *JSouH* 53 (1987): 19-36.

Schweninger, Loren. "Slave Independence and Enterprise in South Carolina, 1780-1865." *South Carolina Historical Magazine* 93 (1992): 101-25.

———. "The Underside of Slavery: The Internal Economy, Self-Hire, and Quasi-Freedom in Virginia, 1780-1865." *S&A* 12 (1991): 1- 22.

Scott, Rebecca J. "Exploring the Meaning of Freedom: Post-emancipation Societies in Comparative Perspective." *Hispanic American Historical Review* 68 (1988): 407-28.

———. *Slave Emancipation in Cuba: The Transition to Free Labor, 1860-1899.* Princeton, N.J., 1985.

Sharp, William Frederick. *Slavery on the Spanish Frontier: The Colombian Choco, 1680-1810.* Norman, Okla., 1976.

Sharrer, G. Terry. "Flour Milling in the Growth of Baltimore, 1750-1830." *MHM* 71 (1976): 322-33.

———. "The Merchant-Millers: Baltimore's Flour Milling Industry, 1783-1860." *AgH* 56 (1984): 138-50.

———. "Patents by Marylanders, 1790-1830." *MHM* 71 (1976): 50-59.

Sheller, Tina H. "Artisans, Manufacturing, and the Rise of a Manufacturing Interest in Revolutionary Baltimore Town." *MHM* 83 (1988): 3-17.

———. "Artisans and the Evolution of Baltimore Town, 1765-1790." Ph.D. diss., Univ. of Maryland, College Park, 1990.

Shore, Lawrence. *Southern Capitalists: The Ideological Leadership of an Elite, 1832-1885.* Chapel Hill, N.C., 1986.

Sisson, William A. "From Farm to Factory: Work Values and Discipline in Two Early Delaware and Maryland Textile Mills." *Delaware History* 21 (1986): 31-52.

Small, Stephen. "Racial Group Boundaries and Identities: People of 'Mixed-Race' in Slavery across the Americas." *S&A* 15, no. 3 (1994): 17-37.

Smith, Billy G., and Richard Wojtowicz. *Blacks Who Stole Themselves: Advertisements in the Pennsylvania Gazette, 1728-1790.* Philadelphia, 1989.

Smith, George W. "Ante-Bellum Attempts of Northern Business to 'Redeem' the Upper South." *JSouH* 11 (1945): 177-213.

Sokoloff, Kenneth. "Was the Transition from the Artisanal Shop to the Nonmechanized Factory Associated with Gains in Efficiency? Evidence from the U.S. Manufacturing Censuses of 1820 and 1850." *EEH* 21 (1984): 351-82.

Soltow, Lee H. *Men and Wealth in the United States, 1850-1870.* New Haven, Conn., 1975.

Stampp, Kenneth M. *The Peculiar Institution: Slavery in the Ante-Bellum South.* New York, 1956.

Stanton, William R. *The Leopard's Spots: Scientific Attitudes toward Race in America, 1815-1859.* Chicago, 1960.

Starobin, Robert. "Disciplining Industrial Slaves in the Old South." *JNH* 53 (1968): 111-28.

———. *Industrial Slavery in the Old South.* New York, 1970.

Staudenraus, P.J. *The African Colonization Movement, 1816-1865.* New York, 1961.

Stealey, John E. "Slavery and the West Virginia Salt Industry." *JNH* 59 (1974): 105-31.

Steffen, Charles G. "Changes in the Organization of Artisan Production in Baltimore, 1790-1820." *WMQ* 36 (1979): 101-17.

———. "Gentry and Bourgeois: Patterns of Merchant Investment in Baltimore County, Maryland, 1658 to 1776." *JSH* 20 (1987): 531-48.

———. *The Mechanics of Baltimore: Workers and Politics in the Age of Revolution, 1763-1812.* Urbana, Ill., 1984.

———. "The Pre-Industrial Iron Worker: Northampton Iron Works, 1780-1820." *LH* 20 (1979): 87-110.

Stone, Richard Gabriel. *Hezekiah Niles as an Economist.* Baltimore, 1933.

Streifford, David M. "The American Colonization Society: An Application of Republican Ideology to Early Ante-bellum Reform." *JSouH* 45 (1979): 201-20.

Swaney, Charles B. *Episcopal Methodism and Slavery, with Sidelights on Ecclesiastical Politics.* Boston, 1926.

Tadman, Michael. *Speculators and Slaves: Masters, Traders and Slaves in the Old South.* Madison, Wis., 1989.

Temin, Peter. *Iron and Steel in Nineteenth-Century America.* Cambridge, Mass., 1964.

Temperley, Howard. "Capitalism, Slavery, and Ideology." *Past and Present,* no. 75 (1977): 94-118.

Terrill, Tom. "Eager Hands: Labor for Southern Textiles, 1850- 1860." *JEH* 36 (1976): 84-99.

Tise, Larry E. *Proslavery: A History of the Defense of Slavery in America, 1701-1840.* Athens, Ga., 1987.

Turner, Edward. *The Negro in Pennsylvania, 1639-1861.* Washington, D.C., 1911.

Verlinden, Charles. *The Beginnings of Modern Colonization.* Ithaca, N.Y., 1970.

Wade, Richard. *Slavery in the Cities: The South, 1820-1860.* New York, 1964.

Walker, Joseph. "Labor-Management Relations at Hopewell Village." *LH* 14 (1973): 3-18.

———. "Negro Labor in the Charcoal Iron Industry of Southeastern Pennsylvania." *PMHB* 93 (1969): 466-86.

Walker, Juliet E.K. *Free Frank: A Black Pioneer on the Antebellum Frontier*. Lexington, Ky., 1983.

———. "Racism, Slavery, and Free Enterprise: Black Entrepreneurship in the United States before the Civil War." *BHR* 60 (1986): 344-82.

Walsh, Lorena S. "Rural African Americans in the Constitutional Era in Maryland, 177-1810." *MHM* 84 (1989): 327-41.

Walters, Ronald G. "The Boundaries of Abolitionism." In *Anti-Slavery Reconsidered: New Perspectives on the Abolitionists*, edited by Lewis Perry and Michael Fellman, 3-23. Baton Rouge, 1979.

———. "The Erotic South: Civilization and Sexuality in American Abolitionism." *American Quarterly* 34 (1973): 177-201.

Ward, David C. "Industrial Workers in the Mid-nineteenth Century South: Family and Labor in the Graniteville (SC) Textile Mill, 1845-1880." *LH* 28 (1987): 328-48.

Wax, Darold D. "The Demand for Slave Labor in Colonial Pennsylvania." *Pennsylvania History* 34 (1967): 331-45.

———. "Preferences for Slaves in Colonial America." *JNH* 58 (1973): 371-401.

Weaver, Herbert. "Foreigners in Ante-Bellum Towns of the Lower South." *JSouH* 13 (1947): 62-73.

Welsh, Peter C. "The Brandywine Mills: A Chronicle of an Industry, 1762-1816." *Delaware History* 7 (1956): 17-36.

———. "Merchants, Millers, and Ocean Ships: The Components of an Early American Industrial Town." *Delaware History* 7 (1956): 319-36.

Wheeler, William B. "The Baltimore Jeffersonians, 1788-1800: A Profile of Intrafactional Conflict." *MHM* 66 (1971): 153- 68.

White, Shane. *Somewhat More Independent: The End of Slavery in New York City, 1770-1810*. Athens, Ga., 1991.

Whitely, William G. "The Principio Company. A Historical Sketch of the First Iron-Works in Maryland." *PMHB* 11 (1887): 63-68, 190-198, 288-95.

Wickham, Chris. "The Other Transition: From the Ancient World to Feudalism." *Past and Present*, no. 103 (1984): 3-36.

Windley, Latham A. *Runaway Slaves: A Documentary History from the 1730s to 1790*. 4 vols. Westport, Conn., 1983.

Wittlinger, Carl. "The Growth of the Small Arms Industry of Lancaster County, 1710-1840." *Pennsylvania History* 24 (1957): 294-313.

Wood, Betty. "Some Aspects of Female Resistance to Chattel Slavery in Low Country Georgia, 1763-1815." *The Historical Journal* 30 (1987): 603-22.

Woodman, Harold D. "Sequel to Slavery: The New History Views the Postbellum South." *JSouH* 43 (1977): 523-54.

Wright, Gavin. *Old South, New South: Revolutions in the Southern Economy since the Civil War*. New York, 1986.

———. *The Political Economy of the Cotton South*. New York, 1978.

———. "Prosperity, Progress, and American Slavery." In *Reckoning with Slavery*, edited by Paul David. New York, 1976, 302-36.

Wright, James. *The Free Negro in Maryland, 1634-1860*. New York, 1921.

Wyatt, Edward A. "Rise of Industry in Ante-Bellum Petersburg." *WMQ*, 2d ser., 17 (1937): 1-36.

Wyatt-Brown, Bertram. "Modernizing Southern Slavery: The Pro- slavery Argument Reinterpreted." *JSouH* 51 (1985): 27-45.

Zilversmit, Arthur. *The First Emancipation: The Abolition of Slavery in the North*. Chicago, 1967.

INDEX